Things Everyone Over

Should Know

Things Everyone Over

Should Know

Constance Schrader

MAIN STREET BOOKS

Doubleday

New York London Toronto Sydney Auckland

A Main Street Book
published by doubleday
a division of Random House, Inc.
1540 Broadway, New York, New York 10036

Main Street Books, Doubleday and the portrayal of a building
with a tree are trademarks of Doubleday, a division of Random House,
Inc.

With grateful thanks to Sandra Earley and Diane Rhodes for helping
this book reach its final form.

Every effort has been made to make sure all the information contained
in this book is current and accurate as of its writing. However, addresses and phone numbers do change, and expert advice in the fields
this book covers may vary in the light of new findings. Please check local directories for current mailing information. Also note that this
book should be used to supplement rather than replace professional
advice.

Book design by Judith Stagnitto Abbate

Library of Congress Cataloging-in-Publication Data

Schrader, Constance, 1933–
        1001 things everyone over 55 should know / Constance
    Schrader.
            p.   cm.
        Includes index.
        1. Aged—Life skills guides.   2. Aged—Health and hygiene.
    3. Aged—Finance, Personal.   I. Title.   II. Title: 1001 things
    everyone over 55 should know
    HQ1061.S3435   1999
    646.7'9—dc21   98-6179
                                                                CIP

ISBN 0-385-48224-8
Copyright © 1999 by The Philip Lief Group, Inc., and
Constance Schrader

All Rights Reserved
Printed in the United States of America
February 1999
10 9 8 7 6 5 4 3 2 1
First Edition

Contents

Part II: Here's to Your Health

Part III: Money Matters Matter

Preface

Has your 55th birthday come and gone? Mine has. And more than 35 million other Americans can say the same. Many of us are active and happy—some happier than ever before.

To be happy, we need to take advantage of new kinds of opportunities. We also need to learn how to deal successfully with life events that may not have concerned us before: health issues, financial issues, moving, and, of course, retiring. But we need something to guide us through the maze of unique benefits that are currently available to us. Where to start? *1001 Things Everyone Over 55 Should Know* can help you evaluate your current situation, locate the necessary information about everything from estate planning to e-mailing your grandchildren, and show you a host of options for a bright future. Now is the time to begin planning the rest of your life.

The 1,001 numbered items are designed to give you nuggets of information that you can use immediately to make your life easier, more pleasant, and more productive. Many of the entries include self-help and self-care information, intended to provide basic facts and to point you in the right direction if you'd like more detailed help. (Of course,

these entries are not intended to take the place of professional medical, legal, and financial advice.) Many entries include an address and phone number where you can write or call for additional information; there are even some entries devoted entirely to listing available resources.

I've divided the book into three sections: "Lifestyles of the Elegantly Aging" contains sections on travel, hobbies—did you know the old-fashioned quilting bee is alive and well?—going back to school, and going back to work. There's also material on volunteering, sorting out your housing options (how about a Crone's Nest?), moving, safety, and relationships—marital and otherwise. The next section, "Here's to Your Health," includes a rundown of what happens to each part of the body as we age, nutritional do's and don'ts, sports (especially those well suited to older adults), information on diseases and conditions most common to seniors, and guidelines on surviving widowhood and paying for funeral expenses. The final section, "Money Matters Matter," provides information on income (Social Security, pensions, tax-deferred retirement plans), managed care and other forms of insurance, taxes, bargains, establishing credit, and frauds you should be aware of. There's an entire chapter devoted to estate planning—it's a crash course in wills, legal lingo, trusts, taxes, and making it easier for your heirs to become your inheritors.

You'll learn how to trace your roots, discover volunteer opportunities that range from executive consulting to helping astronomers catalog the stars, and find out what to look for in a retirement community; there's information on the most talked-about herbal remedies, a listing of Websites pertinent to older adults, and tips on how to cope with empty nest syndrome, elderly parents, or the retired spouse who's getting on your nerves. What should you do when your grandchild has been reprimanded and comes to you for support, or the kids can't come home for the holidays, or your boss has offered you an early retirement package? See items 258, 266, and 741.

Information in the individual entries has been selected because it comes from reliable sources, makes sense, and meets what I think is a widespread need. With the help of the book's comprehensive index, you will be able to find the sections and information most pertinent to you and your family, at the time that you need it.

Every effort has been made to ensure that the contents of this book are as accurate and reliable as possible. Yet, technology and time itself seem to be on fast-forward; some of today's facts may be out of date tomorrow morning. Overnight, new theories and applications are launched; long-accepted methods of dealing with problems are declared obsolete. Perhaps most commonly of all, phone numbers change, phones are disconnected, and organizations move. Be sure to check local listings if you run into these problems.

There is a familiar saying: "Old age is not for cowards." Maturity is an astonishing condition to achieve. Take stock of who you are, examine the resources available to you, and the rest of your life can be better than anything you have known before.

CONSTANCE SCHRADER
Eureka Springs, Arkansas, 1997

Part

1

Lifestyles of the Elegantly Aging

Chapter 1:

Getting Older Is Getting Better

The *New York Times* and the Velveteen Rabbit agree, so it must be true: Getting older is getting better. In March 1997, the *New York Times Magazine* devoted an entire issue to the celebration and investigation of what it dubbed "The Age Boom." It began with a cover featuring thirteen visibly older celebrities, including Mike Wallace, Geoffrey Beene, Eartha Kitt, Ed Koch, George Plimpton, and Helen Thomas. "Funny," the headline noted, "We Don't Feel Old."

In an opening essay, Jack Rosenthal, the magazine's editor, talked about his own mother's joyous approach to the last eighteen years of her life. The editor went on to cite statistics, surveys, and anecdotes that dispelled the major misconceptions about getting older, especially the idea that the process is mostly about illness, poverty, loneliness, and boredom.

In the rest of the magazine, others continued to explode misunderstandings about age. Robert Butler, one of the country's leading gerontologists and a pioneer in the field, now in his 70s himself, noted that he doesn't even begin thinking of patients as "geriatric" until they're in their late 70s or 80s. Swimsuit designer Ann Cole, who gives her age as "between 59 and Forest Lawn," and who to this day wears her own products, told readers, "I haven't become more comfortable with my body. I've just taken an attitude that it's easier not to care or worry." And advertising executive Jerry Della Femina, now in his 50s, railed at his own industry for worshiping youth and writing off its elders, adding, in effect, "just wait until the baby boomers come along."

They all might have taken as their text the 1922 children's book *The Velveteen Rabbit,* by the English writer Margery Williams. In the story, the Velveteen Rabbit wants desperately to be more than a toy; he wants to be Real. He consults the Skin Horse, who is tattered and shabby, but also wise and experienced in the ways of the world. The horse explains to the rabbit, "Real isn't how you are made. It's a thing that happens to you. When a child loves you for a long, long time, not just to play with, but REALLY loves you, then you become Real." The Skin Horse goes on to say that becoming Real takes a long time, that it can hurt, and that you're sort of worn-looking by the end. "But these things don't matter at all," he concludes, "because once you are Real you can't be ugly, except to people who don't understand."

The Facts of Real Life Over 55

1. There are a lot of us over 55 already, and there are going to be noticeably more in the coming years. In 1995 about one in every eight Americans was 65 or over. That's almost 33 million people. By 2000, 65-and-overs will make up more than 12 percent of the population. And, as the country's population ages in general, seniors themselves are getting older. Currently, more than 3 million Americans are over 85. That number is expected to quadruple within the next fifty years, making 85-and-overs the fastest-growing age group in the country.

2. Baby boomers are getting up there, too. The first of those post–World War II children born between 1946 and 1964—including Bill Clinton and Hayley Mills—will reach the age of 55 in 2001. And, true to the societal impact they have had all along the way, boomers are expected to change the face of aging in America. Housing developers are beginning

to wonder what kind of accommodations they'll want when they retire; bankers, what kind of savings and investments they will have; and Disney, what kind of entertainment they will want. Jack Levin, a Northeastern University sociologist and author of *Ageism,* published in 1980, told the *New York Times Magazine* that he has higher expectations for boomers than just living and spending. "The baby boomers have the cultural clout to significantly reduce age discrimination," he said.

3. Life expectancy is moving well beyond the biblical allotment of three score and ten, or seventy years. An American child born in the 1990s can expect to live about twenty-eight years longer than a child born in 1900, to the age of almost 76. Life expectancy increased by 2.4 years between 1900 and 1960 and has raced ahead by 3.2 years since then. The average life span in America is now 70 to 85 years, nearly double that of our great-grandparents and almost triple that of our prehistoric ancestors, who were lucky to make it to 30. On average, women currently outlive men by seven years. By 2010, the average American woman will live to 81.

4. More of us are living better and longer, partly because we have more resources to draw on. Social Security benefits, instituted in 1935, have meant that fewer seniors are poor now as compared with the past. Since 1959, also because of Social Security, the number of old people officially classified as poor has dropped from 35 percent to 11 percent. Medicare, begun in the mid-1960s, has caused a transformation, too. While 15 percent of the general population in America has no health insurance, only 1 percent of people 65 and older is without it. In fact, many Americans get health insurance for the first time when they qualify for Medicare.

5. Living better still isn't living well for many aging Americans, especially women. In 1993 the median income for older people was $14,983 for men and $8,499 for women. About one-quarter of older renters live in publicly owned or subsidized housing. Older people not living with relatives are more likely to be poor than older people living in families.

6. Most of us live with family of some kind. An estimated 80 percent of men and 60 percent of women 55 and older live in family settings, either with spouses, children, or siblings. Only 1 percent of older Americans up to age 74 live in nursing homes; for ages 75 to 84, it's 6 percent, and for those over 85, 24 percent.

7. Contrary to the popular stereotype, most older adults are not depressed.

When they are, it's often treatable. Depression can be treated using a variety of approaches, such as family support, therapy, or antidepressant medications. A physician can determine whether the depression is caused by medication, physical illness, stress, or other factors, and suggest suitable courses of treatment.

8. Almost half of all Americans over 65 live in just nine states. And, no, they're not all warm-weather states. We live where we want as we age and where we have in the past, not just where the sun dictates. California has over 3 million older residents, Florida over 2 million, and there are 1 million each in Illinois, Michigan, New Jersey, New York, Ohio, Pennsylvania, and Texas. Statistics also show that older people are less likely to live in metropolitan areas than younger people are, and are also less likely to change their place of residence.

9. We're better educated and remain in the workplace longer than our predecessors. The percentage of older Americans who completed high school rose from about 25 percent two decades ago to 60 percent today. About 3.5 million seniors—almost 11 percent of us—are either working or actively seeking employment. About half of all workers over 65 are employed part-time, and one-fourth are self-employed. Employers are gradually learning that we're generally steadier and more responsible on the job than younger people and that they don't have to worry about training old dogs to perform new tricks. In fact, research has shown that anyone at any age can improve old skills or learn new ones, whether it's creating handicrafts, using a computer, or running a cash register.

10. We're also pretty healthy, as a class. It turns out that as we age, if we manage to stay clear of disease, the human body works pretty well into its 80s. In addition, we've been participating in the national trend toward better diet and more exercise, and that's helping to preserve us, too. Only 10 percent of Americans 65 and over have a chronic health problem that inhibits major activities. The Center for Demographic Studies at Duke University has pursued a National Long-Term Care Survey since 1982 and has found that over a twelve-year period, disability among the aged has dropped 15 percent. Not only that, when surveyors asked people over 50 when old age began, the consensus was at about 80.

Outlooks on Life Over 55

11. Since the beginning of time, many a man has marveled at aging. The Bible offers a wonderful analogy for age and its subtleties: "No man also having drunk old wine straightway desireth new: for he saith, The old is better." Jonathan Swift, the seventeenth-century English priest, satirist, and poet, observed, "No wise man ever wished to be younger."

12. In modern times, too, age has been a subject for poets and philosophers. Dylan Thomas urged, "Do not go gentle into that good night, / Old age should burn and rave at close of day." By contrast, Robert Browning invited his love along on the road to age: "Grow old along with me! The best is yet to be." Also inspirational is Meridel Le Sueur, an American poet who at age 86 wrote, "I am luminous with age / In my lap I hold the valley." (While in her 70s, Le Sueur rejected a prescription for tranquilizers, insisting that she still had her best writing to do.)

And then there are the thoughts of T. S. Eliot and Casey Stengel. The American-born British poet said, "The years between 50 and 70 are the hardest. You're always being asked to do things, and you are not yet decrepit enough to turn them down." The baseball great observed, "Most people my age are dead."

13. Research has found that personality is one of the few constants in life.

So if you've always been a dynamic go-getter, you will probably continue to be one as you age. If you were a young curmudgeon, you'll no doubt be an old curmudgeon.

14. *Geezerize:* **a verb meaning "to make old."** A word, by the way, only acceptable when used by someone over age 55. Other new terms finding their way into the language include:

Ageism: prejudice against the old. Coined by Robert Butler in 1976.
Crone: a withered old woman, but, in the parlance of many feminists, a wise and independent older woman
Gerontocracy: government by the elderly. This is William F. Buckley, Jr.'s bow to the political clout of people of age.
To be silver: to be older. Used in an ad campaign for a vitamin supplement, but it has a nice ring.

Wellderly and *illderly:* older adults who are aging without disease, and those who aren't. Coined by Harry Moody of the Brookdale Center on Aging at Hunter College.

So Just What Does Make Us Age?

15. Genetics, or wear and tear? Some scientists believe that we age according to a genetically programmed biological timetable; others suggest that aging occurs when cells and organs become damaged over time. The "programmed" theory holds that aging may be a continuation of the process that regulates childhood growth and is a result of:

• The sequential switching on and off of certain genes
• Biological clocks acting through hormones to control the pace of aging
• The decline of the immune system, which leads to an increased vulnerability to infectious disease and thus to aging and death

16. According to the "damage" theory, we grow old because internal and external "faults" advance us in years. To wit:

• Cells and tissues have vital parts that wear out.
• Accumulated damage caused by free radicals—toxic substances produced as a normal part of metabolism—causes cells, and eventually organs, to stop functioning.
• Faulty proteins accumulate to a level that causes damage to cells, tissues, and organs.
• Genetic mutations that accumulate with age cause cells to deteriorate and to malfunction.

17. Our attitude toward life may play a large role in the aging process. Resilience—that is, the ability to bounce back from the stresses of life—seems to be a key to living both long and well. In addition, people who continue to be productive after retirement are more likely to age successfully. "Only about one-third of the characteristics of aging are genetically based," says Dr. John W. Rowe, director of the MacArthur Foundation Consortium of Successful Aging at Mount Sinai Medical Center in New York. In other words, for many, the way you age is your choice.

18. To learn more about the science of aging, contact:

National Institute on Aging
NIA Information Center
P.O. Box 8057
Gaithersburg, MD 20898
800-222-2225
For publications and brochures.

National Institute on Aging
Public Information Office
Building 31, Room 5C27
Bethesda, MD 20892-2292
301-496-1752
For general information.

National Alzheimer's Association
919 N. Michigan Ave., Suite 1000
Chicago, IL 60611-1676
800-272-3900
For information and brochures, and to find a local chapter.

Baltimore Longitudinal Study of Aging
NIA Gerontology Research Center
4940 Eastern Ave.
Baltimore, MD 21224
800-225-2572

Alliance for Aging Research
2021 K St. NW, Suite 305
Washington, DC 20006
202-293-2856
For brochures on age-related ailments.

National Mental Health Association
Information Center
1021 Prince St.
Alexandria, VA 22314
800-969-6642

Accomplishments and Encouragements Over 55

19. When older actors are the stars of Hollywood blockbusters, something special happens. Remember, for example, the compelling depiction of family relationships in *On Golden Pond,* with Katharine Hepburn and Henry and Jane Fonda. In the 1990s Walter Matthau and Jack Lemmon made late-life careers of their hilarious portrayal of Grumpy Old Men, with very real and very strong likes and dislikes. *The Sunshine Boys,* with Matthau and George Burns, was a similar vehicle for older actors. Burns, then 80, won an Academy Award for that performance. His next box-office success was as God in a golf cap in *Oh, God!* (1977). Burns became a national icon for a relaxed style of aging, a style that pokes fun at it all. At his 98th birthday party, Burns noted, "It's nice to be here. At 98, it's nice to be anywhere."

20. Movies that showcase talented, vital women well over 55 have also been a source of delight. Jessica Tandy was 80 when she starred in *Driving Miss Daisy,* and subsequently won an Oscar for the performance. She followed it with prominent roles in *Fried Green Tomatoes* and *Nobody's Fool*—costarring Paul Newman—in 1994, the year she died. *Steel Magnolias,* with Olympia Dukakis and Shirley MacLaine, was another unforgettable film that featured wonderful women of age.

 21. **Older adults have brought texture and wisdom to films.**

Such films have varied from the romantic comedy *When Sally Met Harry,* featuring older couples recounting their love for each other, to Warren Beatty's *Reds,* in which contemporaries of American radical John Reed reminisce about him in and around the telling of his story.

22. Older adults have been known to do things that youngsters would think unlikely. In 1997 alone:

• Former President George Bush, then 72, skydived out of an airplane, saying that he'd always promised himself to jump out of a plane for fun one day after having had to do it to save his life in World War II.
• Strom Thurmond, a Republican from South Carolina, reached age 95 while still serving in the Senate and chairing the powerful Armed Services Committee.
• Actor Tony Randall became a father for the first time at age 77.
• A California woman gave birth to a baby at age 63, making her the oldest first-time mother on record.

23. Here are some more notable accomplishments among the over-55 set. In June 1997 Mary Fasano, 89, became Harvard University's oldest recipient of an undergraduate degree. Harriet Doerr graduated from Stanford University in 1977 at age 66. Doerr went on to graduate school and at age 73 published *Stones for Ibarra,* a critically acclaimed novel telling of an American couple's life in a remote Mexican village. Business executives often make the biggest deals of their careers as they near retirement. The *Wall Street Journal* reported that in the three years from 1995 to 1997, seventeen of twenty-three of the country's largest mergers and acquisitions involved CEOs over age 60.

24. When it comes to the fine arts, aging can enhance creativity. Cervantes, for example, penned the story of the old knight Don Quixote when he was in his 50s; Jonathan Swift wrote *Gulliver's Travels* at age 59. Grandma Moses took up painting when she was 76. Claude Monet was painting at Giverny until he died at age 85. Henri Matisse, too, died at 85 but wasn't able to paint in his last years. Undaunted, he cut brightly colored paper into shapes and arranged them in designs for the windows of the Dominican chapel at Venice, France.

Chapter 2:

Time and How We Spend It

We'll save you the math: If you retire from a forty-hour-a-week job with a standard two-week vacation, you'll have an extra two thousand hours to play with, literally and fig-uratively, every year. And that doesn't count the extra time you pick up once the kids are out of the house permanently.

Now, as any stay-at-home parent or free-lance worker will tell you, extra time can be as much of a challenge as a blessing. The key to enjoying your extra time is *planning*. Yes, it takes work, and it takes thought, but it's well worth the effort.

Bunty Ketcham, a Chevy Chase, Maryland, organizational consultant who herself is in her 70s, has written a handbook for trainers to use to help groups of older adults plan the next thirty years and beyond. Thinking about the past while also looking to the future helps mature adults plan in an organized fashion, she says. The idea, Ketcham adds, "is to give purpose and meaning in the last third of life—to help persons of age under-stand the choices."

Yes, choices. This chapter offers a multi-tude of possibilities for how you live over the next three or four decades and how you re-late to those around you. Here you will find tips and suggestions on travel, hobbies, edu-cation, volunteering, and even new work for pay.

Get Going and Travel

25. "If you want to find the next great travel destination, just follow seniors on the road." So says Cathy Lynn Grossman, travel writer for *USA Today*. "They do everything, and they do it ahead of everyone else. They were in Alaska ten years before the baby boomers. Seniors are the most intellectually adventur-ous of all travelers—they're beyond the beach thing—and these days, they're in-creasingly physical."

Travel industry statistics show that people over 55 don't travel as much as, say, the 35- to 54-year-olds, but when they do go, they stay away from home the longest of any group—an average of 4.3 nights per trip in 1995. They also take more day trips. The upshot is that the travel industry knows we go and that we don't require lots of special facilities. What we do often want is stimulating package deals, tailored to sophisticated tastes and needs.

26. A number of companies specialize in outdoor vacations for mature adults. Check the yellow pages of your telephone book under "Travel" to find one—the companies' names or their ads often indicate their specialities. Other possibilities:

• For women interested in short, same-sex trips throughout the United States and Canada: Outdoor Vacations for Women Over 40, P.O. Box 200, Groton, MA 01450
• For white-water rafting, kayaking, and other trips that cater to seniors (you'll stay in a lodge every night), plus special trips for grandparents and their grandkids: Warren River Expedition, Inc., P.O. Box 1375, Salmon, ID 83467; 800-765-0421

27. Some youth-oriented programs now seek vigorous people of age. Outward Bound has become synonymous with the process of expanding self-awareness through time spent in the wilderness, both as an individual and as a member of a group. If you're interested and in good health, contact: Outward Bound, Route 9D, R2 Box 280, Garrison, NY 10524; 800-243-8520. Wandering Wheels provides organized, long-distance bicycle touring and now seeks vigorous mature adults as well as the younger crowd. Trips can be as near as West Palm Beach or as far away as China. Contact: Wandering Wheels, P.O. Box 207, Upland, IN 46989; 765-998-7490.

28. The national parks of the United States offer a wonderful opportunity to enjoy our country's beauty. The U.S. Bureau of Land Management (BLM) has information on recreation opportunities ranging from stalking the elusive bighorn sheep—with a camera—to tracing the path of the pioneers along the Oregon Trail. National park settings vary from desert to mountains, from alpine tundra to evergreen forests, from expanses of sagebrush to red rock canyons. Many activities, such as white-water rafting, fly fishing, and mountain biking, are available on public lands. You can also organize your travel by topics, such as conservation areas or national historic sites. For more information, contact:

Bureau of Land Management
U.S. Department of the Interior
18th and C Sts. NW
Washington, DC 20240
888-467-8464 (toll-free)
Or call 202-208-3100 for additional information and brochures.

29. Travel for older adults can mean sight-seeing, learning, and doing good all at the same time. The B'nai B'rith Israel Commission, for example, sponsors trips to Israel in which mornings are spent in volunteering at the municipal gardens or at a local hospital, school, army installation, or facility for the elderly and handicapped. Afternoons and evenings are reserved for cultural events. Visits to the Negev Desert, Galilee, and the Golan Heights are made with full-time guides and coordinators. Contact:

Center for Jewish Identities Travel-Line
B'nai B'rith Israel Commission
1640 Rhode Island Ave. NW
Washington, DC 20036
202-857-6584
800-500-6533

 30. Hostels aren't just for youth anymore.

Hosteling provides the lowest travel prices anywhere, since travelers often sleep in dorm-style rooms—although private rooms and efficiency kitchens are sometimes available. For information on the experience, contact:

Hosteling International
733 15th St. NW, Suite 840
Washington, DC 20005
202-783-6161

31. Staying in a private home can save you lots on the cost of lodging. Almost 25 percent, in fact. In France, for example, about twenty thousand rural or village lodgings called *gîtes* rent for anywhere from $250 to $1,000 per week, depending on the location and season. For information, contact:

French Experience
370 Lexington Ave., Suite 812
New York, NY 10017
212-986-1115

Home at First offers a chance to rent a private home in England, Scotland, or Ireland. The homes are in central locations that make them convenient for sight-seeing. You can even stay in the hometown and burial place of the clan hero Rob Roy MacGregor for about $1,800 round trip.

Home at First
P.O. Box 193
Springfield, PA 19064
800-523-5842

32. Or you could exchange your home for one in another country. For most, a rent-free vacation isn't the prime reason to exchange dwellings. Rather, it's the opportunity to adopt another way of life. International at-home exchanges typically last two to four weeks and require several months to set up. In Europe the most popular exchange locations are Britain, France, and Switzerland; in the United States the most popular locations are New England and Florida. Most exchange services charge a fee for registering your home and sending out a directory of listings. Call Intervac at 415-435-3497 and leave a message to receive more information; or contact:

Try Vacation Exchange Club
P.O. Box 650
Key West, FL 33041
800-638-3841

33. You can also take your accommodations with you by driving a recreational vehicle (RV). People over 50 make up more than three-quarters of all RV enthusiasts. Some RVs cost only slightly more than a car, while others are much more expensive because they include amenities such as air-conditioning, heating, wall-to-wall carpeting, a bathroom, and a galley with a refrigerator and range or microwave. Thousands of campsites across the country provide water and power for a fee, and some offer swimming pools, recreation halls, health clubs, and phone hookups. Campsite directories can be had from:

Woodall's Campground Directory of
North America
13975 W. Polo Trail Dr.
Lake Forest, IL 60045
800-323-9076

Wheeler's Campground Guide
1310 Jarvis Ave.
Elk Grove Village, IL 60007
800-323-8899

34. If you're curious about RVs but don't want to buy—you can rent. Many rental companies give seniors a discount. Be prepared to buy insurance in addition to paying the weekly fee. Even if you're sure you want to buy, it's important to rent first to try out RV styles. Rental agencies are located in every area of the United States. A few of them:

Annapolis RV Center
2027 Industrial Dr.
Annapolis, MD 21401
800-327-9668

To order a rental brochure and for other information:

Cruise America/RV Depot
7740 NW 34th St.
Miami, FL 33122
800-327-7778

Recreational Vehicle Dealers Association
for North America
3930 University Dr.
Fairfax, VA 22030
800-336-0355

35. Some seniors are eligible for a Golden Age Passport. If you're 62 or over and plan to visit a national park in an RV, you can apply for a Golden Age Passport—it entitles you to a 50 percent park discount. For more information, write:

National Park Service
U.S. Department of the Interior
Washington, DC 20240

36. There are even special RV groups for women, and for people traveling on their own. Check with:

RVing for Women
201 E. Southern Ave.
Apache Junction, AZ 85219
602-983-4678

Loners of America
Route 2, Box 85E
Ellsinore, MO 63937
573-322-5548

37. Recapture the glamour of cross-country train travel.

These days, deluxe superliners with wrap-around, glass-enclosed, double-decker observation cars speed along at over one hundred miles per hour. Long-distance trains are staffed with expert chefs who serve up specialties in the dining cars. There are two classes of accommodations: Coach transportation is adequate for the day, since most seats recline and have foot or leg rests; longer trips are best in a private mini-room for one or two, with toilet and washbasin. A roomette is larger, but one person will have to climb into an upper berth.

38. Amtrak offers a 25 percent discount for people 65 and over. However, senior fares don't apply to club car travel, sleeping car accommodations, or already discounted fares. Special tours for long trips and sight-seeing are available. For more information, contact:

Amtrak Distribution Center
P.O. Box 7717
Itasca, IL 60143
800-872-7245

39. Take a cruise, and you'll be pampered and indulged as you've never been before. More than half of all cruise passengers are over 50. Older adults have discovered that cruise ships are floating hotels with entertainment, programs, and food, food, food, not to mention varied ports of call—all for one price. (Tips, drinks, shopping, and services such as the barber and beauty salon are extra.) Medical assistance is available twenty-four hours a day on most cruise ships, and doctors will make cabin calls for an extra charge. On longer cruises, there's often a dentist aboard.

40. Several cruise lines offer discounts to mature travelers. And membership in groups such as the American Association of Retired Persons (AARP) often means discounts elsewhere. Even more money can be saved by making reservations from a month to up to a year in advance. For more information, talk to a travel agent or contact:

Cunard Line
28-21 Jackson Ave.
New York, NY 11101
800-221-4770

Holland America Line
300 Elliott Ave. W
Seattle, WA 98119
206-281-3535

41. Older people are traveling for the best possible price. In fact, we're such a large market that most commercial transportation companies know it's in their best interest to make our trips as comfortable and as inexpensive as possible. Almost every airline offers discounted coupon books, money-off yearly passes, and other special privileges to those over 62. Car rental agencies usually have discounts for seniors. Sometimes the cost of renting a car using a combination of an AARP and an agency discount can be lower than the cost of driving your own car.

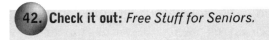

42. **Check it out:** *Free Stuff for Seniors.*

It's a book by Matthew Lesko, a syndicated columnist for the *New York Times,* published by Information USA, Inc. Its travel section has information on goodies like where to see a buffalo herd for free and how to get a free VIP tour of the White House. Other sections include advice on free and low-cost medical and dental care, free financial advice, and free things to do with your free time.

43. Air travel can be the largest expense of your trip, so it pays to plan. Here are some tips.

• By staying over a Saturday night and buying the ticket in advance, you can often lower your round-trip airfare by as much as two-thirds.

• To be sure you have the best deal, even when using a travel agent, call the airlines that fly to your destination and ask what the lowest fare is.

• When making your reservation, ask if it would be cheaper to fly the day before or the day after your originally intended date. If you're traveling to a large city that has two airports, ask which has the cheaper fare.

• Keep an eye out in the newspaper for fare wars. Act quickly when you see one, because tickets sell out fast. If tickets are gone when you call, try again just before the advance-purchase deadline; there may be cancellations.

• Mention your age and affiliation with AARP or any other group of older adults that you belong to, plus any commercial or civic affiliation, and ask if any discounts apply.

• After you've purchased your ticket, call before your departure date to check the fare. If it has gone down, some airlines will refund the difference—but you have to ask.

44. For the truly flexible, here are even more strategies for lowering costs.

• Standby fares are sometimes available if you can risk not flying. Standby means just that—you go to the airport, ask to line up for a standby seat on a specific flight, and then stand by while that flight loads. If there are seats available, you'll get one at the discounted standby fare. If no seats are available, you'll have to go home without flying.

• Ask about off-peak fares that allow travel before or after business hours—typically early-morning or late-evening flights. There are sometimes discounts in slow seasons, like right after a major holiday.

• Consider out-of-the-way airports and circuitous routes to your destination. Nondirect flights take more time, but if you can relax and consider the trip part of the travel adventure, it may be to your financial advantage.

45. **Inexpensive "cyberfares" are starting to get popular, too.**

They are very inexpensive tickets—a $900 round trip for, say, $139—sold by the airlines via their home pages on the Internet every Wednesday or Thursday for travel over the coming weekend. The fares usually require travel on Saturday with a return on the following Monday or Tuesday, and you often have to click on several buttons to jump to them from the home page. Once you find the cyberfares, the page tells you how to book. Some World Wide Web home pages:

• American Airlines: http://www.american-air.com
• Continental Airlines: *http://www.flycontinental.com*
• Northwest Airlines: *http://www.nwa.com*

46. Discounted airfares often come with special rules. For example, many are nonrefundable, and some airlines charge a fee for changing flights or dates once you've booked and paid. In addition, holding a reservation without a ticket does not guarantee a discount fare. You have to buy the ticket to be sure of the savings. Ask about the rules when you book.

47. Plan to avoid the pitfalls of airplane travel. For example:

• If you plan to travel during busy periods such as holidays, make sure you call for reservations early. Don't buy standby fares or open-return tickets—it may be difficult to find an unreserved seat on the plane.
• If on-time arrivals are important to you, ask the reservation agent to give you the on-time performance code for flights you are considering, and to explain them. This one-digit code shows how often the flight arrived on time.
• Look for the following on your ticket: "OK" means you're confirmed; a "through"

flight can have one or more stops; a four-digit flight number may mean you are booked on a commuter airline.
• Take along a photo ID when you go to the airport—it may be necessary for check-in—and be sure your ticket is issued in your name as it appears on that ID.
• Check your ticket as you board to ensure that only the correct coupon has been removed by the airline agent.

48. Get extra protection—pay for your ticket with a credit card. Under federal law, if a refund is requested for a ticket charged on a credit card, the airline must forward the refund to your card company within seven business days after receiving a completed refund application. But remember: Your charge account is billed whether you use your ticket or not; you won't receive credit unless the original unused ticket is returned to the airline. Many credit cards also include automatic free travel insurance when you use them to book tickets.

49. Lost tickets are negotiable documents. You can get a refund only if you can prove the ticket wasn't used. Before you travel, jot down the ticket number on a slip of paper and carry it separately from your ticket during your trip. Your ticket number may be shown on your credit card receipt or travel agency itinerary, and that number can be used as leverage should a refund be necessary.

50. Airlines don't guarantee their schedules. Some delays, such as bad weather, air traffic, and mechanical repairs, are hard to predict and are beyond the airlines' control. If your flight is canceled, most airlines will rebook you on their next flight to your destination on which space is available, at no additional charge.

Each airline has its own policies about what it will do for delayed passengers; there are no federal requirements. If you know you're flying into or out of an area with notoriously bad weather—say, Minnesota in the winter—ask about airline policies before you book. If you are delayed, ask the airline staff if they'll pay for meals or a phone call. Some airlines don't provide any amenities to stranded passengers.

51. Contrary to popular belief, airlines are *not* required to compensate passengers whose flights are delayed or canceled. Airlines almost always refuse to pay passengers for financial losses resulting from a delayed flight, so you may want to allow extra time by traveling earlier than absolutely necessary. When booking your flight, remember that a morning departure is less likely to be delayed than a later flight, due to the "ripple" effect throughout the day.

52. A much-traveled television news producer offers a tip for rebooking when flights are canceled:

Don't stand in line at the airport with all your fellow passengers from the canceled flight. Go to a nearby phone—or use your cell phone—to call the airline's reservation number. The agent on the line can often rebook you on another flight more quickly and easily than the agent behind the counter.

53. Overbooking isn't illegal—in fact, it's customary. Most airlines overbook their scheduled flights to compensate for "no-shows." As a result, a few passengers may be left behind, or "bumped." When overbooking occurs, the federal Department of Transportation (DOT) requires airlines to ask people who aren't in a hurry to give up their seats voluntarily in exchange for compensation.

With a few exceptions, passengers bumped against their will are entitled to compensation. DOT requires each airline to give all passengers who are involuntarily bumped a written statement describing their rights. Travelers who don't get to fly are frequently entitled to an on-the-spot payment.

54. If you can spare the time, volunteer to take the next flight. If you volunteer to take the next flight when a flight is overbooked, the airline may offer to send you free tickets to any of the destinations it serves.

55. Pack essential items in your carry-on bag. Be prepared in case your luggage gets mislaid. Your carry-on bag should contain those items that you'll need during the first twenty-four hours of your trip. They may include:

• Critical items—medicine, cash, credit cards, keys, passport, tour vouchers
• Personal items—eyeglasses, toothbrush and toiletries, a change of underwear
• Small valuables—jewelry, camera

56. Think carefully about what you pack in checked bags. That's because there are limits to luggage liability. Between the time you check your luggage in and the time you claim it at your destination, it may have passed through a maze of conveyor belts and baggage carts; once airborne, baggage may tumble around the cargo compartment if the plane hits rough air. If you plan to check any electrical equipment, appliances, pottery or glassware, musical instruments, or other fragile items, pack them in a container designed to survive rough handling. Professional musicians often buy a seat on the plane for their instruments. The cases ride in the seats, so their owners are sure of their treatment and safe arrival.

57. Relatively few bags are damaged or lost. Most misplaced bags turn up sooner or later. Still, it's a good idea to label all bags, inside and out, with your name, address, and phone number. Add the name and address of a person to contact at your destination. With proper labeling, you can be reunited with your bag in a few hours. If your luggage arrives open, unlocked, or damaged, check immediately to see if anything is missing or damaged. Report any problems to the airline before leaving the airport. If you notice a problem after you get to your hotel, call the airline immediately.

58. Most airlines have a ceiling of $1,250 per passenger on compensation for lost or damaged bags. If your luggage and its contents are worth more than that, consider purchasing "excess valuation" if it's available, or taking out special insurance.

59. Many travelers claim that there's a perpetual cold virus hiding in airplane air circulation systems, waiting to infect travelers. While that's not true, it is true that you are cooped up in close proximity to people who may have colds, and airplane air is dry, thus making you more susceptible to colds. The dryness can also reduce tear volume (especially when coupled with consumption of coffee and alcohol), leading to particular discomfort for contact lens wearers. Drink lots of juice or water, and bring along lubricating eyedrops.

60. Thanks to the Air Carrier Access Act, Americans with disabilities have the same opportunities for air travel as anyone else.

In addition to a provision that a person cannot be refused transportation because of a disability, the act requires the following.

• Airlines must provide assistance throughout the air travel experience.
• Airport terminals and reservation centers must have TDB telephones for hearing- or speech-impaired people.
• Passengers with those impairments must have timely access to the same information given other passengers.
• New wide-body aircraft must have a wheelchair-accessible lavatory and, if a passenger requests it forty-eight hours in advance, an onboard wheelchair.
• Air carriers must accept wheelchairs as checked baggage without requiring passengers to sign liability waivers.

• Carriers must allow service animals to accompany passengers in the cabin, as long as they don't block aisles or emergency evacuation routes.

In addition, most new planes have movable armrests on half the aisle seats and on-board stowage for one folding passenger wheelchair.

The U.S. Office of Consumer Affairs, Pueblo, CO 81009, offers a free booklet entitled "Access Travel: Handicapped Services at Over 500 Airports."

61. You can minimize the effects of jet lag. Here are some hints from seasoned travelers.

• Get several good nights' sleep before your trip.
• Take a flight that arrives at night so you can go straight to bed. If your flight arrives in the morning, try to get outside for a few hours. Sunshine helps to reset your body clock.
• Sleep on the plane.
• Move around during the flight; do isometric exercises; and drink little or no alcohol.
• Reset your watch immediately after takeoff to help yourself get in tune with the new time periods.

62. When passengers complain, most transportation companies listen. As a rule, airlines have troubleshooters at the airports who can take care of many problems on the spot. This includes securing meals and hotel rooms for stranded passengers, arranging

for luggage repairs, and settling small claims for compensation. If you have a larger problem, or are unable to resolve a dispute, call or write the airline's consumer office at its corporate headquarters. At the time of the incident, take notes about what happens and jot down the names of employees with whom you deal. Save your travel documents (tickets, receipts, baggage checks, etc.) as well as receipts for any out-of-pocket expenses.

63. There's an art to writing a letter of complaint. Here are some tips.

• Describe the situation. Include the names of any employees who were rude or who made matters more difficult. Don't bother with petty gripes.
• State exactly what you expect the carrier to do to make amends. Be reasonable.
• Type the letter and try to keep it to one page in length.
• No matter how angry you are, keep your letter businesslike in tone.
• Include your daytime telephone number.

64. If your complaint is about a safety hazard, contact the Federal Aviation Administration.

Community and Consumer Liaison Division, APA-200
Federal Aviation Administration
800 Independence Ave. SW
Washington, DC 20591
800-255-1111

If you need further assistance, call or write:

Office of Consumer Affairs
U.S. Department of Transportation
400 7th St. SW
Washington, DC 20590
888-279-7718

65. Do you need travel insurance? If you book a nonrefundable, nontransferable flight, you might want to consider taking out travel insurance. This protects you if you need to cancel your plans at the last minute because of sickness or some other emergency. Most airlines will require proof of your problem (such as a letter from a doctor) before they will pay out the insurance. As with any other type of insurance, you need to weigh the risks in order to decide whether you want to spend the money. There are also policies available that will cover you in the event of serious illness or injury while traveling, if your current health policy doesn't cover that already.

66. If you're dealing with a charter-flight company or travel packager, read your contract carefully. Don't make any payments without knowing what may be involved. If you have any doubts about a company's reputation, run its name by your local Better Business Bureau. You can also check with the consumer affairs office of the American Society of Travel Agents, 1101 King St., Suite 200, Alexandria, VA 22314; 703-739-2782.

67. If you're traveling abroad for the first time—or haven't gone recently—take some time to prepare in advance.

• Apply for your passport as soon as possible—at least three months before departure.
• If you're headed for remote locales, check the State Department's travel advisories through a local passport office. They warn of serious health or security conditions.
• Check with your travel agent or with the U.S. Public Health Service for information on immunizations that might be needed in countries you will visit.
• Make sure you have enough medicine for the trip, and take it along in its original containers. Bring copies of your prescriptions, and if you have an unusual one, carry a letter from your doctor explaining the need for the drug. For extra security, carry the generic names of your medications, too. If you wear eyeglasses, take along an extra pair.

68. When traveling in foreign countries, carry only a few days' worth of cash. Take most of your money in traveler's checks. Convert your traveler's checks to local currency as you need it rather than all at once. You may also want to bring at least one internationally recognized credit card; leave others at home. If you carry jewelry or other valuables, use hotel security vaults to store them. It's also wise to register such items with U.S. Customs so there's no question of paying duty on them when you come home.

69. Try to buy a small amount of foreign currency before leaving the United States. It will come in handy for incidental expenses such as tips and taxis when you first arrive. Foreign currency can be purchased from major banks or from foreign exchange dealers. A tip once you are abroad: Local banks generally give more favorable rates of exchange than hotels, restaurants, or stores.

70. Take good care of your passport—it confirms your identity and citizenship. Don't carry it in the same place as your money, and don't pack it in your suitcase. Most luggage stores sell a "passport pouch," worn around the neck and under your clothes. But don't be concerned if in some countries you are required to leave your passport with the hotel management; a reputable hotel will return it. If your passport is lost or stolen, report it immediately to the local police. Obtain a copy of that report, and contact the nearest U.S. embassy or consulate to apply for a new passport. If there are any major difficulties, ask to speak to a U.S. consular officer.

71. There's an art to carrying your wallet, purse, or camera bag to prevent being robbed. Tuck totes under an arm rather than letting them dangle from your shoulder. Carry valuables in an inside front pocket or in a money belt, not in a hip pocket. Wrap your wallet with rubber bands to make it more difficult for someone to slip it from your pocket. Money belts or pouches that fit around your shoulder or waist are available through travel magazines and at some luggage shops; skier's wallets that hang around the neck inside the clothes are also good.

72. Traveler's diarrhea is caused by food and water that contain bacteria foreign to your system. We all have bacteria in our intestinal track. But travelers are ingesting bacteria that are new to their digestive systems, and they lack the protective antibodies to fight it. Avoiding the problem is as simple as staying away from:

• Tap water. And don't use it to brush your teeth.
• Ice made from tap water
• Unpasteurized dairy products
• Raw fruit or vegetables unless you peel them yourself
• Lettuce or other leafy raw vegetables
• Rare meat or fish
• Food sold by street vendors

You can generally rely on carbonated soft drinks from a newly opened bottle, and hot drinks such as tea or coffee. Well-done meat and other cooked foods should be safe, too.

73. The Centers for Disease Control recommends a special "cocktail" to combat traveler's diarrhea. Combine the following in one glass: eight ounces of orange, apple, or other fruit juice (rich in potassium, which is lost in diarrhea); one-half teaspoon of honey or corn syrup (useful for absorbing essential salts); a pinch of salt (contains sodium and chloride, which are lost). In a second glass, combine eight ounces of boiled or carbonated water and one-quarter teaspoon of baking soda. Drink alternately from each glass. Supplement with carbonated beverages, boiled water, or tea. Avoid solid food and milk until you have recovered.

74. For more information on travel opportunities and groups that cater to mature adults, contact:

AARP Travel Services
1909 K St. NW
Washington, DC 20049
800-424-3410
Offers about 250 tours for members and their families.

Elderhostel
75 Federal St., 3rd Floor
Boston, MA 02110-1941
617-426-8056
Elderhostel combines travel with education. Its purpose is to join older adults with similar interests for study on college campuses, here and abroad. See page 31 for more on Elderhostel.

Grand Circle Travel
347 Congress St.
Boston, MA 02210
800-221-2610
Grand Circle's escorted tours provide a good balance between structured activities and free time.

75. Another source of free travel information:

Superintendent of Documents
P.O. Box 371954
Pittsburgh, PA 15250-7954
202-512-1800

Booklets include "Your Trip Abroad: Customs, Shots, Insurance"; "A Safe Trip Abroad"; and "Travel Tips for Older Americans."

76. For information about protecting yourself while traveling, call your local Better Business Bureau, or contact:

U.S. Customs Service
1301 Constitution Ave. NW
P.O. Box 7404
Washington, DC 20044
202-927-6724
Ask for its free booklet, "Know Before You Go."

Federal Trade Commission
6th St. and Pennsylvania Ave. NW
Washington, DC 20044
202-326-2222
Offers a free pamphlet, "Telemarketing Travel Fraud."

Hobbies, Pursuits, and Relaxations

77. So what did you do for fun as a kid? Did you collect baseball cards, and are they still in the basement somewhere? Were you once a dab hand with a band saw or a sewing machine? Have you always wanted to read those novels you skimmed in college? With growing blocks of leisure at your disposal as you age, it's time to think back to what gave you pleasure before you worked fifty hours a week and carpooled endlessly, because those earlier memories are a good place to find inspiration for the present and for the future.

78. Collecting can provide pleasure in both the hunt and the acquisition. Collections can range from stamps and coins to ceramic villages and beer cans. In July 1997 the *Wall Street Journal* featured people who collect firecracker labels.

Collections often start with the acquisition of one special piece—often at a tag sale or flea market—and take off from there. There is often study involved as collectors try to find out more about their passion. Many collectors form clubs and publish newsletters. Check with your library or local antique shops for referrals.

79. Collections can appreciate in value over the years. A Barbie doll collection garnered several hundred thousand dollars when sold at auction not long ago, and some stamp and coin collections, started by older relatives and continued over a lifetime, can also be very valuable. We think that collecting is best done for the love of it, but if you want to assess the value of what you've assembled, do a lot of research. Check with your library for books on the items you collect. Consult a professional appraiser or auction house. Check price lists in publications dedicated to your subject (the prices given are often retail ones). Scout antique shows and conventions to get a feeling of value. Dealers can help, too, since they often purchase collections as well as sell them, but be aware that selling an entire collection may fetch less than if pieces were sold singly.

80. Former President Jimmy Carter said that upon retiring to Plains, Georgia, making chairs was the most relaxing of his activities. That's probably because working with your hands, especially if you spent your job-centered years working with your brain, can be surprisingly satisfying as you age. Besides, if you're good at woodworking, throwing pots, or stitching quilts, you've got ready-made gifts for holidays, birthdays, and weddings. Most communities support a number of places where you can get started, and later learn advanced crafting skills—everywhere from adult education programs, to senior centers and local agencies on aging, to artisans groups. Most states also have a central coordinating group for arts and crafts programs that you can contact for information (check with your local librarian for the phone number). Craft suppliers will sometimes provide free supplies to programs for senior craftspeople.

 81. Millions of Americans are interested in genealogy.

It's an enthusiasm that seems to increase with age as we start thinking about where it all began for us. State and city historical societies, back issues of newspapers in the local library, church marriage and birth records, deeds and wills in the local government offices, are the places to start.

The magazine below will help you get started; it's also a good source for locating a professional genealogist.

Everton's Genealogical Helper
P.O. Box 368
Logan, UT 84323
800-443-6325

82. The National Archives in Washington, DC, allows access to all census records up to around 1910. These can be a big help in a genealogical search. The archives maintain extensive military records and immigration and passenger ship arrival records from major ports dating back to the early nineteenth century. The ships' logs, for example, consist of two-by-three-foot sheets listing the passengers' age, language spoken, their height and weight, and the amount of money they brought with them on the voyage. The archives offer a research service if you need the help. The cost for a ship's log research and copying, for example, is $10. Contact:

Reference Services Branch
National Archives and Records
Administration
7th St. and Pennsylvania Ave. NW
Washington, DC 20408-0001
202-501-5400

83. The National Archives can also help you trace your roots. Write:

National Archives Trust Fund Board
Box 129
National Archives and Records Administration
7th St. and Pennsylvania Ave. NW
Washington, DC 20408
Other sources of help and information:

Family History Library
Church of Jesus Christ of Latter-day Saints
35 NW Temple St.
Salt Lake City, UT 84150
801-240-3435
This library is the largest of its kind in the world, and the research staff is well trained. Worldwide branches are open to the public.

U.S. Department of Health and Human Services
6525 Bellcrest Rd., Room 1064
Presidential Building
Hyattsville, MD 20782
301-435-8500
Publishes "Where to Write for Vital Records."

84. Did you love chess as a child, bridge as a college student? Games keep your intellectual skills honed and provide competition along with the fun. To get back into one of these games, contact:

American Contract Bridge League
National Headquarters
P.O. Box 161192
Memphis, TN 38186
901-332-5586
800-467-1623

United States Chess Federation
3054 New York State Route 9W
New Windsor, NY 12550
914-562-8350
800-388-5464

85. Become a filmmaker, with help from the NEA. If they approve of the content of your film, of course. Grant caps range from $20,000 to $37,500 and are available for films documenting everything from traditional bread-baking methods to dulcimer-playing. There are also grants for storytellers, monologists, actors, directors, writers, poets, translators, painters, sculptors, photographers, printmakers, and illustrators. The grants are for both community groups and individuals.

National Endowment for the Arts
1100 Pennsylvania Ave. NW, Room 710
Washington, DC 20506
202-682-5449

86. The most popular hobby in America is gardening. Half of all Americans over 50 say they enjoy it. What's not to like? Gardening gives you a great excuse to be outdoors and rewards your work with beauty and bounty. It's good exercise, to boot.

And you don't have to do it alone. There are garden clubs for enthusiasts. Your local county cooperative extension service probably has a horticulture hotline where you can talk to certified master gardeners; you can even bring in samples of ailing plants for diagnosis. Information about gardening without harmful chemicals is available from:

Environmental Protection Agency
Information Resources Center
401 M St. SW, Room M2904
Washington, DC 20460
202-260-7751

87. Gardens don't just have to be outdoors, either. Ferns, poinsettias, African violets, chrysanthemums, and hundreds of other plants are all suitable for indoor gardening. Get started on making an indoor "jungle" by getting books from the local library or information from nearby garden centers and the county cooperative extension service.

Additional help is available from the Horticulture Services Division of the Smithsonian Institution. It has a series of fact sheets, which include information on fertilization, propagation, and potential problems. Write:

Horticulture Services Division
Arts and Industries Building
Room 2282, MRC 420
Smithsonian Institution
Washington, DC 20560
202-357-1926

88. In 1927 Leo W. Nack entered and won an annual garden contest.

The resulting publicity made his forty-five-by-sixty-foot garden plot an attraction, and he noticed that many of its admirers were men. As a result, Nack formed the Men's Garden Club. The group now publishes a national magazine and provides a lending library, audiovisual rental, and scholarships; it even has an annual convention. It also gets involved with nursing homes and youth gardening. For more information, contact:

The Gardeners of America/Men's Garden
Club of America
5560 Merle Hay Rd.

P.O. Box 241
Johnston, IA 50131
515-278-0295

89. Garden clubs aren't just about flower arranging and backyard plots. They're also concerned with land protection and conservation, and they work actively for those causes. The National Council of State Garden Clubs, Inc., whose motto is "A Force for Good," has 8,488 member clubs and 250,000 individual members who work to protect wetlands, floodplains, and the ecosystem, in addition to pursuing traditional gardening and floral designs. For more information, contact:

National Council of State Garden Clubs
4401 Magnolia Ave.
St. Louis, MO 63110
314-776-7574

90. In many communities, the old-time quilting bee is alive and well. If you're handy with a needle and a sewing machine, you may want to find one and join in. A local fabric or craft shop or the cooperative extension service is the place to begin looking for sewing groups and classes, and they can also be a jumping-off place to all kinds of other crafts. Fabric stores are transforming themselves into craft centers these days, and many offer classes to go along with their products. The extension service also has workbooks and videos about sewing. Call your local office, or write:

Extension Service
U.S. Department of Agriculture

Room 3328
Washington, DC 20250

91. Lightweight, flexible power tools have made woodworking the hobby of choice for men and women alike. Children's toys and small pieces of furniture are among the most popular projects. Several magazines are directed to woodworkers at every level of skill. Libraries also have project books featuring complete sets of plans. Need some training to get started? Watch adult education bulletins from public school systems and community colleges. See what's available at your local hardware store, lumberyard, or big national home-improvement center. Retailers of all stripes are learning that teaching the customer via classes and in-store advice keeps us coming back in and buying.

92. Compile a written record of your life. It isn't necessary to have a photographic memory for names, dates, and facts to record your thoughts, adventures, ideas, and even recipes. You can reconstruct events with diaries, letters, photographs, invitations, announcements, report cards, newspaper items, and anything else you've treasured over the years. Consider the possibilities of old neckties or dresses—photograph them and write notes on when they were worn, by whom, and the significance of the event. A recipe collection can include notes on how the dish is served, who in the family likes it, and how it evolved over the years. A review of your employment history might include your responsibilities and bonuses and promotions as well as memoirs about coworkers who became good friends.

93. A life history, written or compiled, will make a fine keepsake for the family. But more than that, it can help you view—and review—your life as a whole with all its patterns and purposes. A history can help you recognize that your story has unity, uniqueness, and worth. Novelists and playwrights are always doing that kind of review with their characters. John Updike, for example, has aged Harry "Rabbit" Angstrom in his books over the years. Wendy Wasserstein, who wrote about young women when she was young, put women in their 50s on the Broadway stage—successfully—in *The Sisters Rosensweig* as she began to age. Why should you be any different?

94. Set yourself a reading project—how about all those murder mysteries that feature detectives of age? To get you started, here are two we like (a good mystery bookstore can help you find others):

• Agatha Christie's Miss Marple. Although old, Miss Marple is very, very saavy.
• Evelyn E. Smith's Miss Susan Melville. She's a New York heiress and painter whose father taught her to shoot when she was a young girl. In the first novel, she's, well, a paid assassin. The puzzles are good, and the moral justifications interesting. Read the first one, *Miss Melville Regrets* (1986), first. There are three more.

 95. Spend time with people who like to read.

Big bookstores often have cafés inside, as well as comfortable chairs and couches throughout the store, all designed to encourage lounging with books you may end up buying. Most of the larger chains present lectures on topics from finances to New Age spirituality, in addition to hosting book signings, live jazz, and folk music on weekend afternoons. Many have separate book discussion groups for romance, mystery, science fiction, and new fiction. Visit a Borders, Encore, Barnes & Noble, or other large bookstore near you, and pick up a calendar of events.

96. You can have fun on a computer even without knowing how it works. Computers can be a wonderful connection to the world. They can be used successfully by just following step-by-step procedures, as you may have already noticed from using catalog computers at the public library.

Yes, they're a sizable financial investment—from several hundred to several thousand dollars, depending on the systems you choose—and you'll also have to pay for some software, plus monthly fees to one of the services that hook you to the Internet. But there's an almost immediate payback as you stretch your mind and get connected.

97. If you need help with a computer, call a kid. The store where you buy your equipment will help you set it up, and there are dozens of how-to-use-a-computer books. Classes for beginners are available at many places, especially in adult education courses at schools and the local Y. Even copy centers such as Kinko's—who want to eventually sell you computer time—offer classes. If you just want to get your feet wet, many local libraries offer access to the Internet, and the librarian will be happy to get you started on it.

But our best advice is to use a kid—if not for initial training and setup, then for everything else. Young people today are cyber-savvy, and working with them can be a sweet and personal way to connect to a grandchild or a young neighbor.

98. Cruise the Internet or e-mail the grandchildren. You don't have to be a computer genius to get connected and start experimenting. Nothing will break if you push the wrong button, and in most cases, all you waste is time.

You can search for family names in both Vietnam and Civil War archives. You can also buy books via the Internet *(http://www.amazon.com)* and poke around in the New York Public Library files for fun and information *(http://www.nypl.org)*.

E-mail just may revive the art of letter writing, albeit electronically. Many parents keep in touch with their kids at college by using the service; you can keep in touch with friends across the sea without the cost of an international phone call. The on-line directory may even turn up an e-mail address for an old roommate, a long-lost cousin, or a childhood friend.

 99. There are many on-line services for older adults, and chat rooms to talk to like-minded people in real time.

Here are a few addresses to get you started.

• Age of Reason. Information and preselected connections to other Websites of interest to the older age group *(http://www.ageofreason.com)*.
• Guide to Retirement Living Online. Offers information on just that *(http://www.retirement-living.com)*.
• SeniorNet. Designed to help older adults learn to use computers and to enhance their lives by using on-line services such as e-mail, bulletin boards, health information, discounts, and news databases *(http://www.seniornet.com)*.
• Senior Resource. Even more information for older adults *(http://www.seniorresource.com)*.

If you'd rather start by writing or calling, contact SeniorNet at:

University of San Francisco
Computer Services
1 Kearny St., 3rd Floor
San Francisco, CA 94108
800-747-6848

Lifelong Learning

100. Seniors are proving daily that education is not just for the young. While AARP doesn't track older adults returning to school, its representative told the *New York Times* in June 1997 that it is "a growing trend." Several years ago, when the University of Delaware began giving tuition discounts to older students, the number of undergraduates over 60 rose from 76 to 107 over five years, and the number of older graduate students went from 35 to 68. The trend was even the subject of a television sitcom aired during the 1996–97 season. *Pearl* starred Rhea Pearlman as a clearly middle-aged, working-class woman taking a university philosophy class. When Gail Sheehy was preparing research for *New Passages,* her exploration of life cycles from age 40 to 70 and beyond, her surveys found that women who scored high on "well-being" were also well educated. Similarly, among women in their middle years, she found "an almost universal yearning" to go back to school, whatever the level.

101. Many older Americans continue their education by going back to the basics. Seventy years ago, as the Depression approached, many American youngsters started work before graduating from high school. Later, many went off to World War II without finishing school and were never able to complete their education. As a result, according to the National Center for Education Statistics, 36 percent of Americans 55 and over don't have a high school diploma, and one in five older citizens is functionally illiterate.

There are now a number of excellent literacy programs for people over 50. To find out about those in your area, call local high schools and libraries.

102. The best way to earn a high school diploma is by passing the General Educational Development Test (GED). GED preparation classes are offered in most public school systems during the regular school year. Passing the test means earning a high school diploma from your state department of education. For more information, look for "Adult Education" or "Continuing Education" in the local government or school listings in your phone book. Practice books, and more information, can be obtained from:

Southeast Community College
GED—The Learning Line
8800 O St., Room L3
Lincoln, NE 68520
402-437-2716

103. So what about the "old dog, new tricks" syndrome?

Well, it doesn't seem to bother a fair number of older adults who find their names featured in stories in their local newspapers every spring when they don caps and gowns and receive degrees of one kind or another. Studies show that one out of every ten people continues to increase in mental abilities, such as vocabulary, through every decade. While the brain does shrink with age, new imaging techniques show that it doesn't shrink nearly as much as was previously thought. Furthermore, reduction does not necessarily result in loss of mental ability. Studies also indicate that the more you use your brain in challenging ways—such as learning new skills—the less memory loss occurs.

104. Trade and technical schools can be a good place to learn new skills—and to retrain for a new career. These institutions usually have good instructors, modern equipment, and excellent job placement services, and they teach everything from commercial food preparation to computer programming. To find out more about accredited trade and technical schools, check with your state department of education.

105. It's easier these days for older adults to pursue a college degree. Colleges often award credit for the knowledge and experience acquired over a lifetime. One method of acquiring that credit is the College Level Examination Program (CLEP). CLEP tests are administered at numerous locations nationwide during the third week of each month. For information, contact:

Educational Testing Service
P.O. Box 6600
Princeton, NJ 08541
609-771-7865

106. Financial aid is available for adults returning to school. Older students are eligible for a wide variety of scholarships, grants, and loans. Many states even waive tuition to state universities for students over 60 or 65 years of age if those students meet other requirements. To find out what's available in your state, call or write your state department of education. Federal funding may also be available. More than 7 million undergraduates receive some form of federal aid every year,

and minorities, union members, veterans, military personnel and their families, women, and persons with disabilities may qualify for additional help. For information, contact:

U.S. Department of Education
Federal Student Aid Information Center
P.O. Box 84
Washington, DC 20044
800-433-3243

107. From Cicero to computers, politics to poetry, Elderhostel offers an inexpensive, short-term learning and travel adventure. In 1966 more than 323,000 people studied and traveled with the twenty-year-old program, living on college campuses around the world and enjoying the cultural and recreational resources that are part of academic life. Adults 55 or older are eligible. Participants' spouses of any age are welcome; companions of age-eligible participants must be at least 50. The courses are not for credit, so you don't need any specific prior educational background. There are no exams or grades, and no homework or preparatory work, except in intensive programs. For information, contact:

Elderhostel
75 Federal St., 3rd Floor
Boston, MA 02110
617-426-8056

108. Interhostel works in much the way as Elderhostel. It provides an educational and travel adventure with an enhanced awareness of other cultures. Most of its fifty programs are international and last for two weeks—long enough to get a taste of life in a foreign land. Excursions to historic and cultural sites enhance the classroom experience. For more information, contact:

Interhostel
University of New Hampshire
6 Garrison Ave.
Durham, NH 03824
800-733-9753

 109. Delve into Joan Rattner Heilman's *Unbelievably Good Deals and Great Adventures That You Absolutely Can't Get Unless You're Over 50* **(Contemporary Books, 1996).**

While you have to put up with a very long book title, Heilman offers addresses and phone numbers for adult education programs at the likes of Harvard, Duke, American, and other universities. She's got great travel information, too.

110. If you're an art lover, contact the National Gallery of Art. They will provide color slides, films, and more to individuals or groups who want a complete program of art education. These are offered as a long-term loan for noncommercial use to organizations such as schools, resource centers, museums, libraries, and community-access television stations. For a catalog and more information, write:

Department of Education Resources
Education Division

National Gallery of Art
4th St. and Constitution Ave. NW
Washington, DC 20565

111. For general information on education, contact:

Adult Education Association of the United States
810 18th St. NW
Washington, DC 20036
202-624-5250

American Association of Retired Persons
Special Projects Program Coordination and Development
601 E St. NW
Washington, DC 20049
Ask for "The Back-to-School Money Book" (D15400).

National Association of Partners in Education
209 Madison St., Suite 401
Alexandria, VA 22314

CEDAM (Conservation, Education, Diving, Archaeology, Museums)
Fox Rd.
Croton-on-Hudson, NY 10520
914-271-5365; 603-862-1147

Smithsonian National Associates
Smithsonian Institution
1100 Jefferson Dr. SW, Room 304S
Washington, DC 20560
202-357-4700

Work for Pay

112. If you don't want to stop working—or can't afford to—join the not-quite-retired club. It's growing every day. In the decade from 1987 to 1997, the 65-and-older workforce grew by nearly a million, making it 3 percent of the total American workforce. Many people are supplementing their retirement incomes; others are supplementing their psychic incomes, that is, enhancing their emotional well-being. And studies have shown that, with the exception of jobs requiring rough physical labor, older workers perform as well as younger ones.

113. Older workers seem to be popping up everywhere. They're in charge of cash registers at McDonald's as part of its McMasters program; they're the subject of a Wal-Mart commercial as one mature employee, known for good service, teases an older friend. Older workers juggle reservations for Days Inn; they are 25 percent of temp agency Manpower, Inc.'s workforce. The Travelers Corporation has been reemploying retirees since the 1970s, and by the early 1990s it had formed a temp agency within the company using primarily older workers.

At the other end of the income spectrum, the *Wall Street Journal* reported in June 1997 that the rehiring of older executives for high-profile and tough top jobs is a trend. Its chief example was PepsiCo, Inc., which recalled 72-year-old Andrall E. Pearson to run its restaurant business when it prepared to spin off the operation as a separate company.

114. A survey of almost one thousand companies found that 58 percent of them employed retirees.

Some deliberately sought older workers; others took them from the normal labor pool. Almost 72 percent offered pension benefits to the older workers, while 35 percent included health care. According to a 1996 issue of *New Science* magazine, it is "common knowledge" among human resources directors that older workers are exceptionally reliable, have a good work ethic, and have good skills and knowledge. They can be cheaper to employ than younger workers because they cost less to train, cause fewer management problems, and are less likely to resign.

115. If you want to go back to work, ask your old company about part-time employment. There's a good reason that many companies keep older executives on their boards of directors. And line employees can be valuable for their knowledge of the workings of the company in the trenches.

116. Perhaps you'd like to change gears completely. Maybe your neighborhood needs a small repair shop; perhaps the home-based businesses around you could use a computer consultant or part-time secretarial services. You could hire yourself out as a grandmother or grandfather to house-sit, watch children, walk dogs, prepare a freezer full of frozen casseroles for families with two working parents. Seamstress or tailor services seem always in demand. If you're good with a camera and lights, there are children and pets to photograph.

117. It's also worth examining what you already enjoy doing. If you like to garden, you could sell plants, herbs, seeds, or dried floral arrangements. If you farm in any way, you might sell honey, wine, fruits and preserves, or Christmas trees.

Many believe there's a significant untapped market for handicrafts, and if you're clever at what you make, you may be able to sell your crafts. Local fairs and church bazaars are good places to test-market your products. Approach a retail store to sell them on consignment; if you have original designs or patterns, a retailer might buy your work outright. Contact craft magazines or craft newsletters, since they might be a market for your patterns or designs. Native Americans can find outlets for their crafts through the Indians Arts and Crafts Board, U.S. Department of the Interior, Washington, DC 20240.

118. For information about how to sell your creations, contact:

Elder Craftsmen
921 Madison Ave.
New York, NY 10021
212-861-5260
This nonprofit group teaches some crafts such as wood carving and needlework; it manages a retail shop in New York where handcrafted items are sold on a consignment basis; and it advises on selling crafts.

American Home Business Association
60 Arch St.
Greenwich, CT 06830
203-531-8552

Service Corps of Retired Executives
(SCORE)
1825 Connecticut Ave. NW, Suite 503
Washington, DC 20009
202-653-6279

Work for Pleasure— Volunteer

119. Jimmy Carter didn't spend all his time making chairs once he left the White House. In the late 1980s and early 1990s the elder statesman started turning up all over the world as a volunteer negotiator representing the U.S. government and resolving conflicts in Panama, Ethiopia, Nicaragua, Somalia, North Korea, and Haiti. And that's not to mention his work building houses with Habitat for Humanity.

It's a volunteer model to emulate. Perhaps with the previous pressures of work and family, you've not been able to give your church, synagogue, or community the time you would like. Now you can. A good place to start looking for opportunities to help is the government listings for the local office of the Retired and Senior Volunteer Program (RSVP) or your city or county office of human resources or services.

120. Here are some contacts to get you started in volunteering.

Points of Light Foundation
Volunteer Referral Service
1737 H St. NW
Washington, DC 20006
800-879-5400
They will refer you to the Volunteer Center in your area, which in turn will let you know where help is most needed in your community.

AmeriCorps VISTA
1201 New York Ave. NW
Washington, DC 20525
202-606-5000
800-424-8867 (National Senior Service call information hotline)
This federal agency administers domestic volunteer programs, including Retired and Senior Volunteer Program (RSVP), Senior Corps, the Foster Grandparent Program, the Senior Companion Program, and others.

National Health Information Center
P.O. Box 1133
Washington, DC 20013-1133
800-336-4797
Lists organizations and self-help and support groups for getting involved in helping to care for the sick.

121. Hit the brochure rack at the local library.

The need for volunteers is increasing, especially as public money for social services declines. On a recent trip to the library, we found solicitations for school volunteers, for work with children in general, for a local nonprofit thrift shop, and for the local office of SCORE—the Service Corps of Retired Executives, sponsored by the Small Business Administration.

Or work with the organizations or professional societies in your industry. In the summer of 1997 the AFL-CIO recruited retired members to work as volunteers at union organizing sites around the country.

 122. If you're a member of AARP, you can register with its Volunteer Talent Bank.

It's a referral service that matches the skills and interests of people over 50 with the needs of AARP projects and with other national organizations such as Special Olympics International, the U.S. Forest Service, Habitat for Humanity, and Big Brothers/Big Sisters of America. For more information, contact:

Volunteer Talent Bank
AARP
601 E St. NW
Washington, DC 20049
202-434-3219
800-424-3410 x3219

123. If you love animals, help out at your local humane society. Or, find a local organization that cares for the pets of those too sick to do so. If your nursing home or hospital doesn't already have a program whereby animals are brought to visit the residents or the children's ward, you could start one. The sight and touch of a loving animal is a tonic for the spirit.

124. If business is your forte, investigate SCORE. Sponsored by the Small Business Administration, the Service Corps of Retired Executives advises nonprofit organizations, especially in the areas of health care, social services, education, culture, and religion. For more information, contact:

Service Corps of Retired Executives (SCORE)
409 3rd St. SW, 6th Floor
Washington, DC 20024
202-205-6762
800-634-0245

National Executive Service Corps
257 Park Ave. S.
New York, NY 10010
212-529-6660

125. There are many opportunities to help care for children, the sick, and the elderly. Check with your church or synagogue for an idea of what needs doing; local government human services offices or social service agencies will also know. Two national programs with offices around the country:

National Court Appointed Special Advocate Association (CASA)
100 W. Harrison St.
North Tower, Suite 500
Seattle, WA 98119-4123
800-628-3233

Its volunteers support children caught in the foster care system by reviewing case records, interviewing adults involved, and speaking for children at court hearings.

Family Friends
National Council on Aging
409 3rd St. SW, Suite 200
Washington, DC 20024
202-479-1200
Family Friends assists chronically ill or disabled children and their families by doing everything from lending emotional support to providing leisure activities and personal care.

126. Become a Senior Companion. This program offers seniors the chance to assist older people who have physical, mental, or emotional disabilities in daily living skills. Volunteers also aid the homebound, Alzheimer's victims, and people who have just been released from the hospital.

National Health Information Center
P.O. Box 1133
Washington, DC 20013
800-336-4797

127. The scientifically inclined can lend assistance to astronomers and biologists. The American Association of Variable Star Observers uses amateur astronomers to help collect and compile information, and provides volunteers with charts and instructions on how to gauge a variable star's brightness.

Oceanic Society Expeditions is a nonprofit organization concerned with conservation problems and threatened species. Paying volunteers are trained on-site and work alongside biologists in the field.

American Association of Variable Star
Observers
25 Birch St.
Cambridge, MA 02138
617-354-0484

Oceanic Society Expeditions (OSE)
Fort Mason Center, Building E
San Francisco, CA 94123
800-326-7491

128. If you are African American, learn more about your heritage—and help others do so, too. A large collection of photographs of African art and life is available from the Eliot Elisofon Photographic Archives. You can set up a showing in your town. It's a wonderful way to inspire interest in American history and African American identity. A guide to the collection and a catalog and price list are available from:

National Museum of African Arts
Smithsonian Institution
950 Independence Ave. SW
Washington, DC 20560
202-357-1300

129. Organize a group dedicated to Pueblo pottery, Appalachian fiddling, or cowboy poetry. The Folk and Traditional Arts Program of the National Endowment for the Arts (NEA) can help you. It makes matching grants to nonprofit, tax-exempt groups such as community and cultural organizations, tribes, schools, libraries, and professional associations for artists' guilds. Application forms and additional information are available from:

Folk and Traditional Arts Program
National Endowment for the Arts
Nancy Hanks Center
1100 Pennsylvania Ave. NW, Room 710
Washington, DC 20506
202-682-5449

130. Take a group of seniors to an art exhibit or concert. Any arts group that receives money from the National Endowment for the Arts must make low-cost tickets available to people of age. If you know of any local happenings funded by the NEA, call up and ask for the discount.

131. Become a political activist. Individuals can make a difference by working in political campaigns or even running for office. Become informed about local issues, such as new construction, education, or waste removal, by reading and by attending public meetings. Check the "Meetings," "Calendar," or "Events" section of your newspaper for the times and places that various groups will meet.

132. Save the environment. The Sierra Club has several local chapters in every state. Monthly meetings often feature films or speakers on environmental issues. They also have regular outings, usually within an hour of the chapter's locale, which range from bird-watching walks to kayaking, at skill levels from beginner to advanced. Some chapters even offer "Seniors Only" or "Bring Along a Grandchild" hikes. To find a chapter near you, contact:

Sierra Club National Headquarters
85 2nd St.
San Francisco, CA 94015
415-977-5653

133. Save the world. Amnesty International is a Nobel Prize–winning organization whose goal is to end human rights abuses worldwide. It often focuses on cases that involve artists, journalists, and other intellectuals who have been imprisoned for their political beliefs. Because most college campuses have their own chapter, other local groups boast a substantial number of over-55'ers. If you enjoy discussing international politics and want to make a difference, contact:

Amnesty International, USA
322 8th Ave., 10th Floor
New York, NY 10001-0398
212-807-8400

Chapter 3:

Where and How You Live

So where and how do you plan to live for the next thirty or so years?

Chances are, you'll live in several different places and in many different ways as time unfolds. If you're around 55 now, you're prob-ably parked for the near future, but when re-tirement comes, you may want to do what you've always threatened to do—get out of that cold climate; move away from that big yard; toss out that furniture!

You may dream of living year-round at a lakeside cabin or of buying a condo in sunny Florida—with extra space for visiting kids and grandkids. Maybe inexpensive housing in an urban area, close to shopping, public trans-portation, medical care, and friends, is more your style. Or you may want to stay right where you are, in the house that you love.

This chapter is designed to help you think through your options for housing. If you haven't been house- or apartment-hunting in a couple of decades, you may need a re-fresher course. To that end, we've included some general information that would be use-ful to people of any age group.

You'll also find facts, tips, and suggestions on other big issues that relate to how you live—cars, driving, and safety, for example—as you age.

Dwelling on Dwellings

134. A word to the wise: Change is never easy. It can be exciting, stimulating, and necessary, but it is rarely comfortable, and changing where you live is one of the biggest changes you can make. It's among the top ten stress-causers every time someone does a new sur-vey of such things. That ranking in itself is good enough reason to think hard, go slowly, and study up before packing up and moving out.

135. Ponder the financial ramifications of living in a house during the next third of your life. You may want to buy a house for the social as well as the emotional benefits of home ownership, but you're thinking of moving to something smaller and easier to keep up. If so, ask yourself a lot of questions: How will I finance a new house? Can I build equity in my home? Can I project far enough into the future to be sure I want to take on long-term debt? Can I sustain a mortgage payment month after month, year after year? Will owning a home protect me against inflation?

136. Or think for a minute about rentals. The major drawbacks of apartment dwelling are financial (you're not building equity in a home; your rent may go up every year) and personal (there are limits to how much you can customize your living space). On the other hand, you won't be responsible for yard work or home maintenance; moving out is simply a matter of giving your landlord the required notice (no termite inspections, no waiting for someone to buy it).

Maybe you'd like something more than an apartment, but less than a house. If that's the case, you might want to consider owning a condominium, co-op, or mobile home.

137. Location is everything. Would you like to change cities, states, or countries, not to mention climates, at the same time you change housing? Why or why not?

A good reference source to spark your thinking on location, as well as the *kind* of place you want to live, is *A Field Guide to Retirement,* by Alice and Fred Lee (Doubleday, 1991). It discusses options from staying put to snowbirding in a warm climate, from "nomading" in an RV to moving into a planned retirement community.

138. Evaluate your potential new neighborhood, and compare it to your current home. Good neighborhoods for mature adults will be:

• Fast at snow removal; free of flooding; prepared for storms with a good drainage system

• Equipped with reliable public sewer lines and utility lines

• Good at police and fire protection. A low crime rate and a nearby fire department will bring down insurance rates. Trash and garbage collection should be located in a safe, accessible, well-lit area.

• Convenient to banking, shopping, a library, a hospital and/or medical services, to religious services that you might attend, and to a school where you might take adult education classes

139. Ask these questions first:

• Does it have zoning laws to protect the residential area from industrial or commercial intrusion?

• Are there any restrictions on owning pets?

• Are there any regulations about the kind of improvements you can make to your property?

• Is the property tax structure stable, and the rate reasonable? Are there any municipal projects planned (such as highways or sewer enhancements) that might cause an assessment to local homeowners?

• Is there adequate parking for your car and visitors' cars at your property and around shopping and services?

• Are there trees and well-kept lawns and gardens in the neighborhood?

• Are streets well lit?

140. If you're thinking about moving to a new state, look into its taxes first.

Carefully evaluate how that state treats its older residents and what its policy is on retirement income (e.g., Social Security or pensions). Compare that with where you now live. Are there any special provisions for older taxpayers? Every state has its own department of revenue that can answer your questions. Don't forget to ask about any recent legislation that might increase taxes.

141. There are several state taxes you should find out about:

• Personal income tax. Some states allow a personal exemption; some offer an additional exemption for the elderly.

• Personal property tax. Some states tax property, such as cars and other large items.

• State and local sales tax. If the state, county, or municipality has a sales tax, find out the rate for each, and any exemptions that may exist. Many states, for example, have no sales tax on groceries or prescription drugs.

• Source tax. A few states apply a source tax to income earned in that state, no matter where you live. That means that if you worked in a state with a source tax and earned a pension there, you'd pay tax on those pension benefits even if you move to another state. Often the state where you live and pay income tax will let you offset a source tax from another state.

142. Investigate tax credits, too. If you are considering an out-of-state move, ask about:

• Elderly income credit. This nonrefundable credit is subtracted from income tax liability for people 65 and older.

• Exclusions. They encompass income such as public assistance payments that you do not have to report on income tax returns.

• Property tax relief programs. Be sure to ask if there are any programs to alleviate such taxes at the state and county levels.

• Tax deferral programs. They allow some people, usually the elderly and disabled, to postpone paying property taxes until death or the sale of the property. Interest on the deferred taxes can be charged, but generally it is below market rates. The amount of the deferral plus interest charges becomes a lien on the property.

143. A real estate agent can help you sell your house and buy another. In the typical home sale, there are two agents. The listing agent represents the seller; the selling agent represents the buyer. Sellers pay the listing broker a commission—usually between 5 and 7 percent of the sale price of the home—and that broker splits the commission with the selling broker (if there is one). If you are both selling and buying, one agent will probably represent you in both transactions.

144. State laws require that agents treat both buyers and sellers fairly and honestly. However, it's always wise to remember that agents, whether they represent the buyer or the seller, are paid from the proceeds of the sale. If you are buying and your agent takes you to see a house that he or she has also listed, there can be a conflict of interest.

145. To find a good agent, ask around for recommendations. Your friends, coworkers, and family members may be able to give you some names. Interview several agents. Buying and selling is an intense process, so be sure that you feel comfortable both with the services offered and with the agent. Once you've selected an agent, make certain a written agreement spells out his or her obligations as well as your own.

146. The agent will help you set a price on your house. He or she will then prepare marketing materials, put a for-sale sign in your yard, advertise the property in newspapers, hold open houses so potential buyers and/or their agents can view the house, and arrange for private showings. The agent also fields offers for the house, helps you negotiate a final price, and then shepherds you through the process of closing the deal.

147. A good agent will try to find houses that meet your needs. He or she will make appointments for you to see the available houses, will drive you there, accompany you as you look, and point out details you may have missed. When you find a house you're interested in, the agent will help you decide how much to offer for it and will then represent you in any negotiations with the seller. When a deal is made, the agent will help you through the process of closing.

148. When you go house-hunting, go prepared. Take a notebook and jot down as much as you can about what you see. Your notes will help you remember which place is sunny, which has the most closets, and which has the mildewy basement. Check the paint to be sure there is no blistering or peeling. Flush the toilets and turn on the taps to check water pressure. Carry a marble and place it in the center of uncarpeted floors to check for slanting surfaces. Binoculars are good for peering at roof shingles. A flashlight is helpful in basements and other dark spots. Don't let anyone rush you as you look—you're supposed to take time and snoop.

149. Hire a professional inspector to check out major items. Your inspector should check the heating system, air-conditioning system, foundation of the house, insulation, roofing, and structural supports. For a $75 fee, the U.S. Environmental Protection Agency will do a check and let you know whether the house is near a hazardous waste dump or similar site (call them at 800-989-0403). Make your final deal contingent on an inspection of the property.

150. Don't be afraid to ask! Either you or your agent should ask the owner:

• What is the yearly heating cost? Electric bill?

• How old is the roof? Has it ever leaked?

• Was there ever water in the basement?

• When was the house last painted?

• Are there storm windows and screens, and are they in good condition?

• Is there adequate water pressure for two people to take showers at the same time?

• Will the owner provide a certificate stating that the house is termite-free?

• Are there any easements on the property?

 Make sure the house is radon-free.

Radon is a radioactive gas that you can't see, taste, or smell. The Surgeon General has warned that it is a leading cause of lung cancer in the United States. The good news is that houses found to have radon can be fixed. For information on the gas itself, testing for it, and getting rid of it, contact:

U.S. Environmental Protection Agency
Information Access Branch
Public Information Center
401 M St. SW, Suite 3404
Washington, DC 20460
800-557-2366; 800-767-7236

152. You can reduce the cost of selling by working with a discount broker. You can find one by looking in the Yellow Pages under "Real Estate Broker"—the discount ones usually advertise themselves as such. The drawback here is that often discount brokers don't list houses on the Multiple Listing Service (the MLS is a central database, available only to agents, that lists and describes houses for sale) or otherwise expose their properties widely to other brokers and potential buyers. That means the process of finding a buyer can take much longer.

153. If you have both patience and diligence, try selling the house yourself. A house being sold by its owner, without a broker, is called a FSBO (pronounced *fizz-bo*)—from "for sale by owner." Look in the white pages of the phone book under "For Sale by Owner" to find agencies that help with just that. Some agencies do nothing more than rent you a For Sale sign for your yard and offer discounts on newspaper advertising. Others will give you access to the MLS (for a fee) and/or a telephone answering service where potential buyers can book appointments to see your house. Selling your house without an agent can save you the price of a commission—no small amount—but it can also become a long and difficult process.

154. For more information on working with a real estate agent, contact:

Consumer Federation of America
P.O. Box 12099
Washington, DC 20005
202-387-6121
Ask for "Buying a Home: What Buyers

and Sellers Need to Know About Real Estate Agents" (D14783).

155. You can find an apartment without the help of an agent. Many people work with a real estate agent when apartment-hunting, but you don't have to. The classified ads are the first place to look for a place to live. But if there's a neighborhood you like, check the bulletin board of the grocery store, laundry, health food store, or any other public gathering place. Speak with merchants and local residents; community newspapers are often the best source of listings, since their classified advertising rates are so low. If you see a building you'd like to live in, contact the building manager to see if anything is available.

156. Keep these points in mind when considering a specific apartment building:

• The parking area should have enough spaces for both tenants and their visitors. The kinds of cars you see in the lot can give you an idea of who your neighbors will be.
• Look at the landscaping to gauge general maintenance standards. Is the trash disposal area clean and hidden from view?
• Is there a fire exit for those on upper floors?
• Are water hydrants close to buildings?
• Are mailboxes locked and located in safe areas?

The building entrance, corridors, and lobby should be well maintained and brightly lit. The elevators and stairs should be clean, and carpeted to reduce noise. Fire exits should be well marked.

157. When you visit the apartment itself, check these items carefully:

• The entrance door should be solid and have a dead-bolt lock.
• Sounds from adjoining apartments shouldn't be audible.
• Windows should open and close easily, have secure locks, and have screens or storm windows; they should also have shades or blinds.
• Paint or plaster should be smooth, clean, and fresh-looking. Many apartment complexes repaint for each new tenant.
• There should be at least two electrical outlets in every room.
• The thermostats for central air-conditioning or heating should function well. The kitchen and bath should have exhaust fans if they have no windows.
• Make sure all appliances are in good working order.

158. You don't have to buy a house to own your dwelling—you can buy a condominium. Condominiums often provide the same amount of interior space as a small home in the same area—but for less money, and with extra amenities, such as outdoor maintenance, swimming pool, tennis court, and clubhouse. They usually have two kinds of charges: a mortgage and maintenance fees for upkeep of the property. Keep in mind that maintenance fees tend to rise from year to year.

159. Buying a condo means buying into a business. Condo owners typically elect certain owners to represent their interests in the management of the complex. Do you want to participate in the governance of your complex? If not, are you willing to accept decisions made for the good of the majority?

160. A cooperative is more than a rental, but less than a condominium. Co-ops are similar to condominiums in that you have the right to live in a specific unit—but you don't actually own the unit. What you own is a share in the corporation that owns the building and grounds. It's similar to owning a share of stock in a company.

If you find a unit you like, the co-op board will have to approve your application to live there. The co-op board also sets the rules and regulations that owners must follow. If any member of the co-op defaults on payments, the remaining members are financially responsible.

161. Co-ops can be more difficult to sell than condominiums. Lenders are often leery of providing long-term financing for a share in a co-op. However, there is a legal move afoot to give co-op owners a type of deed similar to those provided to condo owners, making co-ops more attractive to potential lenders.

162. Mobile homes—also called manufactured homes and trailers—are increasing in popularity. A mobile home usually costs significantly less than a house built in a conventional way. Some people enjoy the campuslike at-mosphere of a mobile home park; others find the lack of privacy off-putting. Mobile parks usually have regulations about everything—from what you can put in your yard to the type of garbage containers you use. You can avoid all that by setting up a mobile home on property you already own.

163. Before buying a mobile home, know exactly what's included in the price. Ask about any add-on features, service warranties, and setup charges. Where laws permit, some manufactured home communities will sell you the home and the land together as a package, much as with traditional housing. Before deciding to set up in a mobile home park, it's a good idea to check with residents about their experience there.

164. Although they're called MOBILE homes, they're almost always erected on a permanent foundation. That means they are as eligible for a long-term mortgage as a conventional house is. The government insures loans—called Title 1 loans—to finance the purchase of manufactured homes and the lots to put them on, but the loans are processed by private lending institutions.

165. For information about Title 1 loans, contact:

Assistant Secretary for Housing—Federal Housing Commissioner
U.S. Department of Housing and Urban Development
Washington, DC 20410
202-708-3600

166. Florida and California are known for their wonderful mobile home communities. And many other states are developing them, too. For more information, contact:

Manufactured Housing Institute
2101 Wilson Blvd., Suite 610
Arlington, VA 22201
703-558-0400

167. Discrimination on the basis of race, color, religion, national origin, or gender is outlawed by the federal Fair Housing Act of 1968. If you believe you've been discriminated against when trying to buy or rent housing, report it to:

U.S. Department of Housing and Urban Development
451 7th St. SW, Room 5100
Washington, DC 20410
800-424-8590

168. Retirement communities are proliferating. Retirement communities are housing developments geared to adults over 50 or 55. They usually feature extra amenities and are often more affordable than similar dwellings outside the development. Many retirement communities are clustered in the South and Southwest (Florida, California, and Arizona). Some large hotel chains (for instance, the Hyatt and the Marriott) have begun to construct retirement communities.

169. Housing prices in retirement communities vary. Prices depend on the type of housing—garden apartments, condominiums, and single-family houses are all available—and, of course, on the location. The size, quality of construction, and amenities offered also affect the price. There are some communities in which every unit sells for over a million dollars; in others, small houses carry a price tag of about $50,000.

170. Do you really want to live in a retirement community?

Would you feel comfortable living in a place restricted to older residents? If possible, take a vacation near one of these communities and check it out before you buy. Some people find the restrictions of a planned community irritating; others enjoy the social activities it provides. Some experts suggest buying into an established community rather than one that is just developing. That gives you a better idea of what you're getting, and you won't have to wait years for promised amenities.

171. For more information about adult communities, contact:

National Association of Area Agencies on Aging
1112 16th St. NW
Washington, DC 20036
800-677-1116
Ask for the "ElderCare Locator" to help you find a community in a specific location.

National Association of Insurance Commissioners

120 W. 12th St., Suite 1100
Kansas City, MO 64105
816-842-3600
Offers the "Long-Term Care Insurance Buying Guide."

AARP Fulfillment
1909 K St. NW
Washington, DC 20049
800-424-3410
Ask for "Housing Options for Older Americans" (D12063).

172. Independent- and assisted-living facilities offer various degrees of personal care. These options are worth considering if you're worried about illness or disability as you age. An independent-living facility is much like a residence hotel, with housekeeping and other optional services available. An assisted-living facility provides meals and personal care; most also provide limited medical services.

173. Independent-living facilities are for active people who like to be pampered. Like hotels, these facilities offer day-to-day services that often include housekeeping, transportation, emergency medical services, meals and snacks, and recreational and health facilities. Depending on the type of housing, services, and location of the facility, entrance fees to the development can range from $40,000 to over $150,000. In addition, maintenance fees often average between $1,000 and $2,000 per month.

174. Assisted-living facilities offer custodial care services. Residents are assisted with dressing, bathing, and eating. Those who suffer from Alzheimer's disease often do well with the structure and shelter this arrangement affords. At many assisted-living facilities, a medical specialist is on call, physician visits are scheduled, and transportation is available for medical care. Usually, all details of personal care and housekeeping, including meals, are included, and there are a variety of recreational activities. The facilities usually provide either a semiprivate or a private room for individuals and a double room for married couples. There are public areas for all residents. The average cost of assisted living ranges from about $1,500 to $2,500 monthly.

175. Continuing-care facilities, also called life care facilities, offer seniors an assortment of housing options. That often includes independent-living, assisted-living, and nursing home care all in one development. Residents move from one level of care to another, as necessary. A contract for a continuing-care facility is usually intended to remain in effect for life, and some feel it's a form of insurance for the later years. Under this contract, the facility provides housing, services, and nursing care, usually all in one location. Hospitalization, medical services, and physician visits are seldom included in the contract, but the facility will often make the appointments, provide the transportation, and handle the paperwork.

176. Continuing-care contracts often require an entrance fee, plus monthly fees. Sometimes the monthly fee includes all services, but not always. Some communities allow residents to pay for services as needed. At a minimum, the contract guarantees access to nursing care services; at a maximum, it covers the full cost of nursing care.

177. Congregate housing offers the best of both worlds. If you want to live in your own apartment, but like the idea of sharing common areas with others, consider congregate housing. Residents live independently in their own apartments but have access to centralized dining rooms and such support services as transportation, social and recreational programs, and housekeeping.

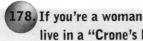 **If you're a woman, maybe you'd like to live in a "Crone's Nest."**

Writing in the January/February 1997 issue of *Holistic Living* magazine, Cynthia Cary explains that a Crone's Nest is a house or duplex shared by two or three women—usually older women, but not necessarily so. Some residents bring cash into the ownership of the dwelling, others contribute what Cary calls "skill and service equity." The women share housework and pool their resources, making everything from energy to money go further. Cary has a book in the works called *A Foxy Old Woman's Guide to Living with Friends* (Crossing Press). Or order her newsletter:

Creating a Crone's Nest
4337C Lanihale Pl.
Honolulu, HI, 96816
808-735-5380

179. For more information about housing options, contact the American Association of Homes for the Aging. They'll send you a free address list of accredited continuing-care homes or a free copy of "Not-for-Profit Housing" and "Care Options for Older People." You can also order *The Continuing Care Retirement Communities: A Guidebook for Consumers* ($10.45, including postage and handling) or *The Consumers' Directory of Continuing Care Retirement Communities* ($28.45, including postage and handling).

American Association of Homes for the Aging
Department 5119
Washington, DC 20061
800-508-9442

Head 'Em Up, Move 'Em Out

180. Get rid of anything you haven't used in two years. Think of it as "downsizing" if you're of a corporate turn of mind, or "deaccessioning" if you're of an artistic bent (the latter is the term museums use when they sell paintings and sculptures). The advice is a little harsh, perhaps, but it's nice to move into the future unencumbered—and it makes for an easier move. This can also be a wonderful way to give children, grandchildren, and friends a part of their "inheritance" now—and accept their thanks in person!

181. Packing is much easier with the proper tools. If you hire a professional mover, the company will sell you all kinds of boxes, such as wardrobe boxes with rods for hangers and dish packs for china and crystal. Ask the movers if they can provide "gently used" boxes at a discount. If you need to save money, you can ask the proprietors of liquor stores and grocery stores for strong boxes.

Boxes and other supplies are also available at the national truck rental companies, but these can be expensive. You may have luck looking up carton manufacturing companies in the yellow pages and asking to buy "seconds."

182. Other supplies to have on hand:

- Bubble wrap for pictures and art
- Indelible markers so boxes can be well labeled
- Stacks of newspapers—or better yet, packages of clean, precut newsprint from your mover or a packing store—for wrapping and padding
- Packing tape and scissors. A handheld tape dispenser, like the ones professional packers use, can be a considerable time-saver over scissors when building or sealing boxes. These are available from your mover or from a U-Haul store.

183. How do you find a moving company? Your best bet is to ask for recommendations from people who have moved recently. If that's not an option for you, listings in your yellow pages under the heading of "Movers" provide detailed information about the kind of services that various companies offer. In that same section, you'll also find a listing for your state's "Board of Public Movers & Warehousemen." You can call them to make sure the company you choose has a valid license in good standing.

184. Professionals pack one room at a time. Following this system is more efficient and makes for fewer loose ends. Label boxes with their contents and the rooms to which they should be delivered in your new place. Number each box and make a note of the contents so when you arrive at your destination you can check to see that everything has arrived safely. Clearly mark fragile items. Put the heaviest items in the bottom of boxes, and get lighter as you go up. It's okay to "waste" a whole box on a lampshade. To save a little money, pack the easy stuff yourself, then let the movers do the rest.

185. Don't pack everything! Keep a separate bag of personal items you'll need during the move, as well as any travel documents and maps. Both a medical kit with bandages and a small tool kit are good to have handy, since nobody ever has a Band-Aid or an Allen wrench when you need one.

186. Be kind to your movers. It makes a potentially stressful day more pleasant for everyone. Remember to put a couple of six-packs of soft drinks in the refrigerator and a stack of paper cups by the sink on moving day so workers can have beverages and water when they need them. A box of doughnuts for quick energy doesn't hurt either.

When the job is done, don't forget a tip if your movers did good work.

Safe Places

187. Be sure you have a safe place to live. We're not talking about burglar-proofing your home—although we will talk about that later. We mean common sense and safety inside your home. The Consumer Products Safety Commission estimates that each year about 750,000 mature adults are treated in hospital emergency rooms for injuries from products they live with and use every day. Microwave ovens, toasters, and vacuum cleaners are just a few items that can be hazardous if used or stored incorrectly.

188. Keep emergency phone numbers at hand. Most urban communities have the 911, quick-call-for-emergencies phone number. If your area doesn't have 911, post the telephone numbers for the police, fire department, and local hospital, along with a neighbor's number, near your phone(s). Write the numbers large and clear so that you can read them easily without having to hunt for your glasses.

189. Electrical cords stretched across traffic paths are guaranteed tripper-uppers. Arrange furniture so that outlets are accessible for lamps and appliances without the use of extension cords. If you must use an extension cord, lay it on the floor along the base of a wall, out of everyone's path.

Furniture resting on electrical cords can damage the wire, creating fire and shock hazards, so make sure that all cords are free. Never put electrical cords under a carpet, and remember that nails and staples can damage cords (use tape to attach cords to walls or floors, if you must). Check wires regularly for damage, and replace all old, frayed, or cracked cords. Unplug appliances if you have any doubts about them.

190. Check for unsafe and overheated wires. Hold your hand over electrical outlets. Warm or hot outlets or switches may indicate that the wiring is unsafe. Unplug cords from these outlets, and don't use the switches. Have a licensed electrician evaluate your wiring.

191. Arrange your home so that you can see well. A light switch near the door will eliminate the need to move through a dark room to get to a lamp. Plug-in night-lights can help you find your way around in the dark and will help prevent trips or falls. Install them in hallways and the kitchen as well as on stairways and in bathrooms. Replace conventional light switches you use at night with a "glow switch" that you can see in the dark.

 Keep your smoke detector in good working order.

There should be at least one smoke detector on every floor of your dwelling, and one at either end of a floor if your home is large. The instructions that come with the product will guide you on placement.

Remember that the batteries need to be replaced regularly—many people change them when resetting their clocks for daylight savings time. Batteries make a peculiar whining or buzzing sound or intermittent beeps when they start to run low.

193. Install a carbon monoxide detector in your home, too. Carbon monoxide is a toxic gas that can't be seen and has no odor—but it can be deadly. Never leave a car running in a closed garage, since it produces carbon monoxide. While you're at it, make sure all fuel-burning appliances are property installed and maintained.

194. Freestanding heaters can be great for cold spots but should be used carefully. Such heaters can cause fires or serious burns if you knock them over or trip over them. Place heaters away from passageways and flammable materials, such as curtains, newspapers, and upholstered and stuffed furniture. Heaters that require proper ventilation but are used unvented can give off dangerous fumes. Never use unvented gas- or kerosene-burning appliances in a closed room.

195. Cook up some safety in the kitchen. Store flammable items such as pot holders, dish towels, and plastic utensils away from the stove. That means getting the dish towels off the oven handle and fixing curtains and towel racks so they don't dangle over cooktops.

Standing on chairs, boxes, or other makeshift items to reach high shelves can result in falls. Buy a step stool, and be sure it's fully opened and stable before climbing onto it. Always place your feet on the center of a step. There are rolling stools available that lock into place when stepped on with full weight.

When working in the kitchen, roll back long, loose sleeves or fasten them with pins or elastic bands.

196. Bathrooms can be slippery when wet. Apply textured strips or appliqués on the bottom of tubs and shower stalls. Or use non-skid mats in the tub or shower—and on the bathroom floor. If you're a little unsteady on your feet, there are stools with nonskid tips on their legs that you can sit on while showering or bathing.

Grab-bars attached over the sides of bathtubs and/or through the tile walls into the supporting studs can help you get into and out of the tub or shower safely. Check existing bars for strength and stability, and repair if necessary.

197. A hot bath feels delightful, but don't turn up the heat too high. Test the water before entering a bath or shower, but remember that aging skin loses some sensitivity, so you may not be able to accurately gauge water temperature in this way. Keep the thermostat on your hot water heater on "low," because temperatures above 120 degrees can cause scalds. A plumber can install a temperature-limiting device on faucets in the sinks, baths, and showers.

198. Bathrooms and appliances don't mix well. If an electrical appliance, such as a hair dryer or electric shaver, falls into a sink or tub full of water, there's danger of electrocution. This is true even if the appliance isn't turned on. Install ground fault circuit interrupters in bathroom outlets—and kitchens—to protect against electric shock. Unplug all small appliances when not in use. Never reach into water to retrieve an appliance until you have first made sure the appliance is unplugged.

199. A surprising number of accidents happen in the bedroom. If necessary, rearrange furniture or lamps so that if you get up in the middle of the night, you can easily turn lights on without tripping over anything. Night-lights can help, too, as can "clap on/clap off" lights.

Never smoke in bed; it's a major cause of burns. If you use a heating pad or an electric blanket, follow the manufacturer's instructions regarding proper usage.

200. Look at stairs from a safety angle. Older people whose eyesight isn't as good as it used to be, and who are less steady on their feet, need to be especially careful on stairs. Stairways should be lit so that each step can be clearly seen while going up or down. Light switches at both the bottom and the top of the stairs are a fine idea. You might also want to keep a flashlight at the top and bottom of the stairs just in case the power goes out.

Handrails should be in good repair, should provide a comfortable grip, and should extend all the way from the top step to the bottom one. Refinish or replace worn treads, or replace worn, loose carpeting. Resist the temptation to leave items on the stairs

that you plan to carry upstairs or downstairs later—they could cause you to trip.

201. Don't forget about outdoor stairs. Outdoor steps are best covered with a rough-textured paint or fit with some abrasive strips. In icy-weather climates, it's a good idea to have small, covered bins of an ice-melt product at the top and bottom of outdoor stairs so that you can toss it ahead of yourself.

202. Many cleverly designed devices—often called accessible products—can make life easier as we age.

Such items include handrails, stools for the bath, and grippers that make opening jars easier. Pharmacies and hardware, department, and medical supply stores carry many of these products.

203. Many organizations sell accessible products. Most will send catalogs of what they have available, and some will provide advice. Federal, state, and private organizations often have programs that provide help in installing safety devices. Contact:

Center for Universal Design
North Carolina State University
219 Oberlin Rd.
Raleigh, NC 27605
919-515-3082

Maxiaids
P.O. Box 3209
Farmingdale, NY 11735
800-522-6294

National Rehabilitation Information
Center
8455 Colesville Rd., Suite 935
Silver Spring, MD 20910
800-227-0216

Yes I Can, Inc.
35-325 Date Palm Dr.
The Esplanade, Suite 131
Cathedral City, CA 92234
800-366-4226

Enrichments for Better Living Catalog
Enrichments
P.O. Box 5050
Bollingbrook, IL 60440
800-323-5547

204. For more information on household safety, contact:

U.S. Consumer Products Safety
Commission
Office of Information and Public Affairs
Washington, DC 20207
800-638-2772
800-638-8270 (teletypewriter for the deaf)

American Association of Retired Persons
601 E St. NW
Washington, DC 20049
800-424-3410
Publishes two very useful booklets: "The Do-Able and Renewable Home: Making Your Home Fit Your Needs" (D12470) and "The Perfect Fit: Creative Ideas for a Safe and Liveable Home" (D14823).

Safe Selves

205. Several factors make older people more accident prone than others. Disease is the largest cause. Arthritis and neurological illnesses can cause unsteadiness and impaired coordination. Reduced hearing can make it difficult to pick up the sound of sirens when driving. Some medications cause drowsiness. Others, including nonprescription cold and sinus remedies, sleeping pills, tranquilizers, sedatives, painkillers, and even aspirin can affect vision.

Falls, burns, and auto accidents are the leading causes of fatal injury among the elderly.

206. Women fall more often than men. That's true up until age 75, but after that, both sexes suffer falls at equal rates. In fact, falls are easily preventable—see the tips offered in "Safe Places" above. Here are a few more suggestions to fall-proof your dwelling.

• Remove any area rugs or runners that tend to slide, or apply double-faced adhesive carpet tape to their backs to make them secure. Cut-to-size rubber matting underneath rugs can also help.

• Remember that rugs with slip-resistant backs become less effective with repeated washings, so check them periodically.

• One handrail on the stairs may not be enough; consider having one installed on the other side.

• Arrange furniture to get rid of any obstacle courses.

• Keep outdoor steps and walkways in good repair.

207. For more information on falls, contact:

National Osteoporosis Foundation
1150 17th St. NW, Suite 500
Washington, DC 20036
202-223-2226
800-824-26637

Johns Hopkins Injury Prevention Center
Keep It Safe
P.O. Box 3717
Washington, DC 20007
800-424-2725

National Council on Aging
Information Center
P.O. Box 8075
Gaithersburg, MD 20898
800-222-2225

208. Burns can be especially disabling. And recovery from them can be slow. Think about what you would do if there were a fire in your home. Plan which emergency exits to use. Check locks to be sure they're easy to open. If you have a lock that requires using a key to open from the inside, hide the key within easy reach of the door. And it's better to install one good, quick-to-open lock instead of many supplemental locks.

In a house fire, don't panic. Stay as close to the floor as possible. If you're on an upper floor and can't jump out, close all doors to the room against the fire and place wet towels or clothes in the cracks to help prevent smoke from seeping in. A sealed room can hold off most fires for some time. Open a window from both bottom and top so you'll have ventilation. Hang a bed sheet or some other large piece of fabric outside the window to attract attention. If smoke seeps into the room, it is even more important to lie on the floor, and if possible, drape a wet towel or cloth around your face.

Safe Driving

209. It's time to talk turkey about cars. The number of drivers aged 65 and over has more than doubled in the last twenty years, and by the year 2020 will reach 30 million people.

The most common cause of accidental death in the 65-to-74 age group is the automobile. In fact, measured by the number of miles traveled, older adults have more crashes and more fatal crashes than any other age group. Drivers between ages 70 and 74 have five fatal crashes for every one hundred miles of travel—more than twice as many as drivers 40 to 49.

210. Yes, we know the car represents freedom. Yes, you've been a good driver for a long time. Yes, Americans are addicted to their autos. But changes in peripheral vision, night vision, and reaction time can make us less than the drivers we once were.

You can compensate by sticking to familiar roads, avoiding night driving, and planning routes that have no left turns at busy intersections. Use caution when parking, and if at all possible, avoid backing up.

211. Consider using public transportation. You may be close to neighborhood bus stops, but never had reason to know exactly where the buses went. Check it out—many suburban bus routes include stops at shopping malls, strip malls, and train stations. Your community may also have vans that will take you to medical appointments or the senior center.

212. The two best things you can do about your driving:

• Give family and friends a standing invitation to be honest about your driving—not while you're behind the wheel, of course—so you can make decisions and changes.

• Enroll in a defensive driving or a driver retraining course. Many are given by public schools as part of their adult education classes. It will perk up your skills and may lower your auto insurance rate.

213. Make sure you're seeing as well as possible when driving. For example:

• Don't wear tinted lenses at night.
• Keep your glasses scrupulously clean.
• Avoid eyeglass frames with wide earpieces, since they can block side vision.
• When driving, watch the big picture on the road ahead. Check either side for vehicles, children, animals, or hazards. Keep your eyes moving; glance frequently in the rearview mirror, at the instrument panel, and at any crossroads.

• Keep headlights properly adjusted, and keep headlights, taillights, the windshield, and side windows clean.
• Choose a clear-glass windshield. Tinted glass can reduce the amount of light entering the eye, and that's hazardous at night. Counteract sun glare with good sunglasses.

214. Twelve states have age-based restrictions on license renewals for older adults. That's *down* from sixteen states a few years ago. The reduction comes because testing is costly, and restrictions on older drivers have been attacked as being ageist. Still, families of accident victims are urging new limitations on older drivers.

215. Some other driving recommendations:

• Keep pace with the traffic flow; slow drivers can cause people to make risky passing maneuvers.
• Concentrate: Don't talk on the phone, drink coffee, or even listen to the radio while driving.
• Minimize noise inside the car by keeping fans, air conditioners, and heaters on low settings.
• Always look behind before putting your vehicle in reverse.
• Check when changing lanes—don't assume your turn signal has alerted those behind you.
• Be aware of your reaction time, and avoid changing lanes when there are children on bikes around or when you're in bumper-to-bumper traffic.

216. Wearing a seat belt reduces injuries if there is an accident. Research has shown that older drivers are at increased risk of injury or death in car accidents because of fragile bones and a reduced ability to withstand trauma. Seat belts distribute impact across the strongest areas of the body and prevent you from hitting the steering wheel, dashboard, or other occupants of the car. They also keep you from being thrown from the car. And they can help you maintain control over the vehicle.

217. Cars can also be trouble when you're a pedestrian. A word to the wise: The same difficulties with peripheral vision that cause problems while driving apply to walking in areas where there's traffic. Take plenty of time crossing the road, especially in bad weather; use crosswalks where available; plan your route to choose the fewest number of road crossings, and then only at the safest intersections. Be especially wary of crossing at traffic lights where right turns on red are permitted.

218. For more information about aging, driving, and accident prevention, contact:

Age Page/Accident Prevention
National Institutes of Health Information
Center
9000 Rockville Pike
Bethesda, MD 20892
301-496-4000

National Safety Council
1121 Springlake Dr.
Itasca, IL 60143
800-621-7615

American Automobile Association
Mature Operator Program
Foundation for Traffic Safety
12600 Fairlakes Circle
Fairfax, VA 22033
202-331-3000

Highway Traffic Safety Administration
400 7th St. SW
Washington, DC 20590
202-366-0123

Crime Prevention

219. To protect yourself against crime, use some common sense. For example, more than 80 percent of the 1 million cars stolen every year were unlocked, and about half had the keys in the ignition. So, to prevent car theft, keep car doors locked whether you're in it or outside it, and take the keys with you when you leave the car.

220. If your car breaks down or has a flat, get off the road. Do this even if you have to drive on a wheel rim. And make sure you're parked as far from traffic as you can get. Turn on your emergency flashers; set flares if you have them; raise the hood and tie a handkerchief to the antenna or a door handle; and then get back in your car. If you have a cellular phone, call for help. Wait in your locked car for assistance. If someone stops, roll down your window just enough to ask him or her to call the nearest police station.

221. Don't be an easy mark:

• Before getting into your car, check to be sure no one is inside.

• Don't approach your car if you see people peering in its windows.

• Before setting out in your car, make sure you know how to get where you're going. Always have a map in your car.

• Stick to roads that are safe, well lit, and well traveled, even if it means taking a little longer to reach your destination.

• When stopping at red lights or stop signs in a neighborhood that makes you nervous, check your mirrors to be sure no one is creeping up on you. In most states, it's legal to run a red light if you feel you're in danger of being carjacked.

• Stow your purse and other valuables out of sight.

• Keep windows rolled up whenever possible.

• Don't hide a spare key under the fender; it's the first place a thief will look.

• If you think you're being followed, don't drive home (it will let the person know where you live). Instead, drive to a police station or a safe place you know will be well lit and crowded. Sound your horn repeatedly. If you feel silly, don't worry about it; it's better to be silly and safe than to be a victim.

222. Don't make it easy for burglars. No home is thief-proof, but most people who steal don't plan ahead—they look for an easy target such as an open garage door, or a front door that you've left open while you're in the backyard. Some security tips:

• Be sure the front of your house or apartment is well lit and that police and other security personnel can find your door easily.

• Never let strangers or people you don't know well into your home. Install a peephole viewer on your entrance door. Make sure repair people are wearing uniforms, and request they show ID.

• Mark valuable equipment such as VCRs, TVs, and computers with identification, such as your Social Security number, to aid in their recovery if they are stolen.

• Take photographs of jewelry or special pieces of furniture for identification if they are stolen.

• Have an alarm system installed in your home. Some come with stickers you can affix in your window alerting would-be thieves that your home is protected—most thieves are less likely to target an alarm-protected home.

223. Modify the outside of your home to help prevent break-ins:

• Trim trees and bushes so they can't conceal anyone outside your house.

• Install lights on the porches and outside walls of your house.

• Entrance doors should have a mounted dead bolt or rim lock.

• Install commercial locks on all your windows.

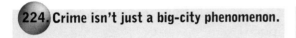

224. Crime isn't just a big-city phenomenon.

Rural homes and farms can be just as vulnerable to property crime, since mischief happens when vandals, thieves, and burglars know they're unlikely to be seen. And one out of every five rural homes is occupied by an older American. Here are some suggestions for securing your property.

- Add outdoor lights everywhere.
- Chain and lock everything you can, especially big tools and equipment.
- Store tools inside a locked barn or storage shed.
- Post No Trespassing and Warning signs to let thieves know you will safeguard your property.
- A watchdog can be a lifesaver.

225. Apartment dwellers and office workers should be cautious, too. If you live in an apartment building or work in a tall office building after hours, be aware of the people around you. If you find yourself alone with a stranger waiting for an elevator, let him or her take the first car that comes, while you wait for the next one. If you're riding an elevator with someone who makes you uneasy, get near the control panel so you can hit the alarm button if necessary. Or get off at the next floor.

226. Being a good neighbor can mean being a nosy neighbor. Watch for any suspicious activity on your block or around your house, and don't hesitate to call the police if you see anything that seems "funny." Join the neighborhood watch in your area. If it doesn't have one, call the police station and get information about starting one. Let a trusted neighbor know when you'll be out of town, and ask him or her to collect your mail and newspapers. Do the same in return.

227. So just what is "suspicious activity"? In general, it's whatever gives you a funny feeling. In other words, trust your instincts. Suspicious activity includes:

- A slow-moving car—particularly one driving without lights at night—pausing in front of houses, playgrounds, or schools
- Property being loaded into a vehicle at an unusual hour
- A parked car whose occupants just sit there, looking around, especially at an unusual hour
- Anyone, but especially a child, being dragged or forced into a car
- A car that seems to be serving as a meeting room or business office, with transactions that seem to involve small parcels or money

228. You can remain anonymous when reporting suspicious activity. If you do call the police, you'll be asked for the location of the activity. Try to describe the event clearly; give the time of the event, a description of the people you saw, a description of their vehicle, including the license plate number, and the direction the people or cars moved in.

229. Keep a phone near your bed for making emergency calls at night. Some other phone safety tips:

• Keep a private number private; don't give it out freely.

• Women used to list themselves in the directory under a first initial rather than a name to avoid receiving crank calls. That trick is now too old. Get an unlisted number instead.

• Report all nuisance or obscene calls to the telephone company. A more immediate and dramatic deterrent is to blow a whistle hard into the mouthpiece.

• Never use a cellular phone to do any business that requires giving out credit card numbers. Thieves can scan cell phone calls to get those numbers. Never use your cellular phone while waiting in line at a tollbooth—it's the most popular place for thieves to scan and "clone" your phone number.

230. Be wary of callers you don't know—especially if they seem too friendly.

In addition:

• If someone calls to "check a wrong number," don't tell him yours. Hang up.

• Take notes and check up on anyone who offers work over the phone, or who suggests a meeting, since luring you away from home may be the goal of the call.

• If a caller you don't know asks for information, don't give it, and never give your Social Security or bank account number to anyone claiming to be checking your identity.

• An occasional wrong number is normal, but several in a row may be worth a phone call to the police.

231. Strolling the city streets can be one of life's great free entertainments—if you don't pay in another way.

• Carry no more cash than you need to, but carry enough to "buy off" a mugger without angering him—$10 to $20 is recommended by some experts.

• Credit cards are just as valuable as cash, so be careful when you take out your wallet. Don't inadvertently advertise how many cards you carry.

• Keep small bills for taxis, buses, newspapers, and the like in a pocket so you don't have to take out your wallet.

• Don't leave your bank before putting away your ATM card and the money you've withdrawn.

• Avoid cashing checks on the first or last days of the month—the days when thieves know people often have cash with them.

• Vary your patterns. Don't cash a check at the same time and in the same place every month.

232. Walk defensively. In cities, keep away from doorways and unlit areas. Walk near the curb if possible, but not so close that your purse or briefcase could be grabbed by someone on a bicycle.

If you see a rowdy-looking group, cross to the other side of the street or enter a store until they've passed. If you come upon a crowd or a fight, leave the area, since bystanders can be in as much danger as participants. Try to find a phone and call the police.

If you suspect you're being followed, don't duck into a strange building, since you can be at a greater disadvantage there than on the street. And don't go directly home, since you don't want to lead someone to your house. Walk to a police station or go into a busy, brightly lit shop.

233. For more information on crime prevention, contact:

National Consumer League
815 15th St. NW, Room 928N
Washington, DC 20005
National Fraud Information Hotline:
  800-876-7060

National Crime Prevention Council
1700 K St., 2nd Floor
Washington, DC 20006
202-466-6272

Federal Trade Commission
Bureau of Consumer Protection
6th St. and Pennsylvania Ave. NW
Washington, DC 20580
202-326-2222

Chapter 4:

Relationships—Ourselves and the People Around Us

The secret to finding new relationships and maintaining old ones seems to be the same as it has always been: putting yourself in the way of people, communicating, and being open to the possibilities. The catalyst for relationships is often simple—you grow close to people because they are physically close to you, as family members, neighbors, coworkers, or classmates. Simple though it is, the resulting connection has a profound effect on how happily we live.

As we age, our connections can be different from what they were in younger years, and sometimes less convenient. Relationships change as roles change. Family can dominate our time in a way it never did before. Some of us in our 50s and 60s find ourselves in "the Sandwich Generation," providing money, support, and care to children not quite finished with school or settled in careers, and also to parents grown very old and fragile. If we've retired or moved, or both, we may be in touch with old friends only by telephone, letter writing,

or e-mail. We need new friends for daily chat and activities.

This chapter is about our loving connections both old and new, physical and mental; some healthy and some not so healthy (sadly, we have had to include information about elder abuse). It's about the joys of grandchildren, grown children, family, friends, and even sexuality in our later years.

Marital Relationships

234. Remember, this is a time of transition. The fifth decade of life can mean the beginning of a lot of changes—physically, mentally, and socially. Family members grow up, move away, and have babies. You may be starting to have more doctor's appointments than you used to. You're probably beginning to plan for your retirement. Don't let these transitions derail your marital harmony. If you recognize change as a normal part of life, you'll find smoother sailing all around.

235. It's okay to give each other space. For the first time in decades, it's just the two of you rattling around the house together. Maybe you're both retired, to boot . . . and starting to feel that too much togetherness is too much of a good thing. It's important to remember that you don't have to do *everything* as a couple. Maintaining separate hobbies and interests is an ideal way to keep a marriage healthy. If you are retired, stay in touch with your ex-coworkers. Meet friends for lunch, shopping, a round of golf, or a movie matinee.

236. There are many activities the two of you can share, too. Taking a stroll around the neighborhood will keep your heart healthy in more ways than one. Try your luck at bingo. Continuing-education classes at high schools and Ys usually offer ballroom dancing and contra (similar to square) dancing. Take a ride out to a farmer's market for fresh vegetables, then come home and cook together. Put in a flower garden. Get a set of binoculars and a field guide book, and see how many different birds you can identify in your own backyard. Investigate local history—there are probably historic houses and sites within ten miles of you that you never had the time to visit before.

237. Welcome to a new era of sexual intimacy. It is true that men's testosterone levels decrease with age, but not dramatically so. The decrease mostly means that arousal and orgasm take longer to achieve, and some men find they need more manual stimulation than they used to. Because the pacing of sex is slowed down, couples have to take more time and pay more attention to what they're doing, thus enhancing their experience together.

By age 50, at least 90 percent of men will have experienced an occasion of impotence. Medications are probably the most common cause. (Even such common over-the-counter preparations as antihistamines have been implicated.) Diabetes, heart disease, and prostate problems can all increase the likelihood of impotence, as can smoking and alcohol abuse. But physicians estimate that in nearly 85 percent of these cases, impotence is correctable. Talk to your doctor about the newest drug, Viagra.

238. When it comes to sex, women are late bloomers. It's been estimated that women don't reach their sexual peak until their late 30s and that they remain there until their 60s. Hormonal changes after menopause can cause a woman's sex drive to actually increase. Besides this, many postmenopausal women find that with the fear of pregnancy gone, they can enjoy sex more completely.

The vaginal dryness that many older women experience can be easily reversed by using over-the-counter lubricants designed for this purpose. Vaginal atrophy can be treated with hormone replacement therapy, although that may have undesirable side effects. One study found that women who had intercourse three times a month or more were less likely to suffer from vaginal atrophy than those who had intercourse fewer than ten times a year.

239. Illness or disability can affect sexuality, but it doesn't have to ruin all the fun.

• Many people who have had a heart attack are afraid sex will cause another one. In fact, the risk is very low.

• Sexual function is rarely damaged by a stroke, and it's unlikely that sexual exertion will cause another.

• Surgery and drugs may relieve the joint pain of arthritis, allowing you to enjoy sexual activity again. Also helpful: exercise, rest, and warm baths.

• In most cases, neither hysterectomy nor mastectomy will affect a woman's sexual functioning physically. But there may be a psychological effect if a woman or her partner believes that the operation has made her less attractive or less "feminine." Counseling—or even simply being aware of the facts—can be a big help.

• For men, a prostatectomy can cause concern about sexuality. It need not, because it rarely causes impotence. In cases of radical prostatectomy (removal of the entire prostate gland), new surgical techniques can save the nerves going to the penis, and an erection may still be possible.

For information on coping with a mastectomy, contact:

Reach to Recovery
American Cancer Society
1599 Clifton Rd. NE
Atlanta, GA 30329
800-227-2345

For information on sex after prostate surgery, contact:

Prostate Health Council
American Foundation for Urologic Disease
300 W. Pratt St., Suite 401
Baltimore, MD 21201
800-242-2383

240. If you want to, you can have sex well into your 90s. Yes, hormonal changes do occur in both women and men as we age, and these can slow down the sex drive and even affect the act itself. While it can be difficult to adjust to alterations in habits that have been acquired over a lifetime, it might be helpful to remember that your sex life is *changing,* not *ending. For more information, contact:*

Sexuality Information and Education
Council of the United States
130 W. 42nd St., Suite 2500
New York, NY 10036
212-819-9770

Society for the Scientific Study of Sexuality
P.O. Box 208
Mount Vernon, IA 52314-0208
319-895-8407

American Geriatric Society
770 Lexington Ave., Suite 300
New York, NY 10021
212-308-1414

241. Getting help for spousal abuse is part of the healing process. When spousal abuse exists, it has usually been a part of the marriage for many years. The physical and emotional difficulties of aging (disability, unemployment, retirement) can cause it to worsen as time goes on. Victims often let their own feelings of guilt, fear, or religious obligation keep them in the relationship. But the longer victims endure abuse, the more difficult it can be, psychologically, to take steps to correct it. Getting help is part of the healing process. Look in the yellow pages under "Social Services" for the names and numbers of shelters and other sources of help.

Family Relationships

242. We did it when they were still small, and we should do it now: Set limits. As you plan the next third of your life, think about how you're going to relate to your adult children—the degree to which you're willing to baby-sit for their children, to lend or borrow money, or to be dependent on them as you age. It may be time for both parties to establish boundaries and to set limits regarding what each is willing or able to do. Communication is important—avoiding misunderstandings will keep your family close-knit as you all enter new phases of your lives.

243. There's a bright side to empty nest syndrome. "Empty nest syndrome" is the term sociologists have given to the negative feelings that arise when grown children have "flown the nest." Your role in life has changed; initially, you may not know what to do with yourself now that there are no children at home to cook for and to clean up after. But some of us find that having the kids gone is not such a bad thing after all. We enjoy a newfound freedom—one that usually includes having more money to spend as well.

244. You thought they were out of your hair! It isn't unusual for adult children to return home these days, due to a shrinking job market, inflation, unemployment, or divorce. Such an arrangement can be taxing to children and parents alike, but if you work out the basics beforehand, you have a better chance of maintaining family harmony. Items to discuss: How much will be contributed toward food and rent? How will household chores be divided? Do they expect you to do their laundry or baby-sit their kids? Other, potentially dicey issues should also be hashed out, such as curfews, and sleeping arrangements for visiting significant others. Working it all out beforehand will make life more enjoyable for everyone.

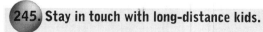

245. Stay in touch with long-distance kids.

Yes, they're busy with their important jobs and unreliable boyfriends or girlfriends—but believe it or not, they still need you. Instead of griping that the kids never call, arrange for a weekly telephone date at a time that is convenient for both parties. Take advantage of two-for-the-price-of-one film processing deals, and exchange photos of vacations through the mail. Snap a few shots of changes to the old neighborhood, and send those, too. Your adult children—and their spouses and kids—would probably get a kick out of receiving copies of their grammar school work, letters from camp, and other items you've treasured over the years.

246. Do yourself a favor—get your hearing checked. Hearing loss is a normal part of aging, and hearing loss *denial* is as common as the ailment itself. To ignore the problem means missing out on conversations as well as television and movie dialogue. You may even be testing the patience of those around you, who must continually repeat everything that's been said. Hearing aids are all but invisible these days; think of them as a tool that will help you remain connected to the world around you.

247. What do you say when . . . your child has lost his job, is filing for divorce, or is having custody problems? Resist the temptation to give specific advice, unless asked. Very often what was good counsel in an earlier decade is unrealistic in our modern, rapidly changing world. Besides, most people in crisis want support more than they want a list of "shoulds." By simply acknowledging the problem, and the pain he or she must be feeling, you'll be doing your child a world of good.

248. What to do when your son or daughter comes out of the closet. With today's greater

acceptance of all members of society, more and more people are living an openly gay lifestyle. While discrimination still exists, it isn't as severe as it used to be (especially in the workplace). If your child has told you he or she is gay, you may be feeling devastated—or furious or guilty. Take it one step at a time, and count your blessings that he or she feels close enough to you to share such an important disclosure—you obviously still play a vital role in your child's life.

If you continue to have trouble coming to terms with your child's sexual orientation, discussing your reactions with a support group can be very beneficial. The largest support group for families of homosexuals is P-Flag. Write or call to find the group nearest you.

Parents of Lesbians and Gays (P-FLAG)
1101 14th St. NW, Suite 1030
Washington, DC 20005
202-638-0243

249. As Shakespeare wrote, "Neither a borrower, nor a lender be . . ." But if you must lend money to your children (not an uncommon occurrence these days), or if you need to borrow from them, treat it as you would any business transaction. Loans should be documented, and an interest rate (if any) agreed upon up front. It may seem cold, but taking care of these nuts-and-bolts details will head off trouble later on.

250. Make family visits fun for everyone. Don't try to reproduce the big family feasts of the past if you're not up to it: This is the time for takeout Chinese or delivery pizza. And it really isn't necessary to dust and vacuum every room in the house. Rent a movie that everyone can watch together, or play an intergenerational game of Uno or Scrabble.

251. You may be a member of the Sandwich Generation. According to a recent *New York Times* article, over 10 percent of the workforce is responsible for the care of an elderly relative (that number is expected to rise to approximately one out of every three people by 2020). Add to that their care of at-home children, and you have millions of people "sandwiched" between pressing duties to two generations of immediate family members. Try to carve out some time to join a caregivers' support group to discover ways in which you might lighten your load. *For brochures and more information, contact:*

> Children of Aging Parents
> 1609 Woodbourne Rd., Suite 302A
> Levittown, PA 19057
> 215-945-6900

252. If you fall ill, think carefully about how you will involve your adult children. Some will want to swoop in and make all the decisions for you, encouraging you to forfeit your independence. Others may become frightened and distance themselves physically and emotionally. Frank discussion of your illness, including the prognosis and your plans for its management, is key. If you have a life-threatening condition, most chil-

dren will appreciate knowing the truth. But you know better than anyone what their emotional reaction might be. If you feel more comfortable not sharing information, then that's okay, too.

253. Abuse of the elderly by younger relatives is a growing problem.

The House Select Committee for Aging has estimated that, annually, over 1 million older Americans are physically, financially, or emotionally abused by their relatives. Elder abuse, also called domestic mistreatment, sometimes occurs because a family mistakenly believes that home care is the only option for an elderly relative. Caregivers can be well-meaning, but easily overwhelmed by the needs of their relative.

254. Protect yourself from domestic mistreatment. Some do's:

• Arrange to have your pension or Social Security check deposited directly into your bank account. (Contact your local Social Security office or call their national hotline at 800-772-1213.)

• Keep in touch with your circle of friends. Develop a "buddy system," and plan to have frequent contact. Ask friends to visit you, even if briefly.

• Have your own telephone; send and open your own mail.

• If possible, take care of your personal appointments with doctors and dentists.

• Don't agree to live with a person who is violent, alcoholic, a drug user, or who makes you feel uncomfortable in any way.

• Don't accept personal care in return for transferral of your property or assets, unless you have contacted a lawyer first.

• Don't allow anyone to hide details of your finances or property management from you.

Glorious Grandparenting

255. There's no substitute for grandparents in a child's life. We older family members give our children's children an invaluable emotional base. We provide continuity with the past. We become trusted guardians when our grandchildren need extra care. And a grandparent's outpouring of love and affection usually comes minus the rules and regulations of parents—we spoil the little ones rotten!

256. The following quotations from grandchildren sum it up:

• Carson, aged 4: "Grandmothers are soft, smell different—and eat a lot."

• Harry, 16: "Grandparents are there when you are in trouble; they can take your side without any risk."

• Alexandra, 9: "My grandfather tells me about when everyone was as young as I am, and they did the same things."

257. A grandparent's role may be difficult to define. Because of our complex society, the role of grandparents may differ from family to family. Here are a few observations and suggestions.

• Child-rearing ideas may differ from generation to generation. Insisting that your ways were better can alienate you from your children—and thus from your grandchildren.

• Overindulgence with grandchildren can lead to being valued just for your material gifts. Balance is the key.

• Adult children can find it tempting to use you as a baby-sitter. Remind your children to ask for, not demand, the gift of your time.

258. Sometimes you have to be a diplomat.

Here are two more suggestions for dealing with adult children and their children.

• When you disagree with a grandchild's parent, don't interject your opinion unless the parent asks for it; never challenge the parent's authority in front of the child.

• If a grandchild appeals to you to take his side against his parents, remind him that his parents have final authority over him and that they have his best interests at heart. You can provide support without undermining his parents.

259. Stay close with your grandchildren, no matter what their age. If they're geographically far, send them postcards from a day trip or a historical site in your own town. Seed packets are fun to receive, too. If they're in college, they'll love receiving care packages of goodies. Older grandchildren will appreciate being given treasured family mementos such as old letters or photos of their parents as children—both are sure to spark a lively discussion.

260. Don't let divorce stop you from seeing your grandchildren. The best way to preserve your relationship with your grandchildren when their parents become divorced is to avoid entering the battles between the children's parents. Don't take sides. Should one parent refuse to allow you to continue a relationship with your grandchildren, you can resort to legal action to obtain visitation rights. Every state now has laws allowing grandparents to petition the court for visitation rights with their grandchildren.

261. In the event of divorce, your grandchildren may gain a new parent. The divorce rate in the United States now hovers between 45 and 50 percent; about 80 percent of those who divorce remarry, usually within three years. Biological grandparents are now more valuable than ever, because they can provide continuity for their grandchildren. Don't let the difficulties of scheduling—or any personal animosity—in new, "blended" families prevent you from nurturing the bond you have with your grandchildren.

Friendships Old and New

262. Your old buddies are more important than ever. As years go by, the people who are closest to you emotionally—that is, children and spouse—begin to leave, due to college, new job opportunities, marriage, divorce, or death. Or you may be single and childless and feeling the lack of family connections. Now is when friends become particularly important to your emotional health.

There are all different types of friends. Some are confidants, and some are people you only do certain activities with—say, golf, bingo, or shopping. There are ex-coworkers, people from your church or synagogue, members of your aerobics, fitness, or yoga group. All of these connections are valuable; and some may even be cultivated into deeper relationships.

263. There are lots of potential new friends out there. Most communities have senior centers (a van may be available to pick you up at home and drive you to the center for a day of activities). Go to religious services, political meetings, senior aerobics, yoga classes. Once you're there, *talk* to people. If you're the outdoors type, join—or start—a hiking or cycling club for adults your age. Ask a neighbor to accompany you on daily heart-healthy walks around the neighborhood. Found an eating club, bridge society, or some other group that fits your interests. Volunteer—see Chapter 2 of this book for details.

264. Get in touch with long-lost pals. Don't be shy about attending high school and college reunions. They provide an excellent opportunity to reconnect with people who used to matter to you, and who can again. Use the Internet's many directories to search nationwide databases of names, phone numbers, and e-mail addresses—you may be able to send a message to an old school chum right on the spot. (You can go on-line at most public libraries; the reference librarian will be happy to get you started.)

265. Reconnect with long-lost relatives. Now is the time to mend that rift with the sister you never speak to or the brother who drifted away into work and new family involvements. Forget the past (except for the good parts). If it feels awkward to call, then send a card. Adult siblings can be a great source of mutual support in later years, especially when you each may be facing weighty issues such as child-rearing concerns, the illness or death of your parents, or the death of a spouse.

266. Bond with others whose families are far away.

If your grown children are farther away than an easy drive—or if you don't have children—you may feel especially lonely during the holidays. This is a good time to begin creating new traditions. Start a birthday lunch club; plan a Fourth of July picnic, seder feast, or Christmas dinner especially for others whose families are not near. There are more of them out there than you may think.

267. Don't underestimate the power of pets. There are all kinds of statistics about the physical and emotional benefits of pet ownership. Pets keep your blood pressure down and your heart beating smoothly. Their gentle companionship is a soothing balm when things aren't going so well. Their unconditional love has even been said to make people live longer.

268. It may be difficult, but it is not impossible, for older women to find suitable partners. Women tend to marry men a few years older than themselves and often outlive their husbands by seven or eight years. As a result, most married women are eventually widowed—and the population of older men is low. However, if you want male friendship, you can probably find it. And keep in mind that relationships between older women and younger men are becoming more and more common these days.

269. Singles groups can be a source of friendship as well as romance. There are dozens of singles organizations these days, both local and national, and many of them cater exclusively to people of age. Check the paper, make some calls, and ask the organization's leader how many people aged 55 and over are in the group. Even if you don't find the mate of your dreams, you will find a group of like-minded people who are having dinner together, going to plays together, and participating in discussion groups. It gets you out of the house and into the world. You'll probably bond with others in your same boat. And if you're really lucky, you may find a new mate.

270. If you do start a new relationship, remember that approximately 11 percent of all new AIDS cases are found in people 50 and over. In the last few years, new AIDS cases rose faster among middle-aged and older people than in those under 40. Because the immune system normally declines with age, AIDS is particularly serious for older adults. HIV in older adults is usually spread through sexual contact; to help avoid infection, always use condoms if you become sexually involved with someone other than a longtime, uninfected partner.

The National AIDS Hotline operates 24 hours a day, seven days a week, and offers general information and local referrals, as well as brochures.

National AIDS Hotline
800-342-2437

SAGE provides HIV/AIDS information and referrals for people 50 and over.

Seniors in a Gay Environment (SAGE)
208 W. 13th St.
New York, NY 10011
212-714-2247

271. For more ideas about expanding your network, contact the local branches of the following national groups.

National Alliance of Senior Citizens
925 15th St. NW
Washington, DC 2005
202-986-0117

American Association of Retired Persons
109 K St. NW
Washington, DC 20049
800-424-3410

To join with other elder activists, contact:

Gray Panthers
2025 Pennsylvania Ave., Suite 821
Washington, DC 20006
202-455-3132

Part

Here's to Your Health

Chapter 5:
The Alphabetical Body

Change is the only constant, especially for the human body. Somewhere in your 30s or 40s, for example, you probably noticed the first "character lines" appearing on your face. Maybe you started to put on weight more easily and began to find a gray hair or two. These days, you may have noticed other changes, too: You don't have as much energy as you once had, your muscles aren't as strong as they used to be, and perhaps you now need glasses for reading or driving. The physiological changes that occur as we age are fascinating ones—interesting in general because they're part of the human comedy and riveting because they're happening to us.

In this chapter you'll find information about what's going on with your bones, brain, feet, heart, and other parts of your body as it ages. It's a kind of quick refresher course in human physiology, mature-style. Subsequent chapters in this section discuss ways to cope with those changes—from good nutrition and exercise to dealing with illness.

The Bones

272. Bones have a public relations problem. The perception is that they stop growing once you reach full height; the truth is that bones are living tissue, and they need good care. From your 30s on, bone mass begins to slowly decline. That means it's important to maintain good nutritional habits (calcium is particularly important for bone strength) as well as exercise. Studies show that just taking daily walks is beneficial to your bones and that weight-bearing exercise can help to slow bone loss.

273. We become shorter and wider in our later years. The shoulders tend to narrow, the chest to grow, and the pelvis to spread. Chest size—that is, the measurement of broadness of the rib cage—reaches its maximum in women between the ages of 55 and 64, and in men, between 45 and 54.

The Brain and Memory

274. There is no change in "crystallized" intelligence as we age.

That is, our grasp of vocabulary, general information, and conceptual understanding remains the same. According to the Johns Hopkins Medical Institutions, that is because blood flow to the brain is the same at 74 as it is at 24. They also report that "fluid" intelligence—the speed at which we process information—does decline, but only marginally: A 70-year-old will take about a quarter of a second longer to respond on memory tests than a 30-year-old. Many researchers believe this is because older people simply have more information stored in their brains to sort through.

275. Older people use their heads better than youngsters do. You could say that brain cells are wasted on the young. Though neurons do begin to die off as we age, scientists believe that this is when our large store of extra, previously unused brain cells kicks in. In other words, younger people may have more neurons, but they aren't using all of them. And recent research strongly suggests that if you keep the brain active (by learning new things, for instance), neurons will once again begin to grow.

276. Remember: Everyone forgets. Memory changes are normal with age and often start at around age 70. We forget what we had for dinner last night, but a random summer day from our childhood comes back in vivid detail. Forgetting can be especially scary after 55 because we worry that memory lapses mean we have Alzheimer's disease. Actually, memory changes are most often caused by temporary—and treatable—medical or emotional conditions. Studies have shown that memory loss in the aged is often a result of depression, loss of estrogen, the side effects of medications, or just plain boredom.

The Cardiopulmonary System—Blood, Lungs, Heart

The Lungs

277. Aerobic workouts can increase your lung capacity, no matter what your age. And so can giving up smoking, of course. The lungs are a pair of elastic organs that take up most of the chest cavity; they're responsible for transporting oxygen to the bloodstream. Their elasticity decreases by about 40 percent from age 20 to age 80, as does their ability to cough effectively, thereby increasing our chance of infection. Smoking appears to age our lungs more rapidly—so stop smoking, and start walking—or go jogging!

278. For more information on keeping your lungs healthy, contact:

National Heart, Lung, and Blood Institute
Building 31, Room 4A21
31 Center Dr.
Bethesda, MD 20892
301-496-4236

American Lung Association
1740 Broadway
New York, NY 10019
212-315-8700

The Heart

279. The heart is a complex pumping device, worthy of admiration. For example, a single heartbeat triggers perfectly timed movements of millions of cells to propel blood from the heart to the rest of the body (about sixty to seventy times a minute at rest). The heart rate during maximal exercises declines about 25 percent between the ages of 20 and 75. Some atherosclerosis (buildup of fatty deposits in the arteries) is normal with aging. To lessen the risk of heart attack, watch your diet, exercise, and if you smoke, quit.

Blood

280. About 7 percent of your body weight is blood. An average-sized adult has about six quarts of the red stuff. The main work of the blood is transportation. It carries everything that needs to be shipped from one part of the body to another. Oxygen breathed into the lungs is carried to all body cells; carbon dioxide is carried away to the lungs, where it is exhaled; and food substances absorbed from the intestines are distributed by the blood to cells throughout the body.

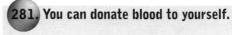

281. You can donate blood to yourself.

Many people who are to undergo surgery choose to do this in advance of the operation. The process, called auto-blood donation, is being used increasingly by those concerned about diseases such as hepatitis and AIDS. For free brochures, contact:

American College of Surgeons
55 E. Erie St.
Chicago, IL 60611
312-664-4050
Ask for "Doctor, What Can You Tell Me About Donating Blood to Myself?"

National Heart, Lung, and Blood Institute
Building 31, Room 4A21
31 Center Dr.
Bethesda, MD 20892
301-496-4236
Ask for "Your Operation, Your Blood" and "Transfusion Alert."

282. Blood pressure goes up nearly 25 percent between the ages of 20 and 75. Blood pressure is the force of the blood pushing against the walls of the arteries. It's normal for blood pressure to go up and down during the day. High blood pressure—also called hypertension—occurs when your blood pressure reading is consistently greater than 140/90. It is very common: About one in four adult Americans has it. Untreated hypertension damages the arteries and is the leading cause of strokes. The good news is that hypertension, once diagnosed, is easy to control. So if you haven't had your blood pressure checked recently, make an appointment.

The Digestive System

283. The digestive system performs the amazing task of changing food into body fuel. The chemical process of digestion starts when you put food into your mouth, and it comes into contact with the enzymes contained in saliva. The food gets chewed, crushed, and mixed with several other enzymes and acids until it's tiny enough to be taken into the blood. The blood then carries the food particles to cells in every part of our body, where they are changed into energy or used to form new body tissue. What isn't absorbed is pushed into the colon for elimination from the body. Digestive organs include the mouth, esophagus, stomach, pancreas, gallbladder, liver, small intestine, and colon.

284. In general, the gastrointestinal system changes less as we age than do other body systems. Still, after a lifetime of meals and snacks, the digestive system may work less efficiently. Digestive disorders are caused by stress, infection, disease, food poisoning, and diet. Digestion can also be hampered by medications, laxatives, reduced exercise, and changes in eating patterns.

The Ears and Hearing

285. Over time, our ears become less sensitive to sound. Hearing is the transformation of sound waves in the air into electrical nerve impulses that are carried to the brain. As we age, the walls of the ear canal thin, and the eardrum thickens. The small bones of the ear can even be subject to arthritis. Our ability to hear high-frequency tones may go down in our 20s, while the ability to hear low-frequency tones tends to decline in our 60s. Between ages 30 and 80, men lose hearing more quickly than do women.

286. Over 22 million Americans have some degree of hearing loss.

It's easy for others to mistake hearing loss in an individual for grouchiness, confusion, or distraction. Some common indications that you may be experiencing hearing loss:

- You don't hear a dripping faucet.
- You find it hard to distinguish individual words, both in person and over the phone.
- Another person's speech sounds slurred or mumbled, especially if there's background noise.
- The higher-pitched voices of women and children are particularly hard to hear.
- If two or more people are talking at once, you find it hard to follow the conversation.
- Certain sounds are overly loud.

• There's a hissing or ringing in the background.

• TV shows, concerts, or parties are losing their charm because you're finding them hard to hear.

The Eyes and Vision

287. We produce fewer tears as we grow older. And our eyelids may get droopy as tissue around the eyes loses tone. The lenses typically begin to lose their elasticity when we're around 40, resulting in presbyopia (see below). This process tapers off by the time we're 70, meaning that your eyeglass prescription shouldn't be changing anymore.

288. Vision does change with age, but not always for the worse. Sometimes nearsightedness improves, and astigmatism lessens. The most common condition of older eyes is presbyopia (also known as farsightedness). Presbyopia actually begins while we're in our 20s, but we usually don't notice it until we're around 40 or 50. It is easily corrected with glasses. Beginning at about age 50, eyes don't deal so well with glare or dim light; older eyes are also subject to harmless "floaters," cataracts, glaucoma, and age-related macular degeneration (the inability to focus properly on objects directly in front of you).

You should pay attention to any changes either in the appearance of your eyes or in your vision. A periodic eye exam is recommended for everyone over 50, especially for those with chronic health conditions. Many eye diseases have no early signs or symptoms, but if they are detected early enough, treatment can prevent loss of eyesight.

289. If you have any of the following symptoms, see your eye doctor.

• Trouble adjusting to dark rooms
• Difficulty focusing
• Abnormal sensitivity to light or glare
• Change in the color of the iris
• Irritated eyelids
• Double vision
• Dark spots in the field of vision
• Lines that seem wavy
• Teary, watering, itchy eyes
• Seeing a cloudy or ghost image around a central image
• Flashes of light
• What seems like a curtain blocking the vision
• Loss of side (peripheral) vision

The Feet

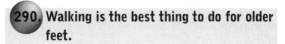

290. Walking is the best thing to do for older feet.

Your feet are often the victims of a host of age-related maladies. Being farthest from your heart, they suffer the most from poor circulation. Their thirty-three joints and over one hundred ligaments and tendons lose their elasticity over time, which may result in aching feet as well as an alteration in your shoe size. Soles and heels begin to lose their protective covering of fat, which means you may get more calluses as you age. And thinning skin makes the feet more susceptible to bacterial and fungal infections.

Podiatrists say that keeping the foot toned by walking or by other exercise—always wearing proper footwear, of course—will alleviate most of these ills. A foot massage also improves circulation (some believe it has other health benefits, too). And it feels just plain wonderful.

The Hair

291. With age, hair changes and thins, but it doesn't have to stop being gorgeous. The entire body, except the palms of the hands and the soles of the feet, grows hair. With age, the hair on our head grows thinner. Conversely, we may find more hair popping up in places we don't want to see it: Men may find more inside their nose and on the ears; women may begin plucking stray hairs from their chin.

If you've worn your hair the same way for more than a couple of years, you may want to put yourself in the hands of a good stylist. The right color and an updated style can take years off your appearance. On the other hand, some people find that a touch of gray adds character to their appearance.

292. Heredity determines if and when your hair will turn gray. Graying is caused by a decline of pigment at the root of the hair; for the most part, whatever happened to your par-

ents in this regard is probably what's going to happen to you. Hair that has turned white has no pigment left in it at all. The result can be rather striking. A mousy-haired friend, now going white, says happily that she's always wanted to be a blue-eyed blonde, and soon she'll be a blue-eyed *platinum* blonde.

293. Balding is hereditary, too. Hair is usually thickest in the teens and early 20s. As time passes, your hair often becomes finer, and the number of follicles in the scalp decreases. For men, balding usually starts at the temples and spreads up to the area above the forehead. Postmenopausal women may experience thinning of the hair. New topical drugs can help both sexes keep the hair that they have.

Joints

294. Joints connect bones to other bones. Well, actually it's the ligaments that do the connecting. The space between is padded with cartilage, and the whole assembly is surrounded by synovial fluid, which keeps the joints lubricated and running smoothly. The bursa is outside of this; it lubricates the muscles. Many older people swear they can feel approaching weather changes in their joints, but scientists dispute the validity of this.

295. Knees and hips feel aging first. Because these joints have been working the hardest throughout your life, they're often the first to feel the effects of aging. Ligaments become less elastic, and muscle mass begins to decrease. Once again, the best way to combat this is by keeping active.

The Mouth, Teeth, and Gums

296. Nearly half of our taste buds are lost by the time we turn 70—it's a blessing in disguise. Sour, bitter, and sweet tastes are less obvious, so a pesky sweet tooth may not need satisfying nearly as often, and spicy foods you may once have disliked suddenly taste better. This is a good thing, since many spicy foods (fresh garlic, hot peppers) are good for you. Salty taste remains the same, so continue to go easy there. Take time to eat slowly, allowing yourself to enjoy the aroma of the food and to distinguish sweet, salty, sour, and bitter tastes.

297. Thanks to fluoride and better dental care, more people are keeping more of their teeth. The mouth, teeth, and gums stay in pretty good shape as we age if we've cared for them over time. Difficulties are often the result of health problems in general. With age, the bottom edges of the front teeth can flatten and become thin. To keep your teeth looking younger, give them a face-lift. Ask your dentist to round the chewing edges of your front teeth. It doesn't take long, it isn't painful, and it's a subtle change that will give you a more youthful appearance. Cosmetic bonding is another popular technique—the dentist applies a thin veneer of plastic to each tooth, filling in chips and deep grooves.

The Muscles

298. Regular exercise is crucial for keeping your muscles young. Muscle mass declines some 5 percent to 10 percent per decade of life. A mature body is generally comprised of more fat and less muscle, partly because muscle cells don't regenerate—once misused or overused, a muscle can't repair itself. Research is now being conducted into the use of hormones, along with exercise, to help maintain muscle mass as we age, but for right now, get out there and exercise.

The Nails

299. Our nails thicken and dry over time. Intercellular glue holds the tightly packed cells of the nail plate together, and when the glue fails, nails split, chip, or break. They may also become marked by ridges from the cuticle to the tip. Split fingernails occur as a result of nails being alternately wet and dry; if your nails tend to split, wear rubber gloves when your hands are in water or apply moisturizing cream immediately after exposure to water. Soaking nails in warm vegetable oil works, too.

300. Tapping your nails is actually good for them. Other healthful practices include typing, and playing a musical instrument. It's also a good idea to keep your nails clipped short, and when filing, to move the emery board in one direction only. If you use polish, acetate-based removers are the way to go—acetone-based products contribute to brittleness. Contrary to popular belief, nothing you ingest—including gelatin, calcium, or vitamins—will improve the health of your nails. But vitamin deficiencies—particularly of A, D, and B_6—may slow nail growth.

301. Nails can signal changes to the body's well-being.

Even ancient physicians relied on them to diagnose disease. If you see these signs, consult a doctor:

- Spots on the nails
- Clubbing or curling around the fingertip (emphysema, cardiovascular disease, or cirrhosis)
- Longitudinal white streaks from the cuticle to the nail's end (kidney failure, Hodgkin's disease, heart attack, or the effect of certain drugs)
- Blue nail beds (diabetes, heart disease, lack of oxygen, or some autoimmune diseases)
- Brown or black discoloration spreading from the nail bed to the surrounding tissue (gastrointestinal polyps or malignant melanoma)
- "Splinter hemorrhages" or red streaks (bleeding capillaries, high blood pressure, peptic ulcer, or heart problems)

The Nose

302. The nose does more than detect aromas. It helps us breathe, and in so doing, filters out irritants and pollutants. The nasal passage even contains an antibacterial agent to help protect us from infection. Smell, of course, enhances the enjoyment of food and is also powerful in triggering long-term memory. In testing, children given smell cues along with a list of words to memorize did better in recalling the words than children who didn't have such cues.

303. Our sense of smell diminishes with age. That means we should use a lighter touch with perfumes, aftershaves, and room deodorizers, since their scents will smell stronger to those around us. More important, it also means that we should check smoke detectors regularly to be sure they're in good working order, since we may not be able to smell something that's smoldering.

The Reproductive System

304. By age 55, most women have entered menopause. As we all know, menopause brings about many changes as estrogen and progesterone production slows. Symptoms of menopause include irregular menstruation, hot flashes, and vaginal dryness. More than 75 percent of women sail through menopause with little or no trouble. Menopause is a gradual process, considered to be over when you have not menstruated for a year.

305. "Women don't have hot flashes, they have power surges!"

Many women welcome the postmenopausal years as a time when they no longer have to deal with menstruation or worry about getting pregnant. Such women typically experience a surge of energy (summed up by the quotation above, taken from Gail Sheehy's *Menopause: The Silent Passage);* they run for political office, write books, start businesses.

306. Most men don't think about their prostate until they pass their 50th birthday. After that, enlargement of the walnut-sized gland is not uncommon. Enlargement can block or irritate the passage of urine; surgery is often recommended to correct the condition. Consisting of two lobes enclosed by an outer layer of tissue, the prostate is located in front of the rectum, just below the bladder, and encircling the urethra.

The Skin

307. No, your skin does not stretch with age. It may seem like it does, especially when you take a look at your eyelids, throat, and cheeks. What's really happening is that the connective tissues of the skin—the collagen and the elastin—are losing strength.

The texture of a woman's skin can also change due to a drop in female hormones. The outer layer thickens and the inner layers become thinner, the result often being an increased sensitivity to cold. Be careful about getting warm, though—the skin burns more easily as we age.

308. Skin becomes drier with the passage of time. Use plenty of moisturizer: When the skin is dry, wrinkles are more noticeable. Dry skin can also mean itchiness, especially on the legs. It's a problem particularly in winter, when humidity is low and moisture escapes from the skin.

309. Liver spots have nothing to do with the liver. As you grow older, you may begin to notice brownish-colored spots, or even small patches, on your face and the backs of your hands. Also called age spots, these are nothing more than oversize freckles. Most people also develop "ruby spots," tiny bumps that can appear almost anywhere on the body, except the hands and feet. Both age spots and ruby spots are harmless. Note: If one of these spots changes color or size in a short period of time, or if the surface texture changes or has irregular edges, check with your doctor.

310. The best way to protect your skin from aging is by using sunblock. Many women are comfortable with the natural aging process. But if you are not one of them, using sunblock is a pretty good way to slow the progress of time. Ideally, sunblock should be used not only when you go to the beach but whenever you are exposed to the sun for any

length of time. The reduction of our ozone layer has resulted in an increase of ultraviolet radiation from the sun, which contributes mightily to wrinkling and sagging of skin, not to mention skin cancer, the most common form of cancer in the United States today.

311. Other ways to apply the brakes to aging of skin:

• Stop smoking right now. It's bad for your health, and it promotes wrinkles. The same goes for excess alcohol consumption.

• Eat a balanced diet, one that includes plenty of vegetables and fresh fruits.

• Drink at least six eight-ounce glasses of water per day. Coffee, tea, and alcoholic beverages actually drain your system of the fluids it needs to stay healthy.

312. For women who wear makeup, it might be time for a change.
Ditch the oil-absorbing powders of your youth, and choose cream products to help get moisture back into your skin. Choose cream instead of powdered blush, which often contains astringents that can make your skin dry and rough. Moreover, powder tends to migrate into creases and accentuate wrinkles. Try using a lip pencil to help prevent the feathering that occurs due to fine lines around the lips. Wondering about wrinkle creams? They usually rely on chemicals that irritate the skin slightly, causing blood to flow and plump up underlying tissue. It may make wrinkles less obvious, but the effect is only temporary.

The Urinary System

313. Urinary incontinence doesn't HAVE to be an inevitable part of growing older.
The urinary system consists of the kidneys, ureters, bladder, and urethra. The kidneys clean the blood, removing liquid waste in the form of urine and passing it down the ureters, to be stored in the bladder and then passed through the urethra.

The idea that we have to endure a breakdown of this system in our later years is a common one. Actually, incontinence is a condition that can be caused by a variety of factors, the most common being medications, infection, and weakened muscles (time to start those Kegel exercises). If you suffer from urinary incontinence, see a doctor. The cure rate is 90 percent.

Chapter 6:

Treating Yourself Well—Nutrition and Exercise

Nothing is as important as exercise and good nutrition for staying healthy throughout our lives. This is something we taught our children when they were young, and now medical research is backing up what we've known all along.

It's never too late to introduce good eating habits, nor for those habits to make a difference. It might seem like all your favorite foods are bad for you, that everything causes cancer, and that nutritionists continually alter health claims for specific foods. The truth is that ongoing research yields new discoveries all the time and that—as you knew all along—using your own common sense is often best (it's no big surprise that baked potatoes are better for you than potato chips, right?).

And it's never too late to begin an exercise regime. Working out, in one form or another, is essential to both physical well-being and emotional balance. It doesn't have to be a formal workout or involve machines and health clubs—although those can be effective, and fun, too. Exercise can be housework and gardening or a half hour's brisk walk-and-talk with a friend.

We know that eating well and exercising can be difficult sometimes. But we hope that this chapter will inspire you to try, despite constraints of time, money—and inclination.

Nutrition

314. Mature adults have special nutritional needs. We need to consume nutrient-dense foods, so that each bite we take packs as much dietary power as possible. Here's why we need such high-quality foods.

• Our ability to extract nutrients from food declines somewhat as we age.
• We need extra nutrients to keep our immune system in optimal condition and to aid recovery after surgery.
• Drugs, both prescription and over-the-

counter, can affect the body's ability to absorb and use various nutrients.

315. Here are some reasons why we may be undernourished. We may not be feeding ourselves as often as we should, because of a diminished sense of taste and smell. And mature adults who live alone may feel it "isn't worth the bother" to create well-balanced meals. Try to create a relaxing, special ritual around mealtime. Eat near a window or with your favorite television show or a book for company. Flowers or candles shouldn't be reserved for guests alone. Indulge in new foods and new recipes. If you feel cooking for yourself every day is a bore, cook in quantity and freeze smaller portions to be heated in the microwave later.

316. Some common medications prevent nutrients from being absorbed by the body—and vice versa. Antacids containing magnesium and aluminum hydroxide may interfere with the body's ability to use vitamin A. Mineral oil, commonly found in laxatives, can hinder the absorption of vitamins A, D, E, and K. If you're taking tetracycline, hold off on dairy products—they reduce the antibiotic's effectiveness.

317. Are you at risk of having poor nutrition? Here's a checklist to find out (total the points as you go along).

• A medical condition has changed the kind and/or amount of food I eat. (2)
• I eat fewer than two meals a day. (3)
• I eat few fruits or vegetables. (2)

• I have three or more alcoholic drinks almost every day. (2)
• Tooth or mouth problems make it hard to eat. (2)
• I smoke. (4)
• I eat alone. (1)
• I take three or more medicines per day. (1)
• I have lost or gained ten pounds in the last six months. (2)
• I don't always feel strong enough to cook. (2)

If your total score is 1 or 2: Good, but take the quiz again in six months to make sure you are maintaining good habits. *For a score of 3 to 5:* You are at moderate nutritional risk. *If your score is 6 points or more:* You are at high risk—consult your doctor or a nutritionist.

318. Clipping coupons isn't the only way to save on your food budget. Here are some tips.

• Buy generic brands. They often taste the same, and they cost less.
• Use unit pricing posted on shelf edges in the store to compare prices.
• Don't assume that buying in bulk is cheaper. Again, check the unit pricing to be sure.
• Buy only what you can use. You may find that single pints of milk, small portions from a salad bar, or single-serving cans of tuna cost more per unit than large containers. But if the contents of large containers go bad before you can use them, then it isn't really a bargain after all.

• Watch for specials on products you know you like and won't go bad. When you see them, buy in bulk.

319. Brochures are available that explain the food assistance and food stamp programs. For information, contact:

Human Nutrition Services
U.S. Department of Agriculture
3101 Park Center Dr.
Alexandria, VA 22302
703-305-2286

320. Nutritional Basic Number 1: Limit fat intake. Dietary guidelines for Americans recommend that of our daily caloric intake, no more than 30 percent should come from fat. Of that, no more than 10 percent, or thirty calories, should come from saturated fats. That's because the cholesterol in fat can lead to high blood pressure and heart disease. Keep in mind that any fried food will raise cholesterol levels in the blood. This is true even when using "heart-healthy" oils to fry with. Read food labels to see how much fat the product contains.

321. That said, fat is still an essential nutrient in the average diet. It is a valuable energy source and also contains vitamins A, D, E, and K. Just make sure you're eating the right kind of fat. Again, read labels carefully: saturated fat, tropical oils (for instance, palm and coconut), and anything hydrogenated all contribute to heart disease. Your best bets are olive oil (it's actually good for the blood), canola oil, and safflower oil.

322. Nutritional Basic Number 2: Eat enough protein. While young people probably consume more protein than they need, many older people do not get enough. In general, our consumption of protein should be about 10 percent to 15 percent of our total daily diet. Protein-rich foods include meat, poultry, fish, and legumes. Other good choices: tofu, nuts, peanut butter, beans (including chickpeas and lentils), cheese, and eggs.

323. Nutritional Basic Number 3: Increase your intake of COMPLEX carbohydrates. That means eating breads, cereals, rice, barley, pasta, oatmeal, and beans. Muffins and cakes are rich in carbohydrates, but their high fat and sugar content make them a poor dietary choice. Whole grains—for instance, brown rice and whole-wheat flour products—are nutritional dynamos, since they have more fiber, vitamins, and minerals than their refined counterparts. A diet rich in whole grains will help you avoid constipation, varicose veins, hiatal hernia, and the formation of calcium kidney stones. Populations whose diet includes lots of rice have lower rates of colon, breast, and prostate cancer.

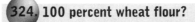 **324. 100 percent wheat flour?**

Bread manufacturers know that people are more health-conscious these days and can be a little misleading in labeling their products. If you're looking for 100 percent whole-wheat bread, flip the loaf over and read the list of ingredients carefully. If it says "100 percent *wheat* flour," that simply indicates the bread is made from wheat flour, as opposed to rye or buckwheat flour. And it almost always means *white* wheat flour was used. If you want the nutritional boost of a whole-wheat product, make sure the package says "100 percent *whole-wheat* flour."

325. Nutritional Basic Number 4: Eat five or more half-cup servings of fruits and vegetables every day. Vegetables and fruits are high in fiber and loaded with antioxidants, so eating them puts you at lower risk for cancer and heart disease. You can have three servings of fruit and two of vegetables, or three of vegetables and two of fruit, and so on (for leafy vegetables, such as fresh spinach or romaine, one cup constitutes one serving). It's best to vary your diet to make sure you're getting the full spectrum of vitamins and minerals, but orange vegetables, dark green vegetables, and citrus fruits usually pack the biggest nutritional punch.

326. Choose an "All-Star" vegetable. The July 1994 issue of the *Mayo Clinic Health Letter* designated five fruits or vegetables as "All-Stars" for good health. The All-Stars are broccoli, mangoes, papayas, strawberries, and turnip greens. They were chosen because a single serving of each met two of the three criteria for helping to ward off disease. Other nutrient-dense choices: cantaloupe, kale, and red bell peppers.

327. Frozen vegetables may be more nutritious than the "fresh" vegetables in your grocery store. As soon as fresh produce is picked, it begins to lose its nutritive value. By the time it gets to the store, sits on the shelves, and then spends another few days in your refrigerator, even more has been lost. By contrast, many large food companies freeze the produce right in the field, directly after harvesting, thus preserving most of the original vitamin content until the food is used.

328. Nutritional Basic Number 5: Get plenty of fiber. A diet high in fiber lessens the risk of heart disease and colon cancer, not to mention constipation and other digestive tract disorders. It reduces the amount of cholesterol in your blood and lowers the insulin requirements of diabetics. Some studies show that women who consume high-fiber diets have a lower incidence of breast cancer. You can get more fiber into your diet by eating more fruits and vegetables (especially raw), whole-wheat products, bran, brown rice, popcorn, and nuts and seeds. Increase your fiber intake gradually, though—your system needs time to get used to the change.

329. What about eggs, red meat, and milk? Most of us grew up learning that these were mainstays of a good diet. It may or may not have been healthful for our parents and grandparents to eat a lot of these foods; scientists now know that these foods, rich in fat and cholesterol, are better suited to a very active, outdoor lifestyle. Additionally, much of our food now carries additives (such as growth hormones, and pesticides ingested through animal feed) that it did not a generation ago, which may increase the risk of cancer. Our greater reliance on processed foods and our relatively sedentary lifestyles are factors to be weighed when making our dietary choices.

330. Nutritional needs have been reorganized from "Food Groups" to the "Food Guide Pyramid." The Food Guide Pyramid puts more emphasis on proportions of certain foods in the diet. Nutritionists now recommend six to eleven servings a day of grains (bread, cereal, rice, pasta); three to five servings of fruits and vegetables; two to three servings of dairy products; and two to three servings of proteins (meat, poultry, fish, beans, eggs, nuts). Fats, oils, and sugars are to be used only occasionally.

331. Sugar can be a nutritional disaster. Ingesting too much sugar contributes to all kinds of diseases and disorders, including diabetes, arthritis, heart disease, high blood pressure, obesity, and tooth decay. A recent study found that women who drink more than an average amount of sweetened beverages are at increased risk for breast cancer. Besides all this, consumption of sugar usually goes hand in hand with consumption of "empty calories"—in other words, you neglect to eat healthful foods because you fill up on junk.

Read labels carefully, because sugar is hidden in all kinds of foods (including ketchup and most peanut butter). Watch for "syrups" and almost any word ending in "-ose" (for instance, sucrose, fructose, glucose)—all are varieties of sugar. Note: Artificial sweeteners are just as bad for you, if not worse—their long-term use has been associated with cancer.

332. Processed foods: another nutritional disaster. Processed foods are usually made with refined white flour (which has been linked to some forms of cancer) and contain an abundance of sugar, saturated fat, salt, and additives. Our bodies are not well equipped to deal with an overload of these substances. Watch out for:

- Crunchy, greasy, salty foods such as bacon bits, potato chips, nacho chips, and some types of crackers, unless the food has been baked instead of fried
- Lunch meats, such as salami and bologna (if you must buy lunch meats, look for brands that are low in fat and sodium)
- Cakes, cookies, and pastries (again, too much refined flour and sugar and fat)
- Bran muffins and granola bars (some of which are as high in fat and sugar as a candy bar)

333. Sodium is hidden in food more often than you think. It's naturally present in most foods, but it's also added to foods to help flavor and preserve them. There is sodium in processed, canned, and frozen foods as well as in lunch meats and cheese.

Sodium helps our bodies to perform many of its vital functions. But too much of it may contribute to high blood pressure, which can lead to heart disease, stroke, and kidney failure. Because our blood pressure rises as we age, it is especially important for older people to keep sodium intake under control. Nutritionists generally recommend no more than 2,400 mg of sodium a day, which is roughly equivalent to a teaspoon of salt.

334. Here are a few ways to reduce the amount of sodium in your diet.

• Eat fresh foods, which usually have less sodium than processed foods.
• Eat chips and pretzels sparingly, if at all (or buy the unsalted versions).
• Avoid cured meats—ham, bacon, sausage, franks, smoked meats, and poultry.
• Remember that ketchup, mustard, relish, pickles, olives, sauces, and dips all contain sodium.
• Flavor foods with lemon, pepper, herbs, spices, onion, garlic, grated horseradish, or small amounts of mustard.

335. Be sure to drink enough water. As we grow older, the signal from our brain that tells us when we need water grows weaker. In addition, many older people cut back on liquids in the hope of avoiding incontinence. As a result, older people often become dehydrated. Water is crucial to the proper functioning of your body's systems. You need to drink between six and eight eight-ounce glasses of water each day—even if you don't feel thirsty.

336. Beta-carotene, antioxidants, and free radicals: Here's a crash course.

Free radicals are substances in our bodies that cause cell and tissue damage (a major cause of aging); antioxidants help prevent this damage; beta-carotene is a powerful antioxidant found in foods such as carrots, yams, and spinach.

Antioxidants help prevent heart disease, cancer, cataracts, and other health problems common to aging. Beta-carotene isn't the only antioxidant, though. Foods (or supplements) containing vitamins C and E, selenium, and zinc are all good sources. Green tea, available at health food stores (but even cheaper in Oriental grocery stores), is an excellent source of antioxidants.

337. Vitamins C and E are especially important for mature adults. Besides being an antioxidant, vitamin C helps our bodies to absorb calcium, which, as we know, keeps bones and teeth strong. Vitamin C also boosts the immune system and lessens the severity of colds and the flu, if taken early enough into the ailment. Vitamin C is found in citrus fruits, peppers, strawberries, raw cabbage, tomatoes, and green leafy vegetables.

Vitamin E—also an antioxidant—appears to lower risk of coronary artery disease, strengthen the immune system, protect against some cancers, slow the progress of Alzheimer's disease, improve blood circulation, and ease the swelling of arthritis. Some cardiologists are now recommending it, along with medication, to their patients. Vitamin E is found in vegetable oils, poultry, seafood, nuts, wheat germ, and eggs.

338. Fish oils have passed scientific testing with flying colors. Fish oils are shaping up as an important nutrient for older adults. They contain omega-3 fatty acids, which are good at fighting heart disease. Fish oils are also beneficial in the prevention and treatment of migraine headaches, asthma, high blood pressure, and kidney disease. And it turns out that fish is "brain food" after all, setting into motion a chemical process that results in an increase of mental energy.

The best source of fish oil is the fish itself, particularly mackerel and salmon. Fish oil capsules and pure cod-liver oil should be used cautiously and sparingly. By the way, improved testing methods have shown that shellfish is *not* high in cholesterol, as was previously believed.

339. Calcium-rich foods are important for bone strength.
Besides being a factor in the prevention of osteoporosis, calcium helps us absorb vitamin D, which is needed for bone strength and development.

Most people look to milk as their main source of calcium. Actually, a tin of sardines with bones contains more calcium than a cup of milk. A cup of yogurt and a cup of collard greens each contain as much calcium as an equal amount of milk. Dark green leafy vegetables, baked beans, and tofu are all good sources of this mineral. If you do choose milk, make sure it's the low-fat variety. And if you're one of the many adults who have developed lactose intolerance in your later years, you should know that this can usually be remedied by getting more exercise.

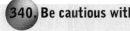

340. Be cautious with calcium supplements.

Too much calcium can lead to a depletion in your levels of iron, magnesium, and zinc. Some nutritionists recommend taking supplements of these minerals along with your calcium; others advise simply going easy on the calcium. Clinical tests have shown that a healthful diet plus multivitamin supplements is much more effective in preventing osteoporosis and in increasing bone density in postmenopausal women than is reliance on calcium supplements alone.

341. Herbal remedies are getting a lot of attention these days.
In recent years, the airwaves have been full of commercials for products containing garlic, ginkgo biloba, and ginseng. A May 1997 *Newsweek* article on St. John's wort was followed a few weeks later by an *NBC Dateline* story on the subject. The same year, *USA Today*'s weekend magazine featured a cover story on a new natural remedies book called *Miracle Cures,* by its "Eat Smart" columnist Jean Carper. The FDA is only now beginning to test the efficacy of herbal remedies, although many have been tested and used in Europe for years. Indeed, most herbs getting attention today have been used as remedies for thousands of years.

342. Echinacea and ginkgo biloba are two "media stars."
In Europe, echinacea is as commonly used as penicillin (and like penicillin, it can cause allergic reactions in a small percentage of people). It's used to ward off, or lessen the duration of, colds and the flu. Take it at the very first symptom of illness, because the sooner you use it, the better it works. Prolonged use reduces its effectiveness, so it is recommended that you take it for three days, skip three days, then start for three days again.

Ginkgo biloba has been tested extensively in Europe and is one of the most commonly prescribed medications in Germany and

France. Gingko is used to improve the memory and to lessen the effects of senility by dilating blood vessels and improving blood flow to the brain. Its relatively rare and mild side effects include headaches and gastrointestinal upsets.

343. Here are some more herbs of note. Ginseng has been used for thousands of years as an overall health tonic. Modern enthusiasts claim it regulates blood pressure and energy levels and boosts the immune system. Different varieties of the root are reported to have different effects—some are calming, some are stimulating. Make sure that what you buy contains the active ingredient of the root. Some doctors believe ginseng can elevate your blood pressure, so you might want to read further on the subject if this is a problem for you.

St. John's wort has been called nature's Prozac. It is used to alleviate depression and anxiety, with little or no side effects (roughly 2 percent of users experience gastrointestinal upset, restlessness, and some allergic reactions).

Saw palmetto is being used for prostate problems. It is said to improve the flow of urine in men with noncancerous enlarged prostates. It has few side effects, but doctors warn that it is not a substitute for conventional medical care.

344. There are no cure-alls. Despite encouraging research, there is no diet or vitamin, mineral, or herbal supplement that can completely ward off disease or halt aging. Manufacturers who make such claims for their products are being downright deceptive. Americans spend at least $10 billion each year on bogus health treatments, and older adults who want to improve their health or prevent aging are prime targets of advertisers. You should be wary of words such as "miraculous," "amazing," "guaranteed," or "effortless" in an advertisement.

345. A well-balanced diet is the best medicine. We've said it before, but it's worth repeating: Researchers have found that eating five servings of fruits and vegetables each day may well reduce the risk of illness and slow the aging process.

346. "Everything in moderation." Is it beneficial to take a daily vitamin and mineral supplement as you age? Some doctors and nutritionists believe you can fulfill all your nutritional requirements by eating a balanced diet (assuming you also quit smoking, get regular exercise, drink alcohol in moderation or not at all, and limit processed foods, sugar, and refined white flour as much as possible). Others feel that due to environmental pollution and the presence of hormones, additives, and pesticides in our food, we need an extra boost.

Studies on the efficacy of supplements are numerous and contradictory. Doctors frequently see older patients who are taking too much of a supplement in their quest for health, not realizing that sometimes these substances can be toxic. If you decide to take additional vitamins and minerals, be aware of proper dosages and of possible interactions with medications.

347. Nutritional information, especially for older Americans, is readily available. Health food stores often carry a variety of books and pamphlets with information on the latest nutritional research. The USFDA maintains the Nutrient Data Bank, which contains surveys and data on the nutrient values of various foods. Over twenty publications on nutrient composition are available. Contact:

U.S. Food and Drug Administration
Office of Constituents
200 C St. SW, HFF-11
Washington, DC 20204
202-205-4317

Obesity

348. Obesity can be hazardous to your health. Yes, our society has practically built a cult around the concept of being thin, and yes, we all have our own ideas about what beauty is. You should try to maintain your proper weight, not so that you can look glamorous, but because being more than 30 percent above your ideal weight puts you at a much greater risk for heart disease, hypertension, arthritis, stroke, and adult-onset diabetes. In long-term clinical studies, animals on a low-calorie diet lived longer, aged more slowly, and were healthier all around than those who were overfed.

349. Here's a guaranteed miracle diet. For almost all overweight people, consuming fewer calories and getting the proper amount of exercise is the most effective way to lose weight; for older adults, the best calories to cut are those that come from fat. Following this regimen not only aids in weight loss but also speeds up your metabolism—that means you'll burn calories more quickly and keep them off more easily.

Generally, men need about 2,300 calories a day after reaching age 50, and women need about 1,900 per day. A steady weight loss of one to two pounds a week is safe for most adults, and a slow and steady weight loss means that pounds are more likely to stay off over the long run.

350. Skipping meals to cut calories may have a boomerang effect. This kind of dieting fools the body into thinking it's starving. In reaction, the body will try to save energy by slowing its metabolism, thus making it even harder to lose weight. In fact, you may even put weight on. Dietary experts advise that eating five or six small meals a day is more effective for weight loss than eating an equal amount of food in three larger meals.

351. Contrary to popular belief, starchy foods are *good* when weight watching. Foods that are high in complex carbohydrates—pasta, rice, potatoes, breads—are good sources of fiber (not to mention vitamins and minerals). Eating fiber helps you to feel full and keeps your digestive tract running smoothly. The caveat is that you should not load those starchy foods with butter, cheese, or rich sauces containing whole milk or cream. These fatty toppings supply many more calories than the complex carbohydrates them-selves.

352. Beware the "fat-free" labeling: Many of these foods are rich in sugars instead. And while sugar-laden foods are not as directly responsible for obesity as fatty foods are, they do have an effect on our metabolism that leads to weight gain.

353. All fats have the same number of calories. That's true whether they are polyunsaturated, monounsaturated, or saturated. And all calories count, no matter what type of fat they come from. So eating less fat will help reduce the number of calories you eat every day, thus reducing you.

For more information about obesity, write:

NHLBI Obesity Education Initiative
P.O. Box 30105
Bethesda, MD 20824

Exercise

354. Exercise is effective in slowing or preventing age-related illnesses. Of course, you should check with your doctor before embarking on any exercise program, especially as you age. But as a rule, any physical activity is good for both your physical and your mental health. In fact, being active—even if you have medical problems—will in all likelihood help you feel better and have more energy.

355. Specific kinds of exercise can have specific health benefits.

• Regular aerobic activities, such as swimming, tennis, and running, raise the heart rate, thus reducing the risk of heart disease and stroke.

• Strength training—lifting weights or exercising against resistance—makes bones stronger, improves balance, and increases muscle strength and mass, all of which can prevent or slow osteoporosis and reduce the risk of falls.

• Strength training can also lessen arthritis pain by strengthening muscles and easing the strain on joints.

• Weight-bearing exercise, such as walking, aerobics, and even stair climbing, is effective in preventing osteoporosis.

356. Even light exercise helps to reduce anxiety.

Many years ago, a famous heart specialist observed that a walk of a few miles was almost as good as some medications. More recently, medical experts have expanded that observation, comparing the effects of exercise with those of tranquilizing drugs. They found that even a fifteen-minute walk produced a measurable relaxation of muscle tension.

357. Here are a few more good reasons to get regular exercise. We burn more calories as we exercise—and we keep burning them for up to six hours after the exercising stops. That's what is known as having an increased metabolic rate. Another good thing that happens as we exercise is that our level of blood sugar drops, setting into motion a chain of chemical reactions—the end result being that our appetite will be less than what it usually is.

358. Commit yourself to a regular regime. An excellent goal is thirty minutes of exercise a day. And it isn't necessary to do all thirty minutes at once—experts say that breaking exercise into three ten-minute periods is just as effective. Skip the elevator and take the stairs, or park your car at the far end of the lot. It's okay to exercise at your own pace and to choose the kind of exercise that suits you best.

359. Gardening is exercise, too. All that digging, bending, and planting burns about four calories a minute. Other activities that burn about four calories a minute include ballroom dancing, golf, table tennis, volleyball, and light calisthenics.

To burn a moderate seven calories a minute, try badminton, bicycling, stationary cycling at 10 to 13 mph, heavy gardening, swimming, singles tennis, brisk walking (4 mph), and fast dancing (including square and contra dancing).

Vigorous exercise burns ten or more calories a minute. Such activities include heavy calisthenics, climbing stairs, cycling at 30 mph, handball, in-line skating, squash, paddleball, jogging, skipping rope, and swimming at fifty yards per minute.

360. The amount and type of exercise you do depends on you—where you're starting from

and what you want to achieve. Don't try to take on too much too fast. If you join a gym, instructors will advise you on a workout regimen. If you're weak, frail, or at risk of falling, begin very slowly (after checking with your doctor first). If you develop sudden pain, extreme shortness of breath, or feel ill while exercising, you should stop immediately.

361. Stop putting it off—join a gym. Or a health club or the Y. All of these have fitness programs geared to mature adults—the aerobics instructors even play songs from the forties and fifties. You can also find exercise programs at senior centers and as part of the local high school's adult education program. Many shopping malls open early to accommodate the legions of "mall walkers" sprouting up in suburban areas. You can also rent or buy workout videos if you'd rather do all this in privacy at home.

 Stretching is the way to start.

It gets your body ready to work out by improving flexibility, thus lowering the risk of injury and muscle strain. Before and after exercise, take at least five minutes for a warm-up and a cool-down period. Stretch slowly and carefully to loosen muscles in the arms, shoulders, back, chest, stomach, buttocks, thighs, and calves. Actually, it's a good idea to keep limber by doing some stretches every morning, whether or not you intend to exercise.

363. Stretching should be geared to your fitness level. If you are weak or frail, limit yourself to finger, hand, and ankle rotations; neck rotations and shoulder shrugs; knee to chest pulls while lying on your back; arm rotations from shoulders; and reaching up.

As flexibility improves, add double knee pulls with both knees to chest; hamstring stretches while sitting on the floor; and sitting stretches—hands to ankles while sitting on the floor. Do calf muscle stretches by leaning forward against a wall; and seal stretches—pulling the head and shoulders up off the floor while on your stomach.

364. Make sure you're getting a proper workout—check your heart rate after you exercise. Your heart rate is the number of times your heart beats in a minute. You want it to be more rapid than usual while exercising, but not *too much* more rapid. A good rule of thumb is that if you have trouble conversing while exercising, you're overdoing it.

1. Immediately after you stop exercising, take your pulse by placing the tips of your first two fingers lightly over one of the blood vessels on your neck or wrist.
2. Count your pulse for ten seconds and multiply by 6 to get your rate for one minute.
3. Compare the number to the table below.

Age	Target Heart Rate Zone
55	83–123 beats per minute
60	80–120 beats per minute
65	78–116 beats per minute
70	75–113 beats per minute

365. To build and restore muscle and bone, try strength training. That would include activi-

ties such as weight lifting and resistance training. It's important to have an expert guide you in working with weights or resistance training machines. Once you know what to do, simple strength training exercises can be done at home. Strength training can be accomplished in as little as a half hour twice a week, taking care not to exercise the same muscles two days in a row. Studies have shown that weight lifting—even light weights—can slow bone loss and raise the metabolism. And these benefits can be enjoyed by anyone at any age.

366. Calisthenics make you strong—they help to maintain muscle tone, too. Starting exercises include:

*   Extend arms and squeeze fingers together; relax, squeeze again.
*   While seated, touch hands to shoulders.
*   While seated, lift legs and extend; then lower slowly.
*   While standing, extend foot and rotate in a circle, using a chair back for support.
*   Using a chairback for support, squat slightly and then rise slowly.
*   Holding on to a chairback, rise up on your toes.
*   Holding on to a chairback, raise your knee to your chest.
*   Lie on the floor, knees bent, and reach forward to touch fingers to knees.

367. Aerobic exercise makes your heart beat faster and increases endurance. It strengthens the heart and improves overall fitness by enhancing the body's ability to use oxygen.

Swimming, walking, and dancing are all low-impact aerobic activities and are easier on the joints and muscles than are high-impact exercises such as jogging and jumping rope.

Aerobic exercise raises the number of heartbeats per minute; the goal is to get your heart rate up and keep it there for twenty minutes or more. If you haven't exercised in a while, start slowly. As you get stronger, you can increase your heart rate. Once you are up to speed, you should do some type of aerobic activity for twenty to forty minutes at a time at least three times a week.

368. If you have arthritis, you can still exercise—underwater.

Many Ys and recreational centers have exercise classes geared toward people with arthritis, replacement joints, or other physical restrictions. The exercises are conducted underwater, in the swimming pool, and are structured to be appropriate to your disability (an on-site physical therapist will work with you to determine this). They range from aerobics, to gentle movements, to simply walking across the pool through the water.

369. Many experts believe that walking is the best exercise for everyone. The conditioning effects take longer to kick in, but walking can be done with little risk of injury. Other advantages:

- It can be done without special training. Even if you're frail or suffer from arthritis,

emphysema, or heart disease, walking will improve your health.

- It costs only the price of a good pair of walking shoes.
- Invite a friend, and it turns into a social experience.
- It can benefit your soul as well as your body. Walking not only relieves stress but can give you time for personal meditation.

370. For optimal fitness, walk at least four times a week. You begin to lose muscle tone after three days without exercise, so it's important to walk regularly. Strive to walk every day. A thirty-minute walking regimen should start with a warm-up period of about five minutes (stretching, walking slowly) and end with a cool-down period of about five minutes (more stretching, walking slowly). Check your pulse rate periodically.

371. Call the National Institute on Aging for a list of publications on exercise and the mature adult. The number is 800-992-0841. Or get AARP's illustrated guide "Pep Up Your Life: A Fitness Book for Mid-Life and Older Persons."

American Association of Retired Persons
Health Promotion Services
601 E St. NW
Washington, DC 20049
202-434-2277

Sports

372. Some sports come highly recommended. The President's Council on Physical Fitness and Sports once asked medical experts to evaluate a dozen popular forms of exercise. Based on the benefits they provided for heart and lung endurance, muscular strength, flexibility, balance, weight control, muscle definition, and digestion, the winners were jogging, bicycling, swimming, skating, basketball, tennis, bowling, walking, golf, calisthenics, and softball.

373. Here are the health benefits associated with your favorite sports.

• Jogging, running, swimming—cardiovascular
• Handball, tennis, boxing—heart and lung
• Downhill skiing, cross-country skiing—leg agility, balance
• Bowling—back and bone strength (also good for vision and coordination)

374. If you take up sports again, you can avoid most injuries by starting slowly. Then progress at your own rate; don't play when you're tired or feel a hurt coming on. If you suffer a sports injury, see a doctor. As a general rule, heat should not be used immediately after a strain or sprain. Apply an ice pack first (a bag of frozen vegetables will work, too). This will help relieve pain and restrict swelling.

375. As we age, cold-weather sports require special preparation. Cycling, skiing, or even walking outside for more than thirty minutes puts you at risk for windburn, chapping, and moisture loss. To prevent this, make sure your face, hands, and head are covered. Apply moisturizer at least fifteen minutes before going out (look for products formulated to protect sensitive areas such as eyelids, lips, and ears). And, of course, don't forget to use sunscreen.

Wear loose, warm layers of clothing—a sporting goods or camping store can advise you on which fabrics are best. Wear two layers of gloves: cotton under wool or leather works well. Staying dry is almost as important as staying warm, since evaporation cools the body very quickly. Wiggle your toes and fingers from time to time, and rotate your shoulders. Change out of damp clothing as soon as possible on your arrival indoors.

376. The National Senior Sports Association (NSSA) holds recreational and competitive golfing events for people 50 and over. Golfers are grouped by skill levels, with pairings changed daily to encourage the development of friendships. Men and women usually play separately.

NSSA events are scheduled during off-seasons, to take advantage of lower rates. The package deal includes everything from accommodations and tournaments to an awards banquet, often at some of the world's most famous courses. For more information, contact:

National Senior Sports Association
301 N. Harrison St., Suite 204
Princeton, NJ 08540
800-282-6772

377. The Senior Sports Classic is for athletes over the age of 55.

There are both state and national competitions in archery, badminton, basketball, bowling, cycling, golf, horseshoes, shuffleboard, softball, swimming, table tennis, tennis, track and field, race walking, racquetball, road racing, and volleyball. For more information and a listing of state branches, contact:

U.S. National Senior Sports Organization
12520 Olive Blvd.
St. Louis, MO 63141
314-621-5545

378. Get more information from the President's Council on Physical Fitness and Sports.
To order a copy of "The Fitness Challenge in the Later Years," contact:

President's Council on Physical Fitness and Sports
450 5th St. NW, Suite 7103
Washington, DC 20001
202-690-9000

379. For more information about specific sports:

Badminton: U.S. Badminton Association, 402-592-7309

Boating: Boat/US, 800-336-2628

Bowling: American Bowling Congress, 414-421-6400

Cycling: U.S. Cycling Federation, 715-578-4949

Hiking: American Hiking Society, 301-565-6704

Horseshoes: National Horseshoe Pitchers Association, 414-835-9108

Running: TAC Masters Long Distance Running Committee, 206-433-8868

Skiing: U.S. Ski Association, 801-649-9090

Softball: Senior Softball USA, 916-393-8566

Tennis: USTA Senior Tennis Directory, 914-696-7000

Chapter 7:

Diseases, Conditions, Repairs, Solutions, and Preventions

Sogyal Rinpoche, in *The Tibetan Book of Living and Dying,* asks his readers to reflect on this statement: "The realization of impermanence is paradoxically the only thing we can hold onto,

perhaps our only lasting possession." It is a worthy sentiment, almost playful in labeling impermanence a possession—and helpful for giving us some objectivity in the face of the physical changes that can come with age.

Life's journey is about change, and about coping with change through knowledge and experience. In this chapter you will find an alphabetical listing of some of the diseases and conditions that many of us have to face. You'll also find suggestions for therapies, remedies, repairs, solutions, and preventions, as well as the occasional inspiration to help deal with it all. We have only included diseases and conditions that are of particular interest to older adults. For example, there's no listing for "colds," because people of all ages get them—but there is a section on "flu," because it can be more harmful to older people. This chapter is not designed to be read

item by item; rather, it is for consulting when you need information on a specific disease or condition.

Acne

380. Welcome back to adolescence, briefly.
Sometimes acne resurfaces unexpectedly in adulthood, often as the result of a reaction to makeup or to a medication like cortisone. Occasionally, it is the result of a hormone abnormality (or in rare cases, a hormone-secreting tumor).

The most effective solution is what the kids use—an over-the-counter gel, lotion, or cream containing benzoyl peroxide. Be careful using it, because it can irritate the skin and increase your sun sensitivity. Start with a

2.5 percent or 5 percent product. If the low dosage doesn't work, and you haven't had a reverse reaction, try a 10 percent solution.

A precaution for acne-prone skin: Use only moisturizers and sunscreens whose labels say they're noncomedogenic—that means the product won't block skin pores.

Alcohol Abuse

381. Researchers say that older people get drunk more quickly than younger people. Sometimes it takes only one drink. Yet those who have been lifelong drinkers often find they drink still more as they age even though the effect increases. Former teetotalers may resort to a drink "just to get to sleep" or to "get through the day." In order to remain as healthy as possible as you age, it is critical that you do not drink to excess.

382. Over time, heavy drinking causes permanent damage to the brain and central nervous system. It also harms the liver, heart, kidneys, and stomach. Its effects can make some medical problems hard to diagnose. For example, alcohol causes changes in the heart and blood vessels that can dull the pain that might be signaling a heart attack. It can cause forgetfulness and confusion, seeming at times like Alzheimer's disease. As a central nervous system depressant, alcohol slows brain activity, affecting alertness, judgment, coordination, and reaction time, increasing the risk of falls and accidents.

383. Alcohol + medication = trouble. Alcohol does not mix well with many common, aging-related medications. When combined with insulin, high blood pressure drugs, antibiotics, or tranquilizers, alcohol may do additional harm. Mixing alcohol with common over-the-counter medicines, such as cough and cold remedies and antihistamines, may lead to extreme drowsiness and impaired coordination, which can lead to accidents—especially if you're driving a car.

384. Here's how alcohol affects vital organs:

• Brain. Alcohol directly affects brain cells. Unclear thinking, staggering, and slurred speech may result. Large amounts of alcohol may cause unconsciousness.

• Heart. Alcohol can increase the workload of the heart, resulting in irregular heartbeat and high blood pressure.

• Liver. Alcohol can poison the liver, since most of the alcohol consumed is processed by the liver.

• Kidneys. Alcohol can stop the kidneys from keeping a proper balance of body fluids and minerals.

385. Alcohol affects other parts of you, too.

• Stomach. Alcohol irritates the digestive system; vomiting and ulcers may result.

• Eyes. Alcohol's effects on the nervous system make it difficult for eye muscles to function, resulting in blurred vision.

• Mouth and throat. Alcohol is absorbed through the mouth and throat and is an irritant to the lining of these passages. It can cause sores and ulcers.

• Blood. Alcohol reduces the body's ability to produce blood cells, resulting in anemia and infections.

• Muscles. Alcohol can cause muscle weakness, resulting in staggering and falling.

• Veins and arteries. Alcohol widens blood vessels, causing headaches and loss of body heat.

386. You may have a drinking problem if:

• You drink to calm your nerves, forget worries, or lighten depression
• You've lost interest in food
• You deny or try to hide your drinking habits
• You drink alone
• You hurt yourself or someone else while drinking
• You need increased amounts of alcohol to feel its effects
• You have medical, social, or financial problems caused by drinking

387. An occasional drink may actually be good for you.

Recent studies have suggested that the body benefits from moderate amounts of drinking. A glass of wine may be good for the heart. People who drink moderately have higher levels of the good kind of cholesterol—the kind that guards against arteriosclerosis—in their blood than teetotalers do.

So should you drink a little or stay away from alcohol completely? Check it out with your doctor, who can give you advice based on your medical history. And let your common sense be your guide.

388. Older problem drinkers have a very good chance for recovery. That's because once they decide to seek help, they usually stay with the treatment program. Help is available via your doctor or through many different social service agencies and organizations. Here are few good places to start:

Alcoholics Anonymous
475 Riverside Dr., 11th Floor
New York, NY 10115
212-870-3400
Check your phone book for a local chapter.

National Institute on Alcoholic Abuse and Alcoholism
6000 Executive Blvd.
Bethesda, MD 20892
301-443-3860

For a referral to a treatment center in your area, contact:
National Council on Alcoholism and Drug Dependence
12 W. 21st St., 8th Floor
New York, NY 10010
800-NCA-CALL

Alzheimer's Disease, Dementia

389. Memory loss and confusion are *not* an inevitable part of aging. In the past, even health care professionals were not aware of this fact. We now know that most people remain mentally capable as they age and that changes in personality, behavior, or skills may signal a brain disease.

The term "dementia" describes a group of symptoms caused by changes in the activity of brain cells; these changes interfere with the ability to carry out daily activities. The two most common forms of dementia are Alzheimer's disease (accounting for about half of all dementia cases) and multi-infarct dementia (sometimes called vascular dementia).

Symptoms of Alzheimer's begin slowly and worsen. The sufferer may experience confusion, personality and behavior changes, impaired judgment, and difficulty finding words, finishing thoughts, or following directions. The disease eventually leaves its victims unable to care for themselves.

Conditions such as high fever, poor nutrition, reactions to medicines, or a minor head injury can all produce symptoms that imitate dementia. A thorough physical, neurological, and psychiatric evaluation is the best way to diagnose dementia.

390. Only about 1 percent of all people aged 65 to 74 have Alzheimer's. The incidence of the disease increases with age. About 7 percent of people aged 75 to 84 have it; it has been diagnosed in approximately 25 percent of the population aged 85 and over. The Alzheimer's Association estimates that about 4 million Americans have the disease.

391. Nearly $300 million in federal grants is spent every year on Alzheimer's research. And the number of investigators is growing. In June 1996, for example, thirteen hundred researchers attended an Alzheimer's meeting in Osaka, Japan—twice as many as attended the same conference the previous year.

392. Scientists believe the disease may be caused by a combination of genetics and lifestyle factors. That is, you may be genetically predisposed to contract Alzheimer's, and other variables—nutrition, injury, infection, exposure to toxins—can increase your risk. The highest incidence of the disease has been found among people who have poor diets and a lower level of education (this last may be because learning stimulates and strengthens brain activity). In the 1970s, a lot of attention was given to the hypothesis that years of inhaling aluminum compounds from spray deodorants contributed to Alzheimer's; it now appears that this theory was correct.

393. Research on Alzheimer's proceeds on six fronts:

• Neuropathology. It focuses on the abnormally twisted protein fibers inside nerve cells in the brains of Alzheimer's patients.

• Biochemistry. Researchers have found

abnormally low levels of some neurotransmitters carrying messages between cells in the brain tissue of Alzheimer's patients.

• Genetics. Scientists are searching for a link to Alzheimer's on chromosome 21, the chromosome related to Down's syndrome.

• Virology. Some scientists have suggested that Alzheimer's could be caused by a slow-acting virus.

• Toxicology. Exposure to toxins may influence the development of Alzheimer's. Several investigators have found elevated levels of aluminum in areas of the brain affected by Alzheimer's.

• Risk factors. While aging is the most clear-cut risk factor, scientists are also examining head injuries and gender.

394. A number of drugs are now being developed for the treatment of Alzheimer's disease. Research is being conducted at the Mayo Clinic on vitamin E and on a drug now used to combat Parkinson's disease; it is possible that these substances may delay the progression of Alzheimer's.

Patient participation in clinical trials is an essential part of all research. For information on becoming a part of a clinical trial, contact:

Alzheimer's Association Information
919 N. Michigan Ave., Suite 1000
Chicago, IL 60611
800-272-3900
In addition to test referrals, it offers "Alzheimer's Disease Fact Sheet," "Multi-Infarct Dementia Fact Sheet," and "Progress Report on Alzheimer's Disease."

395. For free publications, videos, and information on Alzheimer's disease, write:

National Institute of Mental Health
5600 Fishers Lane, Room 15C05
Rockville, MD 20857
301-443-4513

396. Multi-infarct dementia was once mislabeled "hardening of the arteries of the brain." It actually results from a series of little strokes, causing a loss of blood flow to brain tissue, and hence loss of function. Symptoms, which begin suddenly in this kind of dementia, include vision or speech problems and/or numbness or weakness in one side of the body. People with this dementia are likely to improve or remain stable for long periods, then quickly develop new symptoms. It can exist together with Alzheimer's, making accurate diagnosis difficult.

This dementia sometimes responds to blood-thinning drugs, according to Robin M. Henig in *The Myth of Senility*. Its effects can also be minimized with vitamins, medication, and use of a hyperbaric oxygen chamber. For more information, contact:

National Institute of Neurological Disorders and Stroke
Building 31, Room 8A06
Bethesda, MD 20892
800-352-9424

397. Two other, more rare forms of dementia are Huntington's disease and Creutzfeldt-Jakob disease. Huntington's is a genetic disorder that begins in middle age. Its symptoms include personality changes, mental decline, psychosis, and difficulty in movement. Creutzfeldt-Jakob disease is thought to be caused by a viral infection that leads to rapid and progressive dementia.

398. If an irreversible brain disorder is diagnosed, help is available.

• Mental stimulation may slow the progress of symptoms. One way to do this is to keep sufferers informed about the details of their lives—the time of day, where they live, and what is happening at home or in the world around them.

• Memory aids, such as a big calendar, lists of daily plans, signs about safety, and written directions for using common household items are all good stimuli.

• Overall good health—and good nutrition—are important. With multi-infarct dementia, dietary changes may prevent more strokes.

• Medications may relieve agitation, anxiety, depression, or problems sleeping.

• Family members should seek out support groups and not try to treat the problem alone.

Anemia

399. Anemia is common among mature adults.
In fact, it's the most common form of blood disorder. Among its causes are disease, ulcers, malnutrition, vitamin and mineral defi-

ciencies, and medication being taken for other disorders. Women suffer from anemia more often than do men. Anemia can cause paleness of skin and nails, hair loss, and thin skin that bruises easily. Headaches, faintness, spots in front of the eyes, ringing in the ears, loss of appetite, nausea, drowsiness, and exhaustion are other common symptoms.

If you suspect you are anemic, consult your doctor. Treatment varies according to the type of anemia diagnosed.

400. Iron-deficiency anemia is the most common kind.
It is most often caused by blood loss or a poor diet. Blood loss usually occurs in the digestive tract, due to problems such as ulcers. Dietary-deficiency anemia is the result of not eating enough iron-rich foods such as meat, liver, green leafy vegetables, fish, and poultry.

Taking iron supplements—along with vitamin C, for better absorption—will help to replenish the body's store of iron. Believe it or not, cooking in cast-iron pots also helps.

401. For more information about anemia, contact:

Aplastic Anemia Foundation of America
P.O. Box 22689
Baltimore, MD 21203
800-747-2820

Cooley's Anemia Foundation
129-09 26th Ave.
Flushing, NY 11354
800-522-7222

Angina
SEE ALSO HEART ATTACK

402. Angina is heart-related chest pain—but not all chest pain is angina.

Wait thirty seconds; take a deep breath; drink a glass of water: If the pain is gone, then it wasn't angina. The squeezing pressure of angina is felt in the chest, but can also be felt in the jaws, neck, back, arms, and shoulders. Exertion brings on angina, and resting for a few minutes (or taking your medication) should bring you back to normal.

Feeling angina does not mean that you are having a heart attack. With a heart attack, the pain is more severe and does not go away when you rest. However, angina is a symptom of heart disease. If your pattern of episodes changes—if the pain occurs more frequently, is more severe, or occurs without exercise—it is likely that you will have a heart attack within a few weeks.

Lifestyle changes—including exercise, under a doctor's supervision—can help you to control angina. If these fail, nitroglycerin tablets are commonly prescribed (they work by widening the arteries, so the heart doesn't have to work as hard to pump the blood). If the tablets fail to bring relief, surgery may be recommended.

Anxiety Disorders
SEE ALSO PANIC ATTACKS

403. Anxiety evolved as a way to rouse us to action when facing danger. But if it goes unchecked and turns into an anxiety disorder, it works against you.

Having an anxiety disorder means feeling apprehensive most of the time, without any apparent reason, or worrying excessively about health, money, family, or work. The anxiety is often accompanied by symptoms such as trembling, muscle tension, and nausea. The feelings may be so uncomfortable that they interfere with everyday activities. Depression often accompanies anxiety disorders.

For older adults, doctors often recommend nondrug treatment, such as counseling, relaxation techniques, and removal of the stimulus for the attacks. Drug treatments require careful monitoring because the central nervous system is more sensitive as we age, and older adults can experience side effects even at low dosages.

Arthritis

404. The bones of Egyptian mummies show signs of arthritis, proof that this disease has plagued humanity for a very long time. The word "arthritis" means "inflammation of the joints," and that's exactly what this disease is. There are some one hundred different forms of arthritis, and although some forms are better understood than others, the causes of most are unknown (researchers are now investigating a possible food-related link). In older people, the three most common types of arthritis are osteoarthritis, rheumatoid arthritis, and gout.

405. There are a number of warning signs of arthritis. If any of these symptoms lasts longer than two weeks, see your doctor or a rheumatologist.

- Swelling in one or more joints
- Early-morning stiffness
- Recurring pain or tenderness in any joint
- Inability to move a joint normally
- Obvious redness or warmth in a joint
- Unexpected weight loss, fever, or weakness, combined with joint pain

406. Osteoarthritis is the most common type of arthritis found in older adults. Sometimes called degenerative joint disease, it can range from having only mild effects (occasional stiffness and joint pain) to being a serious condition (much pain and disability). It most often affects the hands and the large weight-bearing joints of the body—the knees, ankles, and hips. Early in the disease, pain occurs only after activity, and resting brings relief. Later on, though, pain can occur with even a minimal amount of movement, or while at rest.

Osteoarthritis in the hands or hips tends to run in families; obesity has been linked with osteoarthritis in the knees; injuries or overuse may cause the disease to occur in the knees, hips, and elbows.

407. Rheumatoid arthritis also varies in severity. Signs of it often include morning stiffness, swelling in three or more joints, swelling of the hands and wrists, swelling of the same joints on both sides of the body (for example, both feet), and bumps or nodules under the skin. Rheumatoid arthritis can occur at any age. It affects women about three times more often than men.

The cause of the disease is unknown, but scientists believe it may result from a breakdown in the immune system, the body's defense against disease. People with this kind of arthritis also appear to have certain inherited traits that cause the immune system to go awry.

408. Gout has many of the same symptoms as arthritis. Seen most often in older men and postmenopausal women, gout is an extremely painful inflammation of the joints in the toes, ankles, knees, elbows, wrists, or hands. It occurs when a metabolic imbalance causes levels of uric acid (a normal body waste) to become high, and crystals form in and around the joints.

Gout once symbolized a life of overindulgence in food and drink. It is true that attacks are triggered by binge eating and by excessive alcohol consumption over the years, but these are not the cause of the disease. (Other triggers include stress, sudden weight loss, antibiotics, diuretics, and surgery.) Gout can be controlled by medication, and alcohol intake should be limited.

409. The goals of arthritis treatments are to relieve pain and to get those joints working again. A treatment program may include rest, weight control, heat therapy, exercise, and drug therapy.

Nonsteroidal anti-inflammatory drugs (NSAIDs) are commonly used to relieve pain. They block the production of the chemicals that cause the inflammation, pain, stiffness, swelling, and warmth felt by people with arthritis. Although some NSAIDs are available without a prescription, most require one. It often takes a few days to a week before NSAIDs start to work, and two to three weeks before the full benefits are felt.

410. There are two groups of NSAIDS: salicylates and nonsalicylates. The salicylates include ordinary aspirin, choline salicylate (Arthropan), diflunisal (Dolobid), magnesium salicylate (Magan), and salsalate (Disalcid).

Among the familiar nonsalicylates are ibuprofen (Advil, Nuprin) and naproxen (Aleve, Naprosyn). Others and their brand names are diclofenac (Voltaren), fenoprofen (Nalfon), flurbiprofen (Ansaid), indomethacin (Indocin), ketoprofen (Orudis), and tolmetin (Tolectin).

411. While NSAIDs give much-needed pain relief, they may cause gastrointestinal problems. They can cause heartburn, nausea, stomach pain, vomiting, diarrhea, and occasionally gastrointestinal bleeding. NSAIDs are also associated with headaches, dizziness, and blurred vision. More seriously, they can cause stomach ulcers. Ulcers and other serious stomach problems are more common in smokers and people who drink alcohol. When NSAIDs are taken over a long period at high doses and directions are not followed carefully, there is risk of liver or kidney damage.

NSAIDs should be taken with a full glass of water or milk, food, or antacids. The antiulcer drug misoprostol (brand name Cytotec) can also be used. Adjusting dosage may keep side effects to a minimum.

412. Minor arthritis can be relieved temporarily with the help of aspirin, acetaminophen, or ibuprofen. Use the "extra strength" or "arthritis formula" varieties—they contain more medicine than the "regular strength." Acetaminophen (Tylenol is the most common brand) can help ease the pain, but it does not reduce inflammation. Over-the-counter (OTC) ointments also offer short-term relief, but they don't reduce swelling and shouldn't be used for long periods of time.

Read warning labels: OTC drugs can have side effects, particularly when directions are not followed carefully. Long-term, high-dosage use of acetaminophen, ibuprofen, or aspirin may cause liver or kidney damage. Don't take OTC products for long periods or combine them with other OTC or prescription drugs, unless you consult with your doctor first.

413. Corticosteroids are another treatment for arthritis inflammation—but they have a lot of side effects. They closely resemble cortisone, a natural hormone produced by the body, and can be taken orally or by injection directly into a stiff, swollen joint. Although corticosteroids rapidly relieve pain, swelling, and redness, these are powerful drugs with powerful side effects, and are usually given to older adults in high dosages only when nothing else has worked.

414. The side effects of corticosteroids include:

- Lowered resistance to infection
- Loss of muscle mass
- Loss of strength
- Mood changes
- Indigestion
- Weight gain
- Blurred vision
- Cataracts
- Diabetes
- Thinning of bones
- Increased blood pressure
- Stomach problems when taken with NSAIDs

415. Researchers believe that disease-modifying, antirheumatic agents slow the progress of rheumatoid arthritis. They should be prescribed only by a physician experienced with them.

- Gold compounds are used in mild to moderate cases; many who receive injectable gold notice a metallic taste in the mouth.
- Penicillamine may take two to six months to work and has some possible side effects.
- Hydroxychloroquine and other drugs developed to treat malaria relieve swelling,

stiffness, and joint pain, but can damage the retina, among other side effects.

- Immunosuppressants. Some researchers believe rheumatoid arthritis is an autoimmune disease in which the immune system attacks the body's own tissues. These drugs can cause flulike symptoms.

416. Replacing a natural joint with an artificial one is a common form of treatment for severe arthritis. More than 150,000 joint replacements are performed each year, and over the past few decades, reconstructive surgery has restored mobility and relieved pain for thousands.

This surgery involves removing damaged parts of the joint and replacing them with parts made of stainless steel or alloys or plastic. A bond cement is used to anchor the bone to the new joint component. Recovery can be amazingly swift. In total hip or knee replacement, the patient can stand and walk within a few days. Exercises to strengthen the joint are usually an essential part of the recovery process.

417. As knowledge about the rheumatic diseases has increased, their complexity has become more apparent. Researchers now list many disorders under the heading of rheumatic diseases. Several of the most common:

- Scleroderma is characterized by excessive deposits of collagen in the skin, heart, kidneys, lungs, and gastrointestinal tract. The deposits can cause thickening and hardening of the organs.

• Raynaud's phenomenon results from abnormal changes in the small blood vessels of the hands and feet, preventing proper blood flow.

• Sjögren's syndrome is marked by dryness of eyes and mouth, caused by the destruction of the lymph glands that secrete tears and saliva. It is more common in women than in men.

• Polymyalgia rheumatica afflicts people over 50 and causes stiffness and severely aching shoulders and hips. When prednisone is prescribed, most sufferers can resume normal activities within days. This disease tends to disappear after several months or years.

418. **A word of warning: Americans spend over $1 billion each year on useless arthritis pills and gadgets.**

Because arthritis pain can come and go, many people believe that these phony "cures" work. Beware of any pill or device that promises miracles. If you have questions about the safety and usefulness of a treatment, ask your doctor.

419. For more information on arthritis, contact:

Arthritis Foundation
P.O. Box 19000
Atlanta, GA 30325
800-283-7800

National Institute of Arthritis and Musculoskeletal and Skin Disease
Building 31, Room 4C05

Bethesda, MD 20892
301-495-4484
Ask for "Scleroderma" (AR 140; $6) and "Facts About Raynaud's Phenomenon" (90-2263).

American Academy of Orthopaedic Surgeons
63 N. River Rd.
Rosemont, IL 60018
708-823-7186

American Congress of Rehabilitation Medicine
5700 Old Orchard Rd., 1st Floor
Skokie, IL 60077
708-966-0095

American Osteopathic Association
142 E. Ontario
Chicago, IL 60611
800-621-1773

Asthma

420. Asthma can develop at any age; more than 1 million people 65 and older have it. However, it's often difficult for a doctor to determine whether the problem is asthma or another lung disease (such as bronchitis or emphysema), because asthmalike symptoms are very common. For instance, heart disease may cause breathing problems that resemble asthma.

The breathing tubes of an asthma sufferer are sensitive. They may tighten and become narrow, inflamed, and swollen. They may react to smoke, pollen, dust, or air pollution, among other triggers. Sinusitis, gastroesophageal reflux (heartburn), and even intense emotions can all trigger asthma.

421. There are two major ways to treat asthma.

The first is by avoiding substances that trigger it; the second is by using various medications that keep the bronchial tubes open.

Common items to avoid include cats, pollen (airborne pollen levels are highest in the early morning and on bright, sunny, windy days), and dust, the major asthma irritant. Air-filtering devices, such as air-conditioning and electrostatic air precipitators, can help. Choose one that does not produce ozone, because ozone can increase asthmatic symptoms.

Drug treatments include cromolyn sodium to prevent exercise-induced asthma; bronchodilators to relax the smooth muscles of the airways; anticholinergic drugs to block muscle contractions; corticosteroids to reduce swelling, mucous secretions, and inflammation; and allergy shots.

422. For more information on asthma, contact:

American Academy of Allergy, Asthma and Immunology
611 E. Wells St.
Milwaukee, WI 53202
800-822-2762

American Lung Association
1740 Broadway
New York, NY 10019
800-586-4872

Atherosclerosis

423. Atherosclerosis is a form of arteriosclerosis.

*Arterio*sclerosis (hardening of the arteries) is a chronic heart disease; *athero*sclerosis is the slow buildup of cholesterol and fatty deposits in the arteries. As the deposits build up, the arteries become narrowed, impeding blood flow. If an artery becomes so clogged that an adequate amount of blood cannot reach the heart, heart attack may result; if the blood can't get to the brain, a stroke is possible.

Atherosclerosis is a natural process of aging, but there are things you can do to slow the process: quit smoking, cut down on the amount of fat in your diet, and get more exercise.

Back Pain

424. Back pain is a common sign of the wear and tear of aging.

With the passage of time, and reduced blood circulation, the bone and soft connective tissue in the spine undergo a gradual wearing down.

Degeneration is most likely to occur in the cushioning disks between the vertebrae or in the cartilage of the joints between the vertebrae. One or more disks might actually flatten, causing collapse of the vertebral column. The resulting narrowing of the spinal canal may cause pressure on the nerves that branch out from the spinal cord. There may also be inflammation, sometimes referred to as "degenerative arthritis" or "spondylitis."

425. Imaging tests help doctors diagnose degenerative spine changes. These include, in addition to X rays:

• CT (computerized tomography) scan. The use of a computer along with X rays passed through the body at different angles produces clear cross-sectional images of tissues.
• MRI (magnetic resonance imaging) also produces cross-sectional images with powerful magnetic fields and radio waves that permit a computer to create images of tissue.

426. For sudden onset of back pain, two or three days of bed rest is recommended. The application of heat or cold can help; so can taking nonsteroidal anti-inflammatory drugs or NSAIDs (aspirin, ibuprofen, naproxen).

When major arthritic conditions are suspected, stronger anti-inflammatory medicine, such as cortisone injections, may be prescribed. In cases of severe degeneration, with extensive pain and involvement of the nervous system, surgery may be recommended to remove one or more of the bony arches of the vertebrae and fuse the bones above and below the joints to provide stability.

427. Once your back feels better, gentle stretching and strengthening exercises are advised. Ask your doctor or a physical therapist to recommend suitable exercises. You should start with daily stretching exercises and progress to strengthening exercises. Follow the instructions carefully, and resist the temptation to exceed the recommended repetitions. Doing yoga is another good way to strengthen the muscles in the back.

 Good lifting and bending habits can prevent some back pain.

When lifting, keep your back as straight as possible and the object as close to the body as possible. When bending, use your hips and knees rather than your back. Some other back-smart habits:

• Practice good posture: Sit up straight and walk tall; keep work surfaces at the proper height.
• Exercise regularly.
• Maintain emotional balance. Much back pain is stress-induced, relating to fear and worry.

429. For more information on back pain, contact:

American Academy of Orthopaedic Surgeons
6300 N. River Rd.
Rosemont, IL 60018
800-346-2267
Send a self-addressed, stamped envelope for "Low Back Pain."

North American Spine Society
6300 N. River Rd., Suite 727
Rosemont, IL 60018
708-698-1630

It can provide referrals to orthopedists and neurosurgeons in your area.

American Chiropractic Association
1701 Clarendon Blvd.
Arlington, VA 22209
703-276-8800
It can provide information, as well as referrals to chiropractors in your area.

Arthritis Foundation
1314 Spring St. NW
Atlanta, GA 30309
404-272-7100 (to contact your local chapter)
Send a self-addressed, stamped envelope for its pamphlet on back pain.

Balance

430. If things seem out of balance, it may be more than a figure of speech. Many conditions can affect balance, and too often such problems are chalked up to hypochondria. Diseases of the eye and ear can cause a feeling of dizziness or impede your ability to stay balanced. Diabetes or a vitamin B_{12} deficiency can cause nerves in the feet to malfunction, resulting in difficulty in moving.

431. Balance is controlled in the vestibular ear system. That's part of the inner ear and the brain. Since this system interacts with other parts of the nervous system, problems with it may involve vision, muscles, thinking, and

memory. The most frequent symptoms of vestibular ear problems are dizziness, unsteadiness or imbalance when walking, vertigo, and nausea. People with vestibular disorders may also suffer from headaches, neck pain, motion sickness, and increased sensitivity to light and noise, and often have fatigue, depression, and difficulty with reading and speech. For more information on vestibular disorders, contact:

Vestibular Disorder Association
P.O. Box 4467
Portland, OR 97208
503-229-7705

Body Temperature, Hyperthermia and Hypothermia

432. Over 55, we're cool as cucumbers. That is, as we age, our body temperatures may consistently run one or two degrees lower than the 98.6°F that is normal in earlier stages of life. Body temperature may also vary by as much as two degrees during a day, and is usually slightly higher in the evening. As a result, the absence of a high temperature doesn't necessarily mean that an older adult is not ill.

433. Fevers come in all kinds of packages. For example, did you know that gallbladder disease and kidney disease cause fevers? Many cancer patients complain of feverishness, often before any growth has been discovered—it is one of the ways the body fights off infection.

An increase of even one or two degrees in body temperature results in flushing of the face, aching muscles and joints, and perspiration. You may feel hot and chilled at the same time. Fevers are often accompanied by fatigue. Extremely high fevers can lead to confusion and seizures.

434. The older body is more sensitive to external temperatures and more threatened by extremes of temperature. The two extremes are known as hyperthermia (too hot) and hypothermia (too cold).

Heat exhaustion and heatstroke are two forms of hyperthermia. Of the two, heatstroke is the more dangerous. As we age, our bodies may perspire less, thus cooling us less efficiently. The risk of hyperthermia may also be increased by poor circulation, heart, lung, or kidney disease, high blood pressure, sedatives or tranquilizers, certain heart and blood pressure drugs, and being overweight. Headache, nausea, and fatigue are symptoms of hyperthermia.

To prevent or alleviate heat-related problems:

• Stay indoors on days that are dangerously hot and humid (weather forecasters usually issue advisories).

• Avoid midday heat (no vigorous activity from 11:00 A.M. to 3:00 P.M.).

• Drink plenty of nonalcoholic, noncaffeinated liquids—even if you don't feel thirsty.

• Dress in loose, lightweight garments, preferably made of 100 percent cotton or silk.

• Cool your rooms to eighty degrees or less.

• Avoid hot, heavy meals.

435. In cold weather, hypothermia is a threat. It occurs when the body's temperature falls below about 95°F.

Body heat is lost from the skin and lungs when warm air is expelled during breathing. Extreme or prolonged cold can cause low or inadequate heat production by the body. Because they restrict physical activity, arthritis, muscle weakness, stroke, and Parkinson's disease can also reduce heat production. A stroke that reduces cognitive functioning may also affect the body's ability to heat itself.

To make sure you're as warm as possible, dress in layers (air is trapped between the layers, thus increasing the effect of body heat), and always wear a hat when outside in the cold.

436. For more information about hypothermia, write:

National Institute on Aging
Box HYPO
Building 31, Room 5C35
Bethesda, MD 20892
800-222-2225

Breast Cancer

437. The incidence of breast cancer increases with age. Two-thirds of all breast cancers occur in women over 50. Up to 90 percent of breast cancers can be treated successfully if found early enough and the cancer has not spread beyond the breast. That means it's vitally important to perform breast self-examinations monthly and to have regular mammograms.

A mammogram is an X ray that can detect a minute lump in a breast, one so small that it would have to grow for two years before you would be able to feel it with your fingertips. The mammogram machine uses a low-dose X ray, making the risk of radiation very low. Medicare now helps cover the cost of having a mammogram every other year for women 65 and over. Many hospitals and county agencies sponsor free mammogram screenings.

438. Treatment for breast cancer in older women varies somewhat from treatment for younger women. Surgery is the preferred treatment for breast cancer in most women. With a small tumor—two inches or less—the decision between a lumpectomy (removal of the tumor) and a mastectomy (removal of the breast) usually depends upon whether the breast tissue will allow adequate repair.

Since tumors grow more slowly in older women, and can take a decade to grow to the size of a pea, older women with shorter life expectancies or with very small tumors often receive hormone therapy with a drug called tamoxifen instead of surgery. Tamoxifen impedes the growth of cancer cells and is less toxic than many cancer drugs. With tamoxifen, there is a small increased risk of uterine cancer; some women taking it experience hot flashes and, infrequently, blood clots in the leg.

439. For information about mammograms, contact:

Office of Public Affairs
Health Care Financing Administration
Humphrey Building, Room 435-H
200 Independence Ave. SW
Washington, DC 20201

National Cancer Information Services
800-4-CANCER

Office of Cancer Communications
National Cancer Institute Publications
Building 31, Room 10A24
Bethesda, MD 20892
Ask for "Breast Exams: What You Should Know," "Breast Lumps: What You Should Know," and "Breast Cancer: Understanding Treatment Options."

Bursitis, Tendonitis

440. Bursitis and tendinitis are not arthritis, but they can limit activity as we age. Bursitis is the inflammation or irritation of a bursa, a small fluid-filled sac located in or near joints. Bursas act as cushions between muscles and tendons, or between muscles and bones. They facilitate joint movement. Since they are located near joints, inflammation in these soft tissues is often perceived as joint pain. Often called tennis elbow or housemaid's knee, bursitis is caused by repetitive, vigorous joint movement or by constant pressure on a joint.

Symptoms include pain and stiffness aggravated by movement, and sometimes swelling. Pain is usually located around the shoulder, elbow, wrist, finger, hip, knee, ankle, and feet, and may be more severe at night.

Tendinitis is an inflammation or irritation of a tendon, one of the thick fibrous cords that attach muscles to bone. It is caused by overuse of the tendons, resulting in microscopic tears and painful swelling.

441. Diagnosis of tendinitis and bursitis requires a physical examination and a careful look at your medical history. Blood tests may be done and X rays taken to help rule out arthritis or diabetes.

When tendinitis or bursitis is caused by overuse or injury, rest is essential. Splinting the affected area, moist heat, and physical therapy are helpful, as are anti-inflammatory medications, corticosteroid injections, and antibiotics.

You can reduce your chances of getting bursitis or tendinitis by warming up properly before exercising and by maintaining correct posture. Use of splints or pads to protect vulnerable areas can help, too.

Cancer
SEE ALSO BREAST CANCER; PROSTATE CONDITIONS; SKIN CANCER

442. "Cancer" is a frightening word, but most of us fear it needlessly. The chances of surviving cancer today are better than ever, especially if you are knowledgeable about its detection and prevention.

Cancer occurs when cells in the body's organs become abnormal and keep dividing, producing more cells, without control or order. If cells keep dividing when new cells are not needed, a mass of tissue forms. This mass is a growth, or tumor, which can be benign (harmless) or malignant (dangerous).

443. Benign tumors are not cancer. They can usually be surgically removed, and they usually don't come back. Cells from benign tumors do not spread to other parts of the body.

Malignant tumors are cancerous. Cells from such growths may invade and damage nearby tissues and organs; or they may break away from the malignant tumor and enter the bloodstream or the lymphatic system, forming new tumors in other parts of the body. The spread of cancer is called metastasis.

444. The most common type of cancer in both men and women is skin cancer. Fortunately, it is treatable if caught early enough. And you can vastly reduce your chance of contracting it at all by avoiding prolonged, unprotected exposure to the sun.

Among men, the next most common type

of cancer is prostate cancer; among women, it's breast cancer. In the United States, lung cancer is the leading cause of death from cancer for both men and women.

Cancer is a disease that develops gradually from a complex mix of factors related to environment, lifestyle, and heredity.

445. When cancers are found early, they are more likely to be treated successfully. Cancers are more common in older Americans, so mature adults have the most to gain from regular checkups, self-examinations, and lifestyle changes that will reduce their risk of contracting the disease. Checkups are particularly important—early cancer usually does not cause pain, so unless you are unusually sensitive to your own body's functioning, you may not suspect you have it. You can schedule an appointment with your own doctor, but many local health departments also provide cancer screenings and early-detection programs.

446. You should have regular checkups for these three kinds of cancer:

• Skin. You can check yourself for new growths, sores that don't heal, and moles that change in size, shape, and/or color. If you find any of these conditions, see your doctor immediately.

• Colon and rectum. Beginning at age 50, both men and women should have a yearly fecal occult blood test to check for blood in the stool. If it is found, more tests will be performed. During a regular examination, a doctor should also check the rectum for bumps or abnormalities. Every three to five years, the doctor is likely to order a sigmoidoscopy, in which a thin, flexible tube is used to look inside the rectum and colon.

• Mouth. Your doctor and dentist should examine your mouth at regular visits once you're over 50. Check yourself for changes in the color of your lips, gums, tongue, or inner cheeks, and for scabs, cracks, sores, white patches, swelling, or bleeding. Oral exams are especially important if you use alcohol or tobacco.

447. Older men should have their reproductive organs checked regularly. Since the chance of prostate cancer increases with age, men over 40 should have a yearly blood test to check for prostate specific antigen and a yearly digital rectal exam to check the prostate gland for hard or lumpy areas. Although testicular cancer occurs most often between the ages of 15 and 34, the testicles should also be a part of regular medical checkups.

448. Ditto for aging women. Most breast lumps are not cancerous. But when a lump is malignant and is found early, women have more treatment choices and an excellent chance of complete recovery. Again, monthly self-examination of the breasts can be a life-saver.

Regular pelvic exams and Pap tests, even in the later years, are an important part of detecting early cancer of the cervix. In a pelvic exam, the doctor checks reproductive organs for changes in size and shape. With a Pap test, a sample of cells is collected from the vaginal wall and cervix.

449. There are many different tests that detect cancer. "Imaging" is a technique that produces pictures of the inside of the body; it can help a doctor see whether or not a tumor is present.

X rays are the most common method of imaging. The CT or CAT scan uses a computer linked to an X-ray machine to make a series of detailed pictures. Radionuclide scanning requires a patient to swallow a mildly radioactive substance to allow a scanner to measure radioactivity levels in certain organs.

Ultrasonography uses high-frequency sound waves which enter the body and bounce back, creating a picture that is shown on a TV-like monitor. With the MRI, a powerful magnet is linked to a computer and used to make detailed pictures of areas of the body. Endoscopy is another way of looking inside the body. It employs a thin, lighted tube called an endoscope and allows doctors to collect tissue or cells for examination.

450. Laboratory tests measure the amount of certain substances in our bodily fluids. Levels of these substances may become abnormal when certain kinds of cancer are present.

A biopsy is the only way to know for sure whether or not cancer is present. In a biopsy, a sample of tissue is removed from the abnormal area and examined microscopically. If cancer is present, the pathologist can tell what type it is and how fast it might grow. If cancer is found, further testing is often necessary, because it is important to know how far the disease has progressed.

451. Know your enemy. If there is a diagnosis of cancer, it is important to become well informed about it. Shock and distress may keep you from asking a lot of questions when you first learn the news. Here's a list of questions that should be answered at your next doctor's visit, if they haven't been already.

- At what stage is the disease?
- What is the prognosis?
- What are my treatment choices? What do you recommend and why?
- What are the chances the treatment will be successful?
- What are the risks and possible side effects of each treatment?
- How long will treatment last?
- Will I have to change my normal activities?
- What is the treatment likely to cost?
- Would a clinical trial—an experimental program—be right for me?

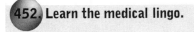 **Learn the medical lingo.**

Discussion with your doctor will be easier if you're familiar with some basic terms. Here are some words you need to know.

Carcinogen: a substance or agent known to cause cancer

Chemotherapy: treatment of cancer with drugs

Immune system: the complex group of cells and organs that defends the body against infection and disease

Interferon: a cellular protein that slows the rate of growth and division of cancer cells

Lymph: a fluid that travels through the lymphatic system of the body carrying cells that help fight infection and disease

Oncologist: a specialist in cancer treatment

Peripheral stem cell support: a method of replacing blood-forming cells destroyed by cancer treatments

Prognosis: the probable outcome or course of a disease

Remission: disappearance of the signs and symptoms of cancer

Systemic treatment: treatment that reaches cells all over the body by traveling through the bloodstream

Tumor markers: substances found in abnormal amounts in the blood and other body fluids, or in tumor tissue of some patients with certain cancers

White blood cells: cells that help the body fight infection and disease

453. If you've been diagnosed with cancer, you may want to get a second opinion. In fact, some insurance plans require one. Hospitals and medical schools can provide you with the names of specialists. You can also call the Physician Data Query service of the National Cancer Institute at 800-4-CANCER.

454. There are five different types of treatment for cancer:

• Surgery is localized treatment to remove the tumor. Nearby tissue and lymph nodes may also be removed.

• Radiation therapy uses high-energy rays to damage cancer cells and stop them from growing and dividing. Radiation therapy is also localized, affecting cancer cells only in the treated area. Radiation can come from a machine or from an implant placed into or near the tumor. Some patients require both kinds.

• Chemotherapy is treatment with drugs. Most anticancer drugs are injected into a vein or muscle; some are given orally. Chemotherapy is systemic, which means the drugs flow through the bloodstream to nearly every part of the body. It is generally given in cycles, with recovery periods following treatment periods.

• Hormone therapy is used for types of cancer that depend on hormones to grow (this includes most breast and prostate cancers). It may mean surgery to remove the organs, such as ovaries or testicles, that make the hormones that cancer cells need to grow. Sometimes drugs stop hormone production.

• Immunotherapy, also called biological therapy, uses naturally occurring substances to stimulate the body's immune system to recognize and destroy cancer cells.

455. Unfortunately, cancer treatments have side effects. The most common:

• Surgery. Side effects depend on the tumor's location, the type of operation, and the patient's general health, among other factors.

Most patients are uncomfortable after surgery. The length of time it takes to recover varies.

• Radiation therapy. Side effects depend on dosage and the part of the body treated. Most common are fatigue, rash, and loss of appetite. This therapy may decrease the number of white blood cells protecting the body, so infections may result.

• Chemotherapy. The drugs used in this treatment generally have a negative effect on cells that fight infection, help the blood clot, and carry oxygen. As a result, patients are more likely to get infections, bruise easily, and become fatigued. Cells lining the digestive tract can also be affected, causing loss of appetite, nausea and vomiting, or mouth sores. Hair thinning or loss often occurs.

• Hormone therapy. Patients may experience nausea and vomiting, swelling, or weight gain. In men, it may cause impotence or loss of sexual desire.

• Immunotherapy. Flulike symptoms can occur, with chills, fever, muscle aches, weakness, loss of appetite, nausea, vomiting, and diarrhea. Some patients get a rash or bleed or bruise easily. With interlukin, a substance that boosts the immune system, there can be swelling. Side effects gradually go away after treatment stops.

456. Chemotherapy or radiation to the head can cause problems with the mouth, teeth, and gums. Before starting such treatment, see your dentist to take care of any necessary dental work. Ask about special care for your teeth and mouth before, during, and after the therapies.

457. If we made the appropriate lifestyle changes, we could prevent up to two-thirds of all cancer cases. Scientists estimate that about 80 percent of all cancers are related to three risk factors: the use of tobacco products; what we eat and drink; and exposure to radiation or other cancer-causing agents. If we applied this knowledge and lived by it, the number of cancer cases would be greatly reduced.

458. The American Cancer Society recommends the following to reduce your risk of cancer.

• Stop using tobacco. Cigarette smoking causes 90 percent of lung cancers among men and 79 percent among women. Smoking accounts for 30 percent of all cancer deaths. Chewing tobacco or using snuff increases the risk of cancer of the mouth, larynx, throat, and esophagus.

• Avoid the sun. Most of the more than 1 million cases a year of skin cancer in the United States are related to exposure to the sun. Sun exposure is a major factor in the development of melanoma.

• Don't drink alcohol to excess. Oral cancer and cancers of the larynx, throat, esophagus, and liver occur more frequently among heavy drinkers, especially when they also use tobacco.

459. The risk of cancer can be reduced with attention to diet and weight.

• If you are more than 40 percent overweight, you have an increased risk of colon, breast, prostate, gallbladder, ovary, and uterine cancers.

• Vary your diet. Including a variety of vegetables and fruits in your diet puts you at a lower risk of developing lung, prostate, bladder, esophagus, colorectal, and stomach cancers.

• Reduce fat intake. A diet high in fat may figure into the development of certain cancers, particularly breast, colon, and prostate.

• Avoid salt-cured, smoked, and nitrite-cured foods. In geographical areas where they are eaten frequently, there is a higher incidence of cancer of the esophagus and stomach.

460. Chances of recovery from cancer keep getting better and better. Researchers are finding new and better ways to detect and treat cancer, so recovery rates keep improving. Some cancer patients take part in clinical research studies that test the efficacy of new treatment methods. To find out about such trials, call 800-4-CANCER.

For more information on cancer and aging, contact:

Cancer Information Service
National Cancer Institute
Building 31, Room 10A24
Bethesda, MD 20892
800-422-6237
*Ask for "Radiation Therapy and You"
and "Chemotherapy and You." A
Spanish-speaking staff is available during
business hours.*

American Cancer Society
National Headquarters
1599 Clifton Rd. NE
Atlanta, GA 30329
800-227-2345

National Coalition for Cancer
Survivorship
1010 Wayne Ave., 5th Floor
Silver Spring, MD 20910
301-585-2616

Centers for Disease Control and
Prevention
Mail Stop K-50
1600 Clifton Rd. NE
Atlanta, GA 30333
404-488-5705

American Lung Association
1740 Broadway
New York, NY 10019
212-315-8700

Cataracts

461. The eye's lens works much like a camera lens. It focuses light onto the retina and the back of the eye, where the image is recorded and sent to the brain. The lens is made of mostly water and protein, and as we age, some of the protein may clump together, causing a cataract. Smoking, diabetes, and the sun are all suspected to be contributing factors to cataracts. Diet also plays a large role.

462. Cataract surgery is very successful in restoring vision.

Cataracts usually start out small and have little effect on vision. To begin with, things may be slightly blurred, as if looking through a cloudy piece of glass. Colors may not appear as bright as they once did.

When cataracts become a problem, they are treated by removing the eye's lens surgically *(not* with lasers, as many believe) and replacing it with a clear-plastic or silicone lens—prescription, if necessary. The procedure takes about twenty minutes. Over 1 million such surgeries are performed each year, making it one of the most common surgical procedures in the United States.

Chronic Pain

463. Chronic pain is persistent pain. Acute pain is the nervous system's way of telling us when there's a problem or an injury; this type of pain subsides once the problem is treated. Chronic pain, on the other hand, doesn't go away. Chronic pain is often triggered by a condition such as arthritis or TMJ (temporomandibular joint syndrome). The nervous system keeps sending "pain" messages for weeks, months, or even years.

The easiest solution for minor chronic pain is the obvious one—take aspirin, acetaminophen, ibuprofen, or naproxen. But because these can have undesirable side effects, or can interfere with medications you are already taking, you might want to look into other pain-management techniques first.

464. Native Americans extracted a form of aspirin from boiled willow bark. In 1897 aspirin in the form we know it today was marketed as a pain reliever by the Bayer company.

Aspirin can cause stomach irritation, although coated or specially treated varieties that minimize this problem are available. Aspirin is not recommended for people with ulcers, uncontrolled high blood pressure, liver or kidney disease, or bleeding disorders. Aspirin can trigger an attack in some asthmatics. Continual high doses can cause hearing loss or a ringing in the ears.

465. By the late 1980s, acetaminophen (Tylenol) was becoming more popular than aspirin for pain relief. Acetaminophen is thought to act on nerve endings to suppress pain. It is the painkiller of choice for people with ulcers and some digestive disorders like colitis. But even at moderate doses, acetaminophen can cause liver damage in heavy drinkers.

466. Ibuprofen (Advil) and naproxen sodium (Aleve, Anaprox) are more potent than aspirin. These are often taken for toothaches, minor arthritis pain, and injuries that are accompanied by inflammation. Taken at the recommended adult dosage, they're also somewhat gentler on the stomach than aspirin. Ibuprofen can cause headaches if used continually for more than a few days.

467. Acupuncture is enjoying increased interest from Western doctors—and insurance companies—for its pain-relieving capabilities. It's an ancient Chinese technique and it's at least two thousand (some say five thousand) years old. Hair-thin needles are inserted under the skin at selected points on the body and then agitated by the practitioner to effect pain relief. Some practitioners use a very weak electrical current instead of manually agitating the needle.

Does acupuncture work? In China it is often used during surgery as an anesthetic. Many American patients report benefits lasting for hours or days when the needles are placed near where it hurts, but not at the body point indicated on traditional Chinese acupuncture charts. Investigators theorize that needling the skin excites endorphins (the body's pain-reducing chemicals), but the most popular theory involves "gate control"—meaning that acupuncture blocks the transmission of pain messages to the brain.

Acupuncture treatments are covered by many insurance companies, including Aetna, Cigna, Fireman's Fund, MetLife, and Prudential.

468. Brief pulses of electricity applied to nerve endings under the skin can also help relieve chronic pain—especially in older adults. The procedure is called transcutaneous electrical nerve stimulation (TENS). Like acupuncture, it works best when applied near where the pain is felt. Its effects may last for a few months, but sometimes it brings years of relief. Care must be taken to avoid skin irritation and burns from the electrodes used in the technique.

469. Mind control can also help you to manage chronic pain. Here are some techniques to investigate.

• Relaxation and meditation therapies enable people to relax tense muscles, reduce anxiety, and alter mental states. The approach may be particularly helpful when pain is associated with fear and dread, as in cancer and back pain.

• Hypnosis has been shown in some studies to reduce anxiety and depression, thereby lessening muscle tension and making pain more bearable.

• Biofeedback is a learned way to control certain body activities such as heartbeat, muscle tension, and bodily warmth. Results with this have been mixed.

• Behavior modification aims to change habits, behaviors, and attitudes that can develop in chronic pain sufferers who are anxious and housebound, if not bedridden. The idea is to reduce pain medication and increase mobility and independence. It can therefore involve the cooperation of family members.

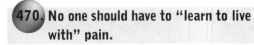
470. No one should have to "learn to live with" pain.

Today, many chronic pain patients are referred to "pain clinics" for treatment. There are more than eight hundred of them nationwide, and their efforts are based on the strides neuroscience has made in tracking and eliminating pain. There will be more such options and better treatments in the future. Check with your doctor for pain clinics in your area.

471. For information on pain relievers and chronic pain, contact:

National Institute of Neurological
Disorders
Information Office
Building 31, Room 8A06
9000 Rockville Pike
Bethesda, MD 20892
800-352-9424
Ask for its headache information packet.

National Chronic Pain Outreach
Association
7979 Old Georgetown Rd., Suite 100
Bethesda, MD 20814
301-652-4948

American Chronic Pain Association
P.O. Box 850
Rocklin, CA 95677
916-632-0922

Chronic Pain Letter
P.O. Box 1303
Old Chelsea Station
New York, NY 10011
The Chronic Pain Letter *is a bimonthly review of new pain treatments, books, and resources.*

Constipation

472. Constipation plagues some of us in our later years. A poor diet, drinking too little fluid, or misusing laxatives can be causes of constipation, as can some medicines, including antidepressants, antacids containing aluminum or calcium, antihistamines, diuretics, and drugs used to treat Parkinson's disease.

But some of us expect too much of our bodies. "Regularity" doesn't have to mean one bowel movement every day. It means whatever is "regular" for you. You may have a problem, however, if you have fewer than three bowel movements per week, have a hard time passing stools, have pain while passing stools, or have other problems, such as bleeding or blood in the stools.

473. Diet has a big effect on constipation. Getting enough fiber is the secret—that means five servings per day of vegetables and fruits and at least six per day of whole-grain products. Consuming too many high-fat meats, dairy products, and eggs can cause constipation, as can rich desserts and other sweets high in refined sugars.

474. Here are some more recommendations that might help.

• Eat slowly, and relax for thirty minutes after each meal.
• Drink alcohol in moderation, if at all; avoid caffeine.
• Exercise.

• Respond to the urge when your body signals—delay is not healthy.

• Avoid laxatives. Some can damage nerve cells in the colon; some interact unfavorably with medications.

475. Mild constipation doesn't require laxatives. A doctor should determine if a laxative is needed and which form is best. People who use laxatives regularly should stop using these medications slowly. In most cases, stopping gradually restores the colon's natural ability to contract. For people confined to bed and who suffer from chronic constipation, medication may be the best solution.

Cosmetic Surgery

476. Cosmetic surgery should not be undertaken lightly. If you are considering it, make sure you understand what is involved, and that your level of expectation is appropriate. Consult with a surgeon who is certified by the American Board of Plastic Surgery. When you're ready to schedule the procedure, look for a physician who is on the staff of a major hospital, even if it means being treated in an office or ambulatory clinic. Ask to see photographs of results, and ask for references you can call. Then call those references.

477. "Lifts" are among the most common type of cosmetic surgery.

• Face-lift. The surgeon makes incisions in the scalp and around the ear; the tissue is then pulled up and back, tightening the facial skin. Excess skin and fat are trimmed away. Because the skin continues to sag with age, many women have another face-lift within two years of the first. The second surgery should last longer than the first.

• Eye-lift. This procedure removes loose skin and fatty tissue from around the upper and lower lids. Note: Crow's-feet will not be eliminated.

• Forehead-lift. Drooping eyebrows and forehead wrinkles are pulled up and away, using an incision in the brow or under the hairline.

• Tummy tuck. Excess sagging skin is removed from the abdomen, and the muscles of the abdominal wall are tightened.

478. Here are some more very popular procedures.

• Breast revision. Reduction removes excess fat and tissue, then repositions the nipple. Breast enlargement, or firming, is done with implants.

• Chemical peels. Caustic chemicals can be used to strip away the top layers of facial skin, removing fine wrinkles. Fruit acids, which are safer and which require less recuperation time, provide a less dramatic peel.

• Dermabrasion. This procedure removes the upper layers of the skin with a diamond stone or wire brush.

• Laser peel. Specially developed high-intensity light removes the thinnest outer layer of the skin. The procedure isn't widely available and should only be performed by a surgeon who has considerable experience performing it.

• Liposuction. Fat deposits on hips, buttocks, arms, or thighs are suctioned out through a device inserted into the body through incisions. Since the body's muscle mass shrinks with age, too much liposuction can leave a person looking gaunt rather than slender.

479. In recent years there has been great concern about breast and other cosmetic implants. The American Society for Aesthetic Plastic Surgery (ASAPS) reports that there is no large increase in the risk of connective-tissue disease (lupus and scleroderma) in women with breast implants. But some feel that such a report—coming from ASAPS—would be biased.

Meanwhile, many women who received silicone breast implants have filed class-action lawsuits against the manufacturers, claiming that they have suffered auto-immune disorders as a result of the implants.

For many women and their doctors, the jury is still out. Until there are conclusive findings, how about a Wonderbra?

480. Lunchtime surgery achieves small changes in short order. Many new procedures can be done very quickly and on an outpatient basis. A surgeon can make small changes—shortening earlobes, say, or tilting up a drooping nose—in less than an hour or two. Check with your surgeon, or contact:

American Society for Aesthetic Plastic Surgery
444 E. Algonquin Rd.
Arlington Heights, IL 60005
708-228-9274

Depression
SEE ALSO MENTAL ILLNESS

481. Diagnosing depression in older adults can be tricky. Those who suffer from it often act confused and have trouble concentrating—the very symptoms exhibited by people on some medications or by those who have Alzheimer's disease or some other disorder of the brain.

Among adults 65 and over, probably about three out of one hundred suffer from clinical depression; for nursing home residents, that number rises to at least sixty out of one hundred. Over the course of a lifetime, the incidence of depression is higher in women than in men, but men are more at risk once they pass the age of 55.

482. There are two types of clinical depression: major and bipolar. People suffering from major depression find it almost impossible to carry on their usual activities. They may be unable to eat and sleep (or may eat and sleep too much) and are incapable of enjoying life. This type of depression can occur once in a lifetime or several times. Major depression should not be confused with the normal feelings of sadness or anxiety that occur as reactions to certain events and that pass within a week or two.

Bipolar disorder depression (also called manic-depressive illness) is characterized by severe mood swings, ranging from extremely low feelings to unrealistic highs. This depression usually shows up for the first time during one's early twenties, although it can start later in life.

483. The causes of depression in mature adults include:

- Chronic disease
- The side effects of medications, such as those prescribed for high blood pressure
- Heredity. There may be a genetic component associated with depression, especially bipolar disorders.
- Personality type. Different people react to the same set of circumstances in different ways. People who depend on others to an extreme degree, and those who have low self-esteem, seem to be especially prone to depression.
- Life events. Any event that brings a lot of change can trigger depression. For older people, that often includes the death of a loved one, illness, or money problems.

484. You may be suffering from major depression if several of the following symptoms have lingered for more than two weeks.

- Feelings of sadness and emptiness
- Anxiety
- Tiredness; lack of normal energy
- Loss of interest or pleasure in ordinary activities, including sex
- Sleep problems, including waking very early in the morning or sleeping too much
- Problems with eating; weight gain or loss
- Crying often for unexplained reasons
- Aches and pains that won't go away
- Difficulty in concentrating and remembering or in making decisions
- Feeling that the future looks grim
- Feeling guilty, helpless, worthless
- Irritability
- Thoughts of death or suicide; suicide attempts

485. If you are having suicidal thoughts, seek professional help immediately. Look in the yellow pages under "Social Service Organizations"—almost any one of them can either help you or refer you to someone who can. (A friend or family member may not take your feelings seriously or may not know what to do.) Statistics show that the rate of completed suicide is 25 percent higher in older people than in the general population.

486. The pain of depression can be treated successfully in most people. Most depressions are treated with antidepressive medication, psychotherapy, or both.

If antidepressants are prescribed, your doctor will choose one whose side effects are compatible with your symptoms (in other words, if insomnia is a problem, you'll be prescribed a drug that causes drowsiness). It can take some trial and error before you and your doctor hit upon the proper dosage; effects probably won't be felt for at least two weeks, and medication will be continued for a few weeks after the episode has passed.

487. Prozac is probably the best-known antidepressant today.

Physicians call it a "selective serotonin re-uptake inhibitor" (other drugs in this class include Zoloft, Paxil, and Luvox). Prozac is popular for a variety of reasons. One is that it elevates the mood—although many patients praise it because it simply makes them feel "normal" again. Other positive attributes: It requires only one dose a day, can be taken with other drugs, and has relatively minor side effects (nausea, headaches, diarrhea, and insomnia).

However, Prozac can cause a decline in sex drive and make it difficult to achieve orgasm. It has been reported to lower the immune system. Prozac has also been criticized for causing "suicidal thinking," but many doctors believe that such a reaction is extremely rare. Some people who suffer from depression take capsules of the herbal supplement St. John's Wort, also called "nature's Prozac" for its ability to elevate moods without the side effects of Prozac.

488. Psychotherapy—talking with a trained therapist—can be very effective.

Short-term therapies developed to treat depression focus on specific symptoms. There may be anywhere from twelve to twenty sessions. Therapy falls into one of two categories: cognitive or interpersonal. Cognitive therapy aims to help the patient recognize and change negative thinking patterns that contribute to depression. Interpersonal therapy focuses on dealing effectively with other people, which improves relationships and can reduce symptoms. You can find a good therapist by asking your rabbi or clergyperson or a trusted friend. Or check the yellow pages under "Psychologist," "Psychiatrist," or "Social Service Organizations."

489. The D'ART (Depression Awareness Recognition and Treatment) Program offers a free pamphlet. The pamphlet is called "If You're Over 65 and Feeling Depressed ... Treatment Brings New Hope." To obtain a copy, contact:

National Institute of Mental Health
D'ART Public Inquiries
5600 Fishers Lane, Room 7C02
Rockville, MD 20857
301-443-4513

Diabetes

490. The risk of contracting diabetes mellitus increases with age. It occurs when the body can't properly convert food into energy.

When sugars and starches are ingested, the body changes them into a form of sugar called glucose. In diabetics, the mechanism that controls the amount of glucose in the blood breaks down, thus allowing the substance to build up to dangerous levels. Specifically, this buildup occurs either because the body doesn't have enough insulin to regulate glucose levels in the blood or because its insulin isn't fully effective.

491. There are two types of diabetes. Type I, or insulin-dependent diabetes, usually asserts itself in youth. But Type II—also called adult-onset diabetes—accounts for about 90 percent of all cases found in older people. Most people with Type II don't need insulin injections and can keep blood glucose levels near normal by controlling weight, exercising, not smoking, and following a sensible diet; sometimes oral medication is necessary.

Diabetes is the seventh leading cause of death in the United States and is the leading cause of kidney disease. Therefore, it is important to maintain proper blood glucose levels. Long-term complications include stroke, blindness, heart disease, kidney failure, gangrene, and nerve damage.

492. The first sign of adult-onset diabetes is often found during a routine medical exam. While for many adults insatiable thirst is the first sign of diabetes, that's not always the case with older people, whose thirst mechanism may have declined somewhat with age. Older adults may first experience numbness or tingling in the feet or lower leg. Some feel run-down, or have vague symptoms, including blurred vision, skin infections or itching, or slow-healing cuts and bruises. If diabetes is the cause, a blood test will reveal the presence of excess sugar in the urine or the blood.

493. Being overweight can trigger diabetes in some older people. In fact, 80 percent of all people with Type II diabetes are overweight. It also tends to run in families and is more prevalent in some populations than in others. In the United States the incidence of diabetes among African Americans is 60 percent higher than it is for whites; among Hispanics it is 110 percent higher. Among the Pimas, a Native American group, half of the tribe's members over age 35 develop the disorder— they have the highest incidence in the world.

People who are at risk for diabetes due to a strong family history of the disease can lower their chances of getting it—or delay its onset—by sticking to a nutritious, low-fat diet and by getting plenty of aerobic exercise.

494. The form of diabetes most often found in older adults can be controlled by lifestyle changes. Diabetes can't be cured, but it can be controlled. Besides giving up smoking and avoiding alcohol, a carefully planned diet can help to lower blood glucose levels (your doctor will provide you with more details about which foods to choose; lists are also available from the American Diabetes Association). A regular fitness program, performed consistently each day, also lowers blood glucose levels. Oral drugs or insulin injections may be prescribed when diet and exercise plans fail, or when they aren't enough.

Some very elderly diabetics may be unable to feed themselves properly or forget to take their medication. Because these lapses can result in serious problems, such patients are often encouraged to wear a medical alert device.

495. Diabetics can and should take responsibility for their own care. If you have diabetes, it is important to keep your skin clean and to protect it against injury. A minor cut can lead to a serious infection. Cuts should be treated quickly, and plenty of moisturizer used to combat dryness. Diabetics can monitor their blood sugar levels using home-testing kits.

496. The feet require special care. Diabetics should check their feet daily for redness, sores, blisters, breaks in the skin, infections, or buildup of calluses. They should soak their feet often, choose well-fitting shoes and socks, and *never* go barefoot.

497. Diabetics need to be particularly careful about their eyes. Diabetics need to schedule regular eye examinations because they are at increased risk for diabetic retinopathy (damage to the blood vessels in the retina), cataracts (the clouding of the eyes' lenses), and glaucoma (increased fluid pressure inside the eye). This is because diabetes can affect the balance of fluid in the eye and can damage nerves and blood vessels within the eye.

498. Teeth and gums should also receive special attention. Diabetics should make their dentists aware of their disease and schedule a checkup every six months. This is because they are more susceptible to gum infections than are nondiabetics.

499. Some additional dental tips:

- If you wear dentures, make sure they fit properly.

- Brush with a very soft bristle brush; firm up gums by using a rubber-tipped dental tool between the teeth, in a circular motion.

- Watch for bleeding of the gums when you eat or brush your teeth—it may mean the beginning of an infection.

- Notify your dentist if your gums look pale or if you notice any other changes in your mouth.

500. For more information about living with diabetes, contact:

National Diabetes Information Clearinghouse
1 Information Way
Bethesda, MD 20892
301-654-3327

American Diabetes Association
1660 Duke St.
Alexandria, VA 22314
800-232-3475
Ask for "Seniors: Diabetes and You."

National Institute of Diabetes and Digestive and Kidney Diseases
Building 31, Room 9A04
31 Center Dr., MSC 2560
Bethesda, MD 20892
301-496-3583

Diarrhea

501. Diarrhea is the body's way of ridding the digestive system of toxins. Interestingly, it is also a common response to antibiotics, making drug-induced diarrhea a particular problem as we age.

Most episodes of diarrhea clear up on their own, especially with some attention to diet. During a bout, avoid gastrointestinal stimulants, including caffeine, anything very hot or cold, beer, milk, and fried or spicy foods. Many doctors recommend the BRAT diet until symptoms ease: Consume only bananas, rice, applesauce, and tea.

Most important of all is replacing fluid. Drink at least ten glasses of water or nonacidic fruit juice per day. This can be supplemented by broth and gelatin. Getting enough fluid will help to prevent complications that stem from loss of electrolytes such as sodium and potassium.

502. Here's a good recipe for replacing fluid and electrolytes.

In one glass, combine eight ounces of orange, apple, or other potassium-rich fruit juice, half a teaspoon of honey or corn syrup (useful in absorbing essential salts), and a pinch of salt (replaces essential sodium and chloride). Fill another glass with a carbonated beverage, water, or tea. Alternate sipping from both glasses.

503. Sometimes diarrhea is the sign of a more serious illness. It can also lead to complications. Call your physician if the condition lasts more than four days, or if you have severe abdominal or rectal pain, fever, or blood in your stool. Other symptoms to pay attention to are excessive thirst, feeling unusually weak, and feeling either dizzy or restless.

Diverticulosis and Diverticulitis

504. In the United States most people over 60 have diverticulosis. Diverticulosis is the formation of small sacs in the wall of the large intestine. The condition usually causes no symptoms other than occasional pain in the lower left side of the abdomen and, sometimes, rectal bleeding. It is only a concern when it develops into *diverticulitis,* which happens when the sacs become inflamed. Diverticulitis causes pain and fever and requires a trip to the doctor. Diverticulitis requires antibiotics, but once the bout is over, a high-fiber diet is recommended to prevent both diverticulitis *and* diverticulosis.

Dizziness

505. Unexplained dizzy spells are not uncommon as we age, but they should not be ignored. Dizziness can be a feeling of poor balance, a spinning sensation, faintness, weakness, or a loss of coordination. It is usually caused by poor vision, hyperventilation (overbreathing), or emotional distress. But it can also be the result of a more serious medical or drug-related condition. Viral infection, stroke, and heartbeat irregularities can all cause feelings of dizziness. If you have two dizzy spells in a week, or if you have dizziness accompanied by hearing loss, blackouts, or headaches, call a doctor immediately.

Dry Mouth

506. Its medical name—xerostomia—sounds exotic, but dry mouth is very common. It's so common in older people that for a long time it was considered to be normal. Nowadays, we know that mature adults produce as much saliva as younger ones.

Dry mouth can be triggered by anything from stress and fear to various diseases and medical treatments. It's a side effect of more than four hundred commonly used drugs, both prescription and over-the-counter, including drugs for high blood pressure, antidepressants, and antihistamines.

Dry mouth is uncomfortable and can contribute to tooth decay and gum infections. It can also make it hard to eat, swallow, taste, and speak. But its remedies are simple: Drink more fluids, and suck on sugarless candies to stimulate the salivary glands. Avoid sugary snacks, caffeine, alcohol, and tobacco. You might also want to run a humidifier in your bedroom at night.

Emphysema, Chronic Bronchitis

507. Emphysema is a serious lung disease that is usually related to smoking. It is a condition that develops gradually over a period of years. As we grow older, it becomes harder to distinguish emphysema and chronic bronchitis from asthma, which is more treatable. Often people have a blend of emphysema and chronic bronchitis.

Shortness of breath can be an early symptom of emphysema. As the disease develops, breathing becomes more of an effort. People who suffer from chronic bronchitis cough up phlegm daily over a period of years and sometimes have difficulty expelling air from their lungs.

Medication can help ease the symptoms of both of these diseases. And it is critical that sufferers quit smoking.

Eye Conditions
SEE ALSO CATARACTS; FLOATERS;
GLAUCOMA; MACULAR DEGENERATION

508. Presbyopia is most people's introduction to aging eyes. The word comes from the Greek for "elder" and "eye," and refers to the slow loss of ability to see close objects or small print. It's a normal process that occurs over a lifetime as the lens of the eye grows less elastic.

Presbyopia usually goes unnoticed until

after age 40, when most of us begin holding reading material at arm's length or develop headaches or tired eyes. These symptoms can usually be remedied simply by picking up a pair of nonprescription, magnifying reading glasses. They're available from optical shops and drugstores and often come in three-packs (one for the desk, another for the bedside, and a third for the car).

509. As we age, our eyes are sometimes too dry and sometimes too wet. When sluggish tear glands don't produce enough fluid, eyes get itchy or burn. A humidifier will help alleviate the condition, as will specialized eyedrops called artificial tears.

Wet eyes can be caused by light sensitivity or by a reaction to wind or temperature changes. Wearing sunglasses often helps. Excessive tearing can also mean an infection or a blocked tear duct, requiring a doctor's visit.

510. The ultraviolet rays in sunshine can damage our eyes all year round.

This, we think, is a wonderful reason to wear very cool sunglasses, but be sure they give sufficient protection, too. Sunglasses that block 99 percent of ultraviolet B (UVB) rays are adequate to protect the eyes in moderately bright sunlight. Sunglasses that screen out 99 percent of both ultraviolet A (UVA) and UVB rays are necessary for intensely bright sunlight (wear these when you're on the beach). Such sunglasses should block 60 to 90 percent of visible light, in order to reduce glare and to increase visual comfort. Check the label or sticker that comes with the sunglasses for information on the amount of protection they offer.

511. The eyelids protect the eyes, distribute tears, and limit the amount of light entering the eyes. They are also subject to pain, itching, tearing, and sensitivity to light. As you age, your eyelids may droop (ptosis), have blinking spasms (blepharospasm), or get inflamed at the outer edges near the eyelashes (blepharitis).

Eyelid problems can be caused by environmental conditions and sometimes by disease. They are usually treated with medication or surgery. Consult with your eye doctor if you experience discomfort.

512. Have a comprehensive eye exam every year to detect, diagnose, and treat any problems. In addition to testing your ability to see and focus, the procedure should include a general health history (including medications you take), an interior and exterior eye examination, and glaucoma tests. A check for eye muscle coordination and focus-changing ability should also be part of the exam.

513. Eye care professionals are not all the same, although their titles sound alike. The following should help you sort out any confusion.

• An ophthalmologist is a doctor of medicine (M.D.) or osteopathy (D.O.), licensed to practice medicine and perform surgery. Ophthalmologists prescribe glasses and contact lenses.

• An optometrist is a doctor of optometry (O.D.), licensed to practice in areas of eye and vision care. Optometrists screen patients for vision problems and prescribe glasses, contact lenses, or exercises to correct muscle imbalances. In some states, they use diagnostic and therapeutic drugs. If surgery or medication is needed, the optometrist will refer you to an ophthalmologist.

• An optician fits, adjusts, and sells glasses, contact lenses, protective eye wear, and other optical devices prescribed by ophthalmologists and optometrists.

514. At some point, bifocals are likely to enter your life. They are, of course, those eyeglasses with split lenses. The upper part corrects for distance vision, and the lower part corrects for close-up sight.

For many people, bifocals are a symbol of aging; they might therefore take getting used to emotionally as well as physically. Wearers must adjust to looking through the right part at the right time—and the midrange can sometimes be blurry. But if you stick with it, it will soon become second nature—even while lying down to watch TV.

Seamless bifocals are now common. Some people find they take a little longer to adjust to, but wearing them makes them feel better about their personal appearance.

515. Yes, there are bifocal contact lenses. In fact, there are two kinds. "Simultaneous vision" lenses require you to look through the distance *and* the close-up portions at the same time; the brain and eyes learn to adjust appropriately. "Translating bifocal" lenses

have a thicker lower edge for reading (much as with bifocal eyeglasses), and the remainder of the lens is used for distance. Bifocal contact lenses require a lot of light in order for you to be able to see well.

516. Another modification of contact lenses lets each eye work independently. It's called monovision, and with it, one eye is fitted with a lens for distance and the other with a lens for close-up work. The brain learns to switch to the eye needed for the task at hand. Until you're used to wearing them, these lenses can cause blurred vision, dizziness, and headaches. It's best to avoid visually demanding tasks until you've adjusted to them.

 517. **One of the consistent best-sellers in large print is** *Sex After Sixty,* **by Robert N. Butler and Myrna I. Lewis.**

Most best-sellers are available in large-print editions. The works of Mary Higgins Clark, Deepak Chopra, John Grisham, Michael Crichton, and Dean Koontz, for example, can all be found in this format.

If reading is still too difficult, you can listen to books on tape. Best-sellers and classics can be obtained in cassette form, either from a bookstore or from the public library. Some libraries will even lend you a cassette player.

518. Here are some tips for a lifetime of healthy eyes.

• Use adequate light for reading and other close tasks; light should fall on the work, not in your eyes.

- If you wear glasses, clean them often.
- Keep car windshields and headlamps shining, too.
- Eat healthfully. Studies show that antioxidants, such as vitamins C and E, help to combat cataracts and macular degeneration.
- Make sure your eyes are protected when playing sports.
- Don't smoke.

519. If your vision is failing, spread color boldly around your home.

- Paint the stair handrail a bright color so it's easy to see when you grab for it. The edges of stair steps should get similar treatment.
- Keep your keys on a large, brightly colored key chain so they'll be easier to find. Colored key tops, available at hardware stores, help to distinguish individual keys.
- When cooking, use graduated measuring cups rather than one big cup with the hard-to-see scale painted on its side.
- Choose brightly colored drinking glasses, since clear glasses can disappear against the background and be hard to spot when you reach for them.
- Choose boldly colored gardening tools that are easily visible against grass.

520. To learn more about the effects of aging on your eyes, contact:

National Eye Institute Information Center
31 Center Dr., MSC 2510
Building 31, Room 6A32
Bethesda, MD 20892
301-496-5248

Lighthouse Information and Resource Service
111 E. 59th St., 11th Floor
New York, NY 10022
800-334-5497

National Association for the Visually Handicapped
22 W. 21st St.
New York, NY 10010
212-889-3141

Vision Foundation
818 Mt. Auburn St.
Watertown, MA 02172
617-926-4232
For information on special products and services for people with visual impairments.

National Library Service for the Blind and Visually Handicapped
1291 Taylor St. NW
Washington, DC 20542
800-424-8567
Provides free library services and offers braille and large-print materials, recorded books, and other periodicals.

For information from the AARP via a hotline, call 800-232-5463.

Fatigue

521. If you feel drained, it's a good time to get up and get moving. About half of all older adults experience weakness and fatigue. Don't think of it as an inevitable part of aging—it's often the result of living a sedentary lifestyle. Try to get more exercise than you usually do, whether it's in the form of a structured workout, sports, or simply a daily walk around the block.

Exercise not only gives you more energy, it makes you feel better psychologically. One reason: It increases the brain's output of endorphins, which produce a sense of well-being. This is good to know if depression is causing you to feel drained.

Sometimes, of course, fatigue has a pathological basis. Often, one of the first signs of a cold or the flu is a feeling of being unusually tired; metabolic difficulties, untreated diabetes, kidney disease, and heart problems are frequently accompanied by overwhelming fatigue. Consult with your doctor if weakness and fatigue linger.

Floaters

522. You probably first started seeing floaters before you turned 55. Those specks that drift across your field of vision usually appear for the first time when you are in your 30s and are sometimes accompanied by tiny flashes of light. Floaters are caused by shadows on the retina made by bits of a jellylike substance behind the lens of the eye. Wearing sunglasses helps make floaters less noticeable and irritating.

While floaters are not unusual, you should see your doctor if you experience a sudden change in the type or number of spots.

Flu

523. For older adults, a flu can be life-threatening. Influenza lowers the body's ability to fight off other infections like pneumonia, which is one of the five leading causes of death among people 65 and older. It is also dangerous for anyone who has a chronic illness such as heart disease, emphysema, asthma, bronchitis, kidney disease, or diabetes.

A flu shot every autumn—before flu season really sets in—can prevent the illness. The injections can cause a low-grade fever or redness at the injection site; if you're allergic to eggs, you'll have to skip the shot. It is necessary to get a flu shot every year because new strains of viruses appear annually.

Foot Conditions

524. Some of the more common foot troubles that appear as we age are also the most easily remedied.

• Blisters are liquid-filled enlargements of the skin. They are caused by friction that results from ill-fitting or new shoes or from taking a long walk. Apply moleskin padding to the area and keep it clean and dry. If the blister bursts, leave the top skin in place as a protective cover, but also apply an antiseptic and a small bandage.

• Bunions are an inflammation or misalignment of the joint at the base of the big toe. They are an inherited tendency, aggravated by arthritis or by wearing shoes with unnaturally high heels or narrow toes. Surgery is necessary to correct painful bunions; wearing a specially designed arch support can help to control their growth.

• Corns are hard patches of skin found over the joints of the toes. They develop when friction continues beyond blistering, and irritated skin protects itself by thickening and hardening. For temporary relief, use a padding product. Corns can be remedied by soaking the foot for about thirty minutes, then using a pumice stone to work away the hardened skin.

• Calluses are cousins to corns; they occur in wide areas of the foot, such as the ball. Except in extreme cases, calluses can usually be treated the same way as corns.

525. Heel pain may result as the pads of the feet grow thinner with age. It happens when there is too much stress on the heel bone, perhaps as a result of a bruise or because of poorly constructed footwear. Arthritis and gout can also cause heel pain.

Pain in this area may also be due to heel spurs—calcium growths that occur on the heel bone. They are usually painless until they are fully formed, when inflammation develops at the site of the spur formation.

Whatever the kind of heel pain, common sense can help. Rest when you need to, and be especially sensitive to the pressure that exercise puts on your feet. Make sure you're wearing the proper footwear for walking, jogging, or exercising.

526. Swollen feet could signal a problem. We have all growled about swollen feet on airplane trips, during pregnancy, or when we don't wear shoes for a while. But in our later years, persistent swelling of both feet may signal a systemic problem such as kidney, heart, or circulatory disease. Increased or periodic swelling in the lower extremities may be a symptom that hypertension has contributed to heart disease.

527. For more information on feet and foot care, contact:

American Podiatric Medical Association
9312 Old George Town
Bethesda, MD 20814

American Orthopedic Foot and Ankle
Society
222 S. Prospect
Park Ridge, IL 60068

Gallstones

528. About 20 percent of Americans over 60 have gallstones. These are formed from bile that has become concentrated into a stone stored in the gallbladder. If you're lucky, you'll have "silent gallstones," which cause no symptoms and require no treatment. However, a severe and steady pain in the upper right portion of the abdomen may mean that the stone has "migrated" out of the gallbladder.

Surgery is often required for migrating gallstones, although there are some nonsurgical options, such as drugs that dissolve the stones. Maintaining ideal body weight, eating a balanced diet, and drinking one glass of alcohol per day all seem to have preventive value.

Gas

529. People of all ages get gas. Gas is caused by a combination of swallowed air and the normal breakdown of undigested foods in our gastrointestinal systems. The unpleasant odor results from intestinal bacteria that contain sulfur. Changes in diet—along with over-the-counter medications—can help reduce the problem. Here are some tips.

• Don't chew gum or eat hard candy, since you swallow a lot of air doing so.
• Eat fewer gas-causing foods. Culprits include onions, raw apples, radishes, beans, cucumbers, milk, melons, chocolate, coffee, lettuce, peanuts, and eggs.
• Avoid foods that contain a lot of air, such as soufflés, beaten omelets, fresh-baked bread, and meringues. Cut down on carbonated drinks.
• "Beano" works. It's an antigas food enzyme product available at drugstores and health food stores.
• Over-the-counter antacids work, too. Activated charcoal tablets may provide some relief for gas from the colon.

Glaucoma

530. It's important to catch glaucoma early.

Glaucoma occurs when the normal fluid inside the eyes slowly rises. This causes an increase in pressure; left uncontrolled, the pressure may cause damage to the optic nerve and other parts of the eye, resulting in loss of vision. By the time symptoms occur (pain, blurry vision, narrowed field of vision) serious damage may already be done. Glaucoma is a leading cause of blindness in the United States. It affects 3 percent of all people over 65. Make sure you see your eye care practitioner regularly; testing for glaucoma is part of the routine exam.

531. If glaucoma is found, several treatment options are available. Medicated eyedrops may reduce pressure by slowing the flow of fluid into the eye and improving drainage. Laser surgery that focuses a strong beam of light on the eye can be used to open an exit for the fluid. Traditional surgery, or a combination of surgery, eyedrops, medication, and laser surgery, is also effective.

Hair Loss and Hair Growth

532. Ancient Egyptians used unguents in an attempt to hold on to their hair. They also used bronze tweezers to pluck strays. Hannibal wore a toupee, and Louis XIII of France introduced his court to wigs in an attempt to hide his receding hairline.

There is nothing new about our desire to disguise baldness, or to dye, transplant, or otherwise transform our hair. Its appearance plays a major role in other people's perceptions of us. Hair that is thinning or graying is a giveaway to the aging process, as are runaway nose, ear, and eyebrow hairs in men and whiskery chin hairs in women.

533. Most hair loss is genetic. In men, it's called male pattern baldness, and it can be inherited from either side of the family (not just from your mother's father, as was previously believed). It starts at the temples and continues above the forehead. Women who are past menopause may begin to experience an overall thinning of the hair.

Chemotherapy can cause loss of hair, as can taking certain medications (although this reaction is very rare). Emotional stress, surgery, high fevers, and severe infections can cause it, too. Crash diets—especially those low in protein—and iron-deficiency anemia are also culprits. Hair abuse doesn't help, either. Perming, dyeing, chemically straightening, and overuse of hot curlers and blow-dryers can all cause breakage and hair loss. In all of these cases, hair loss is reversible.

534. Get rid of unwanted body hair. Tweeze it, bleach it, shave it, or use a depilatory. Most beauty salons do waxings. A permanent solution for excess body hair may be electrolysis, although this type of treatment has its limitations. Unwanted hair growth is a problem in postmenopausal women due to hormonal changes, but excessive hairiness should be closely monitored by a doctor, since it may signal a more serious problem.

535. Hair regrowth treatments may help some people. Minoxidil, known commercially as Rogaine, is the first proven method of hair regrowth. It is a clear liquid that is sold over-the-counter in drugstores, discount stores, and supermarkets.

Minoxidil works best for women with thinning hair and for men who have just begun to go bald. It regrows hair in some people and also helps to retain what is already there. According to the Rogaine information hotline, among studies of white women aged 18 to 45, 59 percent reported "moderate to dense" hair regrowth (40 percent had only "minimal" regrowth). Among white men aged 18 to 49, only 26 percent reported "moderate to dense" regrowth.

Minoxidil must be applied twice a day and

used continually—that is, if you stop using it, you will lose whatever hair has grown back, and you will continue to go bald. It will take at least three months before any regrowth can be noticed. Because minoxidil is effective only at the *first sign* of hair loss, older men who started going bald years ago will not see any results, and anyone on high blood pressure medication should not use it. Depending on your budget, treatment can be expensive.

Interestingly enough, while studying the effects of Rogaine, researchers found that 20 percent of the test subjects who had been given a placebo also experienced hair regrowth—a clear case of mind over matter.

Rogaine has not been tested on people over the age of 49, so you might want to think twice about using it.

536. Hair transplants are also a possibility if you're really serious about regaining your hair. Here are the different methods.

• Hair transplants involve moving follicles from the lower fringe of the scalp, where hair usually remains full, to the top of the head. This is rarely a viable option for women, since their hair loss tends to be diffuse, leaving no "full" area to draw from.

• Transposition flaps correct large areas of hair loss by moving entire strips of hair-bearing skin, rather than individual follicles. Flaps can produce good results, but are costly and require complicated multiple surgeries.

• Scalp reduction entails the removal of areas of the scalp that no longer grow hair so that areas with hair are pulled closer together.

 537. Consider joining a Bald Pride organization.

Bald-Headed Men of America has about twenty thousand members nationwide. They refer to themselves as Hairless Hunks, and their rallying cries are "Bald Is Beautiful," "Bald Is Bold," and "The Few! The Proud! The Bald!" The group promotes "National Rub-a-Bald-Head Week" and publishes a newsletter called *Chrome Dome*, which informs members of conventions and other items of interest to bald men. By the way, most women consider baldness to be more attractive—and a sign of healthier self-esteem—than wigs and toupees, no matter how skillfully they have been manufactured.

For more information, contact:

Bald-Headed Men of America (BHMA)
102 Bald Dr.
Morehead City, NC 28557
919-726-1855

538. For more information on hair loss, contact:

American Hair Loss Council
100 Independence Pl., Suite 315A
Tyler, TX 75703
A nonprofit organization that provides information on safe hair replacement products.

Information Center for Rogaine
Upjohn Company
P.O. Box 166
Beltsville, MD 20704
800-635-0655

National Alopecia Areata Foundation
710 C Street, #11
P.O. Box 15070
San Rafael, CA 94901
415-456-4644

Headache

539. The incidence of migraine headaches usually diminishes with age. But we're still susceptible to the types that result from indigestion, hunger, or stress.

When a headache is accompanied by weakness, numbness, speech difficulty, confusion, balance problems, or impaired vision, seek help immediately. Ditto for an acute headache on one side of the head that is accompanied by tenderness or swelling of the scalp.

The types and causes of headaches are still not fully understood by the medical community. If you're suffering from a "normal" headache, relaxation is usually the best thing for it. Try deep, slow breathing in a darkened room. By the way, sex helps.

540. High blood pressure frequently causes headaches. This type is characterized by a generalized throbbing pain, often accompanied by nausea and vomiting and sometimes a drooping eye. A CT scan or MRI may be required to make a diagnosis.

Headaches can also be caused by depression, arthritis in the neck, blockage or inflammation of the arteries, glaucoma or eye inflammation, a brain tumor, or medication.

There are many kinds of headaches, and doctors still aren't sure what causes all of them.

541. To catch up on the latest headache information, contact:

National Headache Foundation
5252 N. Western Ave.
Chicago, IL 60625
800-843-2256
Send a stamped, self-addressed business-size envelope for a free copy of "The Headache Handbook."

American Association for the Study of Headache
P.O. Box 5136
San Clemente, CA 92672
Send a stamped, self-addressed envelope for a list of headache specialists and clinics in your area.

Hearing Loss

542. About a third of all people over 65 have trouble hearing. As much as you may be resisting it, you might need to consider the possibility of wearing a hearing aid. An otolaryngologist—that is, a doctor with special training in ear, nose, and throat problems—will make the diagnosis of a hearing problem. He or she will then refer you to an audiologist, a health care professional who will identify and measure your hearing loss and advise you on the best types of hearing aid for your situation.

543. The most common hearing problem over age 50 is called presbycusis. It is a gradual loss of high-frequency hearing in both ears and is caused by changes in the inner ear.

With "conductive" hearing loss, sounds are blocked between the eardrum and the inner ear. Earwax, fluid in the middle ear, abnormal bone growth, or an infection can cause this loss. "Sensorineural" hearing loss happens when there is damage to parts of the inner ear or nerves. Head injuries, tumors, illness, certain medicines, poor blood circulation, or high blood pressure may cause this type of hearing loss.

544. Do you hear a ringing sound? Tinnitus—a ringing or roaring sound inside the ears—is a common problem, and its origin is a mystery. It may be caused by earwax, an ear infection, the use of too much aspirin, certain antibiotics, or a nerve disorder. Tinnitus can come and go, or it can stop completely.

545. Hearing aids can't completely restore hearing, but they can help a lot. It can take about a month to adjust to the device, but after that, your brain and your ears will cooperate to understand which sounds you want to hear.

Most hearing aids are very small devices, which nonetheless include a microphone to pick up sound, an amplifier to make sound louder, a receiver to deliver sound to the ear, batteries, volume controls, and an ear mold that channels sound into the ear and holds the aid in place. The American Speech-Language-Hearing Association has an excellent brochure that describes how hearing aids work. Call it at 800-638-8255.

Hearing aids can range in price from $450 to about $800. Financial assistance is sometimes available for those on limited budgets. Your local dispenser or clinic may be able to provide details.

 Nowadays, hearing aids are all but hidden within the ear.

The traditional "behind-the-ear" style is what most people think of when they think of hearing aids. But 80 percent of the aids worn today are much smaller, and are custom-designed to fit *within* the wearer's ear. The basic models work best in small, quiet settings, but more advanced, "programmable" versions of each style are available. These are more sensitive to each wearer's needs, making speech more audible—even with background noise. Here are the three most popular hearing aids.

- In the ear. This is the most commonly worn type. It is durable, and its controls are easy to use.
- In the canal. This smaller, less noticeable model fits into the ear canal. It is slightly less durable than the in the ear model, and because the volume controls are also smaller, they are a little more difficult to manipulate.
- Completely in the ear. It's all but invisible. The drawback is that the tiny controls can be hard to work. This style will not be beneficial for those with severe hearing loss.

547. Advances in technology are beginning to provide other hearing-assistance devices.

• Personal listening systems carry sound from the speaker or other source directly to the listener and minimize or eliminate environmental noises.

• TV listening systems help the wearer to hear a TV, radio, or stereo system without interference from surrounding noise or the need for high volume.

• Direct audio input hearing aids are equipped with audio input connections that can be attached to a TV, stereo, tape recorder, radio, microphone, auditory trainer, and personal systems.

• Many standard telephone receivers come with a coil that can be activated when the receiver is picked up by a person with a hearing aid. Specially designed telephone receivers that amplify sound are also available.

548. If someone you know has a hearing problem, you can help.

• While speaking, face the person and talk clearly.

• Stand where there is good lighting and low background noise.

• Speak clearly and at a reasonable speed; don't hide your mouth, eat, or chew gum.

• Use facial expressions or gestures to give clues.

• Reword your statement.

• Be patient; stay positive and relaxed.

• Include the hearing-impaired person in all discussions about him or her.

549. For information about hearing loss, contact:

American Academy of Otolaryngology—
Head and Neck Surgery
1 Prince St.
Alexandria, VA 22314
703-836-4444
Offers physician referrals.

American Speech-Language-Hearing
Association
10801 Rockville Pike
Rockville, MD 20852
800-638-8255

American Tinnitus Association (ATA)
P.O. Box 5
Portland, OR 97207
800-634-8978
Provides information about support networks and materials on prevention and treatment; also makes professional referrals.

Self Help for Hard of Hearing People
910 Woodmont Ave., Suite 1200
Bethesda, MD 20814
301-657-2248

American Association of Retired Persons
601 E St. NW
Washington, DC 20049

Ask for "Have You Heard? Hearing Loss and Aging."

International Hearing Society
20361 Middlebelt Rd.
Livonia, MI 48152
800-521-5247

Heart Disease

SEE ALSO ANGINA; ATHEROSCLEROSIS

550. Heart attack is the death of a portion of heart muscle. It occurs when an obstruction in one of the coronary arteries prevents adequate oxygen from a portion of the heart. You may hear heart attacks referred to in terms of "obstruction" (coronary thrombosis) or the "damage" done (myocardial infarction).

Heart failure occurs when the heart is unable to pump the amount of blood needed by the body. Heart failure can develop from heart and circulatory disorders, such as high blood pressure and heart attack. It often leads to congestion in the body tissues, with fluid accumulating in the abdomen, legs, and/or lungs. This condition, which may develop over a period of years, is often called congestive heart failure.

551. Chest pain—angina—or shortness of breath may be an early sign of heart disease. Other symptoms include a feeling of heaviness, tightness, pain, burning, pressure, or squeezing, usually behind the breastbone, but sometimes also in the arms, neck, or jaws.

Angina happens when the heart isn't getting enough oxygen, usually due to narrowed arteries. The pain can last for a few minutes and usually occurs after exertion, stress, or a heavy meal. Angina should not be ignored, because it is often the warning sign of a future heart attack.

Eating a low-fat diet, exercising, and giving up tobacco can help to control angina, as can prescription medications. However, if medication and lifestyle changes don't help, or if symptoms get worse, surgery may be required.

552. Coronary heart disease (CHD) is the most common form of heart disease. Also called coronary artery disease, it is the number one killer in the United States.

It is caused by a narrowing of the coronary arteries that feed the heart, thereby restricting blood flow, and the oxygen and nutrients available to the heart. The arteries narrow when cholesterol and fat, circulating in the blood, build up on their walls.

If you have high blood pressure, or if you smoke, you are doubling your chances of contracting CHD. Obesity and physical inactivity are also risk factors; obesity increases the likelihood of high blood cholesterol and high blood pressure, and physical inactivity increases the risk of heart attack. Other risk factors include diabetes, diet, stress, and heredity.

553. For American women, heart disease is the number one cause of death. It wasn't always so; researchers believe that the diet and lifestyle of modern women make them just as likely as men to die from this disease. It is responsible for one-third of all deaths among American women.

As a woman ages, her risk increases: By age 64, one in nine has heart disease, but fully one-third of all women aged 65 and over have it. This may be due in part to hormonal changes after menopause; replacing estrogen via hormone replacement therapy (HRT) has proved successful, but because HRT can itself cause serious problems, it shouldn't be looked to as a cure-all.

554. Statistics indicate that lifestyle changes and medical interventions appear to be having a positive impact on coronary heart disease.

Although it remains the leading cause of death in people over 65, the percentage of heart disease deaths has *decreased* 44 percent for those between ages 65 and 70 over the last thirty years and 30 percent for those over 80. There's a similar statistic for stroke: During the same period, it's gone down 40 percent in older people.

555. There is no one simple test for coronary heart disease.
A group of tests establishes the extent and severity of CHD, ruling out other causes of symptoms:

• Electrocardiogram (ECG or EKG) is a graphic record of the heart's electrical activity as it contracts and rests. It detects ab-normal heartbeats, some areas of damage, inadequate blood flow, and heart enlargement.

• Stress test (treadmill test or exercise ECG) records heartbeat during exercise. Some heart problems show up only when the heart is working hard. It is coupled with an ECG and breathing rate and blood pressure measurements. Exercise tests are useful but are not completely reliable.

• Nuclear scanning shows damaged areas and problems with pumping action. Radioactive material is injected into a vein. A scanning camera records the dispersal of the material in the heart.

• Coronary angiography (arteriography) explores the arteries and is the only certain way to assess damage. A fine tube called a catheter is inserted into an artery and passed through it to the heart. Fluid is injected through the tube into the arteries; the heart and blood vessels can then be viewed using X rays while the heart pumps.

556. For many people, heart disease is managed with lifestyle changes and medications.
We've said it before, but it bears repeating: "Lifestyle changes" means getting enough exercise, maintaining a healthful diet, and not smoking. Although great advances have been made in treatment, controlling these facets of your lifestyle remains the single most effective way to stop heart disease. And even if you're on medication for the disease, you must still adhere to these lifestyle changes. Once heart disease develops, it requires lifelong management.

557. Changing your diet to one low in fat—especially saturated fat—and cholesterol will help reduce the buildup of fat in the arteries. You want to keep your cholesterol low after a heart attack to decrease your risk of having another one. Eating less fat should also help you lose extra weight, another cause of high blood cholesterol. Weight loss is the most effective lifestyle change for reducing high blood pressure that leads to heart disease.

558. Here are some quick definitions of different types of fats.

Cholesterol: a chemical compound manufactured by the body and used to build tissue. Dietary cholesterol is found in animal food products—egg yolks, liver, meat, and some shellfish.

Fat: a chemical compound whose function is to store energy in the body

Fatty acid: molecules of mostly carbon and hydrogen atoms

Hydrogenated fat: a fat that has been chemically altered by the addition of hydrogen atoms. Vegetable shortening and margarine are hydrogenated fats.

Lipoprotein: a chemical compound made of fat and protein. Lipoproteins carry cholesterol in the blood. High-density lipoproteins (HDLs) are healthy, while low-density lipoproteins (LDLs) are not.

Monounsaturated fatty acid: found in olive oil and peanut oil; tends to lower levels of bad cholesterol (LDL)

Polyunsaturated fatty acid: found in vegetables and seafood

Saturated fatty acid: found in animal products such as meat, whole milk, butter, and lard; associated with bad cholesterol (LDLs)

559. It would seem reasonable that eating less cholesterol would reduce a person's cholesterol level. Not necessarily so. As it turns out, eating less cholesterol has less effect on blood cholesterol levels than eating less saturated fat. But that doesn't mean you can binge on cholesterol-rich foods; some studies have found that eating cholesterol still increases the risk of heart disease, even if it doesn't raise blood cholesterol levels.

Some studies show that eating foods containing polyunsaturated and monounsaturated fats can reduce levels of the bad cholesterol (LDL) in the blood. Polyunsaturated fats—most liquid oils—tend to lower both kinds of cholesterol. Oils such as olive and canola—rich in monounsaturated fats—however, tend to lower bad cholesterol without affecting good levels (HDL).

560. When you reach for a snack, take some advice from the American Heart Association.

• Crunchies: apples, pears, carrots, celery
• Hot stuff: clear soups, cocoa made with nonfat milk
• Munchies: unsalted sunflower seeds, flavored popcorn, bread sticks
• Quenchers: tomato or vegetable juice, nonfat milk
• Sweet stuff: raisins, fresh or dried fruits, gelatin

561. Even moderate amounts of exercise are associated with lower death rates from heart

disease. That can mean, for example, walking for thirty minutes three or four times a week. (See Chapter 5 for more exercise suggestions.) If you have severe CHD, you may have to restrict your exercise somewhat, so check with your cardiologist first to find out what kinds of exercise are best for you.

562. Medications for heart disease are prescribed according to the nature of the illness. Angina symptoms can generally be controlled by beta-blockers (drugs that decrease the workload on the heart), nitroglycerin and other nitrates, and calcium channel blockers (they relax the arteries).

For those with elevated blood cholesterol who are unresponsive to dietary and weight-loss measures, cholesterol-lowering drugs may be prescribed. Digitalis is given to aid impaired heart pumping function. High blood pressure and fluid retention can also be treated with drugs.

563. If you think you're having a heart attack, take two aspirins.

Of course, you should go to the emergency room, too. But studies show that people who managed to take aspirin at this critical time had a better chance for recovery.

Aspirin is generally recommended as a blood thinner to cardiac patients. Blood cells contain platelets that can clump together, clot, or plug tiny blood vessels. Aspirin keeps the blood thin and prevents the platelets from blocking the arteries. In study after study, a daily dose of aspirin was found to reduce by half the incidence of both fatal and nonfatal heart attacks (but

don't take aspirin every day unless your doctor has advised it).

564. For some, surgery will be needed to alleviate coronary heart disease. Angioplasty (dilating of the blood vessels through use of a balloon) and bypass surgery are the most common treatments for coronary heart disease. With bypass surgery, a blood vessel—usually taken from the patient's leg or chest—is grafted onto a blocked artery, bypassing the blocked area. The blood can then go around the obstruction to supply the heart. Several bypasses are often done at the same time.

Bypass surgery relieves symptoms of heart disease but does not cure it; medication and lifestyle changes are required as a follow-up in order to maintain the work of the surgeon.

565. Several new procedures for unblocking coronary arteries are under study. Though their safety and effectiveness have not yet been established, they include:

• Atherectomy. Surgeons shave off strips of plaque blocking the artery.
• Laser angioplasty. Instead of using a balloon to open blocked arteries, doctors insert a catheter with a laser tip to burn out or break down plaque.
• Stents. A metal coil is permanently implanted in a narrowed part of an artery to keep it propped open.

566. Gene therapy—still in the experimental stages—increases the number of small arteries carrying blood to the heart. Gene therapy is based on the body's ability to generate new blood vessels when certain "growth factors" are introduced to it.

Scientists know which genes are responsible for the growth factors. They have found ways to copy those genes and add the copies to heart muscle. Gene therapy has been successful in rats; the next step will be to test it in larger animals. If experiments continue to be successful, then scientists will consider clinical trials in humans.

567. Some good sources of free information on heart care:

American Heart Association
National Center
7272 Greenville Ave.
Dallas, TX 75231
214-373-6300
Ask for "An Older Person's Guide to Cardiovascular Health and Disease."

National Heart, Lung, and Blood Institute
Building 31, Room 4A21
31 Center Dr., MSC 2480
Bethesda, MD 20892
301-496-4236
Ask for "Check Your Health Heart IQ" (92-2724), "Check Your Smoking IQ" (91-3031), "Check Your Weight and Heart Disease IQ" (90-3034), "Eat Right to Lower Your High Blood Pressure" (92-3289), "Facts About Angina" (92-2264), "Facts About Coronary Artery Bypass Surgery" (92-2891).

Heartburn

568. Heartburn has nothing to do with your heart. It's caused by stomach acid backing up into the esophagus, the tube that connects the mouth and the stomach. It's a burning pain behind the breastbone that occurs after meals and can last anywhere from a few minutes to several hours.

To avoid heartburn, don't eat spicy foods, tomatoes, chocolate, fried foods, and peppermint; smoking also aggravates heartburn. An antacid can provide relief, as can sleeping with the head of the bed raised about six inches on blocks or bricks. (Extra pillows usually don't work, because of position-changing during sleep.)

Hemorrhoids

569. The primary cause of hemorrhoids (weakened and enlarged rectal veins) is straining during bowel movements. They're also caused by pregnancy and childbirth, constipation, obesity, or prolonged standing or sitting.

Frequent warm baths and medicated creams or suppositories will ease hemorrhoids in their early stages. Ice packs help reduce swelling. Eating a high-fiber diet and drinking at least eight glasses of water per day are good preventive measures.

570. Sometimes hemorrhoids must be treated surgically. The surgery is performed under anesthesia, during an office or hospital visit.

There are two techniques to repair internal hemorrhoids. The first is "rubber band ligation," in which a band is placed around the base of the hemorrhoid, cutting off circulation so that the hemorrhoid withers away within a few days. In sclerotherapy, a chemical solution is injected around the blood vessel to shrink the hemorrhoid.

Other techniques used for both internal and external hemorrhoids include using electrical or laser heat or infrared light to burn hemorrhoidal tissue, and hemorrhoidectomy, in which extensive or severe hemorrhoids are excised.

Hiatal Hernia

571. Hiatal hernia occurs in one out of four people over the age of 50. The condition isn't as serious as it sounds. A hiatal hernia is a protrusion of the stomach into the chest cavity through the diaphragm. Being obese increases your chances of developing one.

The condition can allow stomach acids to flow back to the esophagus, causing a burning sensation. (Heartburn and hiatal hernia are not the same things, although they exhibit similar symptoms; hiatal hernia can cause heartburn.) Most hiatal hernias, when small, cause no symptoms. Occasionally, they get large enough to interfere with breathing and to cause chest pain, difficulty swallowing, or iron-deficiency anemia. In such cases, surgery is required.

High Blood Pressure, Hypertension
SEE ALSO ATHEROSCLEROSIS; HEART DISEASE; STROKE

572. Blood pressure goes up as we age, because blood vessels become less elastic and are less able to dilate. Blood pressure is too high when readings go over 140/90.

At that level—and when blood vessels are clogged with fatty tissue—doctors begin to worry about the possibility of heart attack and stroke. About 70 percent of strokes in older women and 40 percent in older men are related to high blood pressure.

573. Here's a rundown of medical problems related to high blood pressure.

• Heart disease. When arteries are blocked as a result of high blood pressure, the heart can't get enough oxygen. Reduced blood flow causes chest pain, and if the flow is stopped completely, a heart attack will result.

• Enlarged heart. High blood pressure causes the heart to work harder. Over time, the heart thickens and stretches, and functions less efficiently.

• Kidney damage. Over time, high blood pressure causes blood vessels in the kidney to narrow and thicken and thereby filter less fluid. Waste builds up in the blood, causing kidney damage.

• Stroke. Narrowed arteries resulting from high blood pressure make it difficult for blood to reach the brain. If a blood clot blocks one of the narrowed arteries, a stroke may occur. A stroke can also occur when very high pressure causes a break in a weakened blood vessel in the brain.

574. Diuretics (water pills) are the drugs most commonly prescribed to reduce high blood pressure. They work by flushing out extra sodium from the body and allowing the blood vessels to dilate, thereby reducing pressure.

Another group of drugs, called inhibitors, prevents production of a chemical that causes blood vessels to constrict. Calcium blockers and similar drugs dilate blood vessels by blocking the action of calcium in the vessel wall. Many of these drugs are not given alone, but in combination with others.

575. Some doctors recommend restraint in prescribing medication for older adults, because they are so susceptible to side effects. The elderly, for example, may lose too much sodium and potassium with diuretics. Other antihypertensive drugs can cause depression and confusion. Your physician may want to get your blood pressure under control with drugs, but then taper off on using them once lifestyle adjustments are in place.

576. People with mild or borderline high blood pressure can often reduce it without medication. That means losing weight, exercising, and avoiding salt, alcohol, and smoking.

Being overweight can make you two to six times more likely to develop high blood pressure; exercising at least three times per week, for at least thirty to forty minutes at a time, will help control both your weight and your blood pressure. Limit salt intake to no more than 2,400 mg (about one teaspoon) a day. (Read labels carefully: It's easy to get more than that each day when you eat processed foods.)

You should have no more than two alcoholic drinks per day, if that much. (One drink is one ounce of 100-proof whiskey, five ounces of wine, or twelve ounces of beer.) And stop smoking. Smoking injures blood vessel walls and speeds up hardening of the arteries.

 577. Eating salmon helps to reduce high blood pressure.

It contains omega-3 fatty acids, which researchers believe fight hypertension. Other promising subjects of study:

• Potassium. Potassium-rich foods include lean pork, catfish, cod, flounder, milk, yogurt, dried peas, green beans, peaches, prunes, oranges, tomatoes, spinach, squash, plantains, and bananas.

• Calcium. People with low-calcium diets often have high blood pressure. Low-fat milk, cheese, yogurt, and green leafy vegetables are all high in calcium.

• Magnesium. A diet low in magnesium may make blood pressure rise, but doctors don't recommend taking it as a supplement. Whole grains, green leafy vegetables, nuts, seeds, and beans are all better sources.

578. For more information on high blood pressure, contact:

American Association of Cardiovascular and Pulmonary Rehabilitation
7611 Elmwood Ave., Suite 201
Middleton, WI 53562
608-831-6989

American Heart Association
7272 Greenville Ave.
Dallas, TX 75231
800-AHA-USA1

National Heart, Lung, and Blood Institute
P.O. Box 30105
Bethesda, MD 20824
301-251-1222

Incontinence

579. Let's lay this one to rest right here: You won't necessarily become incontinent as you age. Despite what TV commercials and drugstore shelves imply, if you do suffer from urinary incontinence, it can usually be cured, or at least substantially lessened.

Urinary incontinence—the leaking of urine from the body—occurs when pressure in the bladder overwhelms the urethra's ability to resist. Sometimes it is caused by changes in body function resulting from disease. For example, incontinence can be the first and only symptom of a urinary tract infection. It can also be a side effect of medication. But it usually occurs as a result of the controlling muscles growing slack with age.

580. There are several types of incontinence:

• Stress incontinence occurs during exercise, coughing, sneezing, laughing, lifting, or other movements that put pressure on the bladder. It occurs more often in women.
• Urge incontinence is the inability to hold urine long enough to reach the toilet. It often follows a stroke, dementia, Parkinson's disease, and multiple sclerosis.
• Overflow incontinence is leakage from a full bladder. It may occur in men when an enlarged prostate blocks the urine flow.

581. There are several ways to treat incontinence. The simplest are:

• Scheduled voiding, pelvic muscle (Kegel) exercises, and biofeedback (for stress and urge incontinence)
• Medication, although it has side effects
• Surgery in which collagen is implanted in the tissues around the bladder to help support it and to minimize pressure
• Surgery to improve structural problems, like an abnormally positioned bladder or blockage due to an enlarged prostate

582. Incontinence support groups can help. For information and assistance, contact:

Help for Incontinent People (HIP)
P.O. Box 544A
Union, SC 29379
803-579-7900
800-252-3337

Simon Foundation for Continence
P.O. Box 835
Wilmette, IL 60091

National Kidney and Urologic Diseases
Information Clearinghouse
P.O. Box NKUDIC
Bethesda, MD 20892
301-468-6345

Alliance for Aging Research
2021 K St. NW, Suite 305
Washington, DC 20006
202-293-2856

Continence Restored
785 Park Ave.
New York, NY 10021
212-879-3131

Jaw Pain
SEE ALSO TEETH AND DENTURES; TEMPORAL ARTERITIS

583. Temporomandibular joint syndrome, or TMJ, is a real jawbreaker for the pain it causes in the joints of the jaw. The jaw joint connects the lower jaw, or mandible, to the temporal bone on the side of the head. A soft disk lies within the jaw joint.

This disk, as well as the bones surrounding it, can be damaged by arthritis or by grinding or clenching of the teeth. Often the first symptom of such damage is a clicking sound heard when chewing. Other symptoms include limited jaw movement, a radiat-

ing pain in the face, neck, or shoulders, headache, dizziness, hearing problems, or a sudden change in the way the upper and lower teeth fit together.

TMJ affects about twice as many women as men. A doctor may prescribe gentle relaxing exercises or muscle-relaxing or anti-inflammatory drugs.

Kidney Disease

584. Generally, the kidneys continue to work pretty well as we get on in years. Kidney disease among older adults is similar to that in younger people—the body retains fluid, blood pressure rises, and not enough red blood cells are produced. It is then necessary to undergo special medical treatments that perform the work of the kidneys. These treatments include:

• Hemodialysis, which cleans and filters the blood through the tubes of a machine
• Peritoneal dialysis, which uses the lining of the abdomen to filter blood after a special cleansing fluid has been introduced
• Kidney transplantation, in which a failed organ is replaced with a healthy one

For more information, contact:

American Association of Clinical Urologists
955D N. Plum Grove Rd.
Schaumburg, IL 60173
708-517-7229

Kidney Stones

585. Scientists have found evidence of kidney stones in a seven-thousand-year-old Egyptian mummy. Kidney stones continue to plague humankind, with the first attack usually coming before age 40. Ten percent of all Americans will suffer from kidney stones at some point in their lives. Men are particularly susceptible. The condition has been on the increase over the past twenty years.

Kidney stones develop from crystals that grow on the inner surface of the organ. While kidney stones are common, they are also relatively harmless, medically speaking. The only trouble is that you *feel* as though you'll die from the pain. Most kidney stones pass from the body on their own.

586. The first symptom of a kidney stone is usually sudden, extreme pain in the back or lower abdomen. If a stone is too large to pass easily, the muscles of the ureter try to push it into the bladder.

Treatment for kidney stones has improved vastly in recent years. Medical treatment now includes the creation of shock waves outside the body. The waves travel through tissue, and when they hit the dense stone, pulverize it into easily passable "sand." Another procedure involves passing a small instrument into the kidney to capture the stone and shatter it.

People with a family history of kidney stones are more prone to them; tests can determine if you're at risk. Drinking plenty of liquids, especially water, appears to help ward them off. There is also medication that prevents kidney stones from forming.

Lactose Intolerance

587. Some 50 million Americans are lactose intolerant—that is, they are unable to digest milk products comfortably. And the condition seems to grow worse with age. By the time we hit our teenage years, we have about 10 percent less of the enzyme needed to digest milk than we had when we were infants, leading some researchers to theorize that milk is an appropriate food only for babies. Symptoms of lactose intolerance include cramps, gas, bloating, or diarrhea within fifteen minutes to three hours of consuming a milk product.

It is a disorder that rarely needs treating. Women at risk for osteoporosis can meet most of their needs for calcium with greens, fish, and other calcium-rich foods, as well as calcium supplements; yogurt, because of its enzymatic content, is also well tolerated. People who are bothered by dairy food sometimes find they can eat small, easily digestible amounts of it—a half cup of milk or three-quarters of a cup of ice cream. Others use over-the-counter lactose aid tablets or drops.

Liver Disease

588. The liver tends not to be affected by aging. But some people do contract cirrhosis, a disease that impairs the function of the liver. Cirrhosis has a host of symptoms, including fatigue, gastrointestinal complaints (pain, nausea, loss of appetite, constipation, diarrhea), easy bruising, bleeding gums, and frequent nosebleeds. It is caused by nutritional deficiencies, poisoning of the system (including by alcohol), and bacterial and viral infections (especially hepatitis).

People with cirrhosis are very sensitive to medications, since the disease slows the liver's normal cleansing and filtration processes. The effects of drugs are longer-lasting, and they can build up in the body to dangerous levels.

Treatment is aimed at stopping or delaying the progress of the disease, minimizing damage, and reducing complications. In some cases, steroids or antiviral drugs are prescribed. A low-protein, salt-reduced diet can also be helpful.

589. For more information, contact:

American Liver Foundation
1425 Pompton Ave.
Cedar Grove, NJ 07009
201-256-2550
800-223-0179

Macular Degeneration

590. Macular degeneration is the most common eye disorder in people aged 50 and over. Scientists don't know what causes it, other than the simple process of aging. It is most prevalent among white women who smoke and among women who have a family history of the disease.

If left untreated, this condition can lead to loss of central vision; a rarer version can cause blindness. Your eye doctor will check you for the condition during your regular checkup (straight lines that appear wavy will be a clue). The disease progresses faster in some people than in others but can usually be treated successfully with laser surgery.

A diet high in beta-carotene has been found to be beneficial in preventing macular degeneration. In other words, carrots are good for the eyes after all.

Male Menopause

591. The jury is still out on whether there is such a thing as male menopause. Men do experience a gradual decline in testosterone levels starting at about the age of 50. The key word here is *gradual*—the corresponding hormonal decline in women happens suddenly, accounting for some of menopause's more obvious symptoms.

The hormonal decline in men may mean a

slight decrease in muscular strength and in bone density, and a tendency to gain weight more easily. It doesn't necessarily affect sexual functioning.

Memory Loss

592. More people are worried about memory loss these days. One reason: That large segment of the population known as baby boomers is approaching the age of 50 and beginning to wonder if it will affect them. Another reason is the increasing public attention paid to the memory loss associated with Alzheimer's disease. However, the changes that affect memory in an Alzheimer's patient are different from memory changes in a normal but aging brain. And statistically, most people will *not* be struck down with Alzheimer's.

Memory loss in older people is very often caused by depression, stress, fatigue, insomnia, and medication—all treatable and often temporary conditions.

593. Set up systems and strategies to help you remember what you need to know. Write appointments on a calendar or in a daily diary. Keep a small notebook with you to make lists of things that need doing as you think of them. And putting things in the same place all the time makes them easy to find.

Maintain a well-balanced diet—poor nutrition makes it harder for the mind to work. Exercise increases blood flow to the brain. Walk tall and straight; some researchers think

slumping reduces the brain's blood supply. Keep medications, even over-the-counter ones, to a minimum.

594. Exercise your mind by playing cards, working crossword puzzles, reading, and meeting new people.

Learning a new language—perhaps the one that your immigrant forebears spoke—is fun, too. A recent study trained some 230 people aged 64 to 95 to learn mental skills that would help their memories. Nearly half of them regained the acuity they had had fourteen years earlier. Nearly half of the rest, whose thinking hadn't slowed, became sharper than ever.

595. Changes in outlook and behavior can help, too. Don't let anxiety make you forget. If you find yourself at a loss for information when someone is questioning you, ask for a moment to get your thoughts together, and take several deep, slow breaths. Or take a friend along if you're going to be in a situation where you're afraid you may forget vital information. Pace yourself when you need to learn something new. Take on mental activities in the morning when you're fresh and alert.

596. No matter what your age, certain incidents that are part of a normal life can make concentrating difficult. Events such as moving, being ill, and the death of someone close are likely to affect your ability to focus on tasks at hand. This will pass as you adjust to your new life situation. If you continue to feel "out of it" for more than a few weeks, you might benefit from seeing a counselor. If you have episodes of total loss of memory of any recent events, or if you experience dangerous mishaps, such as driving on the wrong side of the road or forgetting traffic signals, it's time to seek help.

Menopause
SEE ALSO HEART DISEASE; OSTEOPOROSIS

597. By age 55, chances are that most women have been through menopause. It is, of course, the time when menstruation ends, as the production of ovarian estrogen is severely reduced. The reduction in estrogen causes hot flashes and changes in the vagina and uterus, including thinning of the walls and dryness that can make sexual intercourse uncomfortable. Breasts can develop cysts and lose muscle tone.

Menopause is actually the last stage of a gradual biological process. Starting three to five years before the final menstrual period, hormone production changes, and periods do, too. Many women become less regular, and periods may become lighter or heavier. They stop altogether on the average at around age 50, but the end can also occur at any time from the mid-30s to the mid-50s.

598. Here's the word on hot flashes. They get all the publicity when it comes to menopause. A hot flash is a sudden feeling of heat in the upper part, or all, of the body. The face and neck become flushed, and red blotches may appear on the chest, back, and arms. Heavy sweating and cold shivering can follow.

Hot flashes are the earliest and most common sign of menopause. They can be as mild as a light blush, or severe enough to wake you from a sound sleep. Most last from two to five minutes, but some may last up to half an hour.

Speaking of menopause mythology, some people believe that women are more moody, irritable, or depressed during menopause. The truth is that some are, but others are not. One study found that many cases of depression relate more to stress than to menopause.

599. Postmenopausal women are at greater risk for osteoporosis and heart disease, because estrogen production is reduced. But hormone replacement therapy (HRT) can protect against both, as well as against stroke and, according to some recent research, Alzheimer's disease. Such therapy also eases the effects of menopause.

The female hormone estrogen can be replaced using transdermal patches, pills, shots, or a cream applied directly to the vagina. Often, another female hormone, progestin, is given along with estrogen to protect against endometrial cancer. Progestin is usually taken in pill form.

Once hormone replacement starts, the normal thickness of the vaginal walls returns. Within a few days to a week or two, the symptoms of menopause disappear. Many doctors recommend that women take estrogen until age 65.

600. Although millions of women take HRT, it may not be the right choice for everyone. Only about 20 percent of women who are candidates for hormone replacement actually receive it.

Many experts believe that the benefits of HRT outweigh its side effects, especially for women who are at high risk for osteoporosis or heart disease. But the risks of long-term HRT have not yet been fully studied.

You should probably *not* take estrogen if you have a personal history or strong family history of breast or uterine cancer, high blood pressure, diabetes, liver disease, blood clots, seizures, vaginal bleeding, or gallbladder disease. HRT may worsen lupus, migraines, fibroids, depression, and fibrocystic breast changes in some women.

601. Hormone replacement therapy has a number of known side effects. They include vaginal bleeding, headaches, nausea, vaginal discharge, fluid retention, swollen breasts, and weight gain. HRT is also associated with:

• Endometrial cancer—that is, cancer of the uterus. Taking a combination of estrogen and progestin guards against this kind of cancer. If a woman takes estrogen alone, she should have an endometrial biopsy every year to check for cancer.

• Breast cancer. The jury is still out on this one. Some studies have shown that HRT increases the risk of breast cancer with age and duration of use, but other studies show *no* increased risk.

The American College of Obstetricians and

Gynecologists recommends that all women taking HRT have a yearly medical checkup that includes a blood pressure check, pelvic and breast exams, and a mammogram.

602. HRT is not the only way to deal with the symptoms of menopause. Certain drugs can reduce hot flashes. Over-the-counter vaginal creams that combat dryness are readily available. Lowering the room temperature may help you sleep better and ease uncomfortable hot flashes.

Experts suggest that after menopause, women not taking HRT should have at least 1,500 mg of calcium each day, and calcium supplements should be enhanced with 600 to 800 IU of vitamin D daily. Weight-bearing exercises, such as walking or lifting weights, make your muscles work against gravity and are of great help in strengthening bones and preventing osteoporosis.

603. Fibroids usually stop growing after menopause—and some actually shrink. So if you've made it this far without getting a fibroid—that is, a growth on the uterine wall—you probably won't get one now.

Every year about 175,000 American women, most of them between 35 and 55, undergo hysterectomy, the surgical removal of the uterus, as treatment for fibroids. Guidelines from the American College of Obstetricians and Gynecologists say that a fibroid that makes a woman's uterus bigger than it would be at twelve weeks of pregnancy is an indication for a hysterectomy, even if she has no other symptoms.

By age 60, more than a third of American women have had a hysterectomy. But the practice of routinely recommending hysterectomy for fibroids in young women has come under increasing scrutiny from both consumer organizations and physicians concerned about the high rate of the surgery in the United States. So be sure to get a second opinion if you receive a recommendation for a hysterectomy.

604. If you need information on menopause, contact:

North American Menopause Society
University Hospitals Department of
OB/GYN
2074 Abington Rd.
Cleveland, OH 44106

National Women's Health Network
1325 G St. NW
Washington, DC 20005
202-347-1140

Older Women's League
666 11th St. NW, Suite 700
Washington, DC 20001
202-783-6686

National Women's Health Resource
Center
2440 M St. NW, Suite 201
Washington, DC 20037
202-293-6045

Mental Illness
SEE ALSO ANXIETY DISORDERS; DEPRESSION; PANIC ATTACKS

605. The term "mental illness" is used to describe a broad range of mental or emotional problems that interfere with life. Mental illness is not, as some believe, a form of self-indulgence.

Like many health problems, mental illness results from a combination of causes.

• Biological factors. Often genetic in nature, these factors include problems in the chemistry of the nervous system and a structural defect of the brain that changes behavior.
• Psychological factors. These stem from an individual's personal history. A traumatic event or lengthy exposure to stress can make people vulnerable to mental health problems.
• Social factors. Good nutrition, shelter, personal safety, and a support network of family and friends are as important to mental health as to physical well-being. People who lack these basic needs are likely to experience mental health problems.

Whatever the cause, mental illness crosses lines of race, wealth, and social status and affects one in every four American families. There are more cases of diagnosable mental illness than of heart disease, lung disease, and cancer combined.

606. Symptoms of mental illnesses generally show up in a person's behavior and personal

habits. When changes become frequent or last several weeks, pay attention. Some warning signs:

- Marked personality change
- Confused thinking; strange or grandiose ideas
- Prolonged, severe feelings of depression or apathy
- Extreme highs and lows in emotions
- Excessive anxieties, fears, or suspiciousness; blaming others
- Social withdrawal; abnormal self-centeredness
- Denial of obvious problems; strong resistance to help
- Dramatic, persistent changes in eating or sleeping habits
- Numerous, unexplained physical ailments
- Anger or hostility out of proportion to the situation
- Delusions, hallucinations, or hearing voices
- Abuse of alcohol or drugs
- Growing inability to cope with problems and daily activities
- Sudden, unexplained feelings of panic or terror
- Thoughts or talk of suicide (which should always be taken seriously)

607. If you or someone you know has symptoms of mental illness, help is available from a variety of sources. Psychiatrists, psychologists, social workers, and counselors are all listed in the yellow pages. Or you can get referrals from community mental health centers, hospitals, family service agencies, and local medical and/or psychiatric societies.

There are many ways to manage the symptoms of mental illness. Often the help of a psychotherapist or professional counselor is needed, and sometimes tranquilizers or antianxiety drugs are prescribed. Ideally, drugs are used only in combination with counseling.

608. Tranquilizers depress the central nervous system. Minor tranquilizers, used to treat anxiety disorder, slow down the central nervous system, sometimes causing a feeling of drowsiness. Users may become dizzy, unsteady, and confused. If taken at night, the effect of the tranquilizers may continue into the next day. If taken at the same time as other drugs that depress the central nervous system—antihistamines, some pain relievers, or muscle relaxants—the effect of the tranquilizers is greatly increased. Ulcer drugs may also affect the body's use of tranquilizers. Mixing tranquilizers and alcohol can cause unconsciousness or even death.

609. Some safety tips if you take tranquilizers:

- Ask your doctor about possible side effects; let him or her know if you begin to experience any of them.
- Make sure your doctor knows about all of your medications, including over-the-counter drugs.
- Follow the doctor's instructions exactly. Take only the amount specified, and take it only as often as prescribed.
- If you miss taking a prescribed amount,

don't "make it up" by doubling the next dose.

• Some tranquilizers can make you feel chilly.

• Avoid caffeine while taking tranquilizers.

• If you think you've taken an overdose by mistake, get help immediately.

• Withdraw from tranquilizers gradually to avoid symptoms such as muscle cramps, sweating, and vomiting, and even convulsions.

610. For more information on mental illness, contact:

National Alliance for the Mentally Ill
2101 Wilson Blvd., Suite 302
Arlington, VA 22201
800-950-6264

National Mental Health Association
Information Center
1021 Prince St.
Alexandria, VA 22314

National Institute of Mental Health
5600 Fishers Lane, Room 15C05
Rockville, MD 20857
301-443-4515
Ask for "Plain Talk About Physical Fitness and Mental Health," "Caring for People with Severe Mental Disorders," "Just Like You and Me," "Plain Talk About the Stigma of Mental Illness."

Office of Clinical Center Communications
Building 10, Room 1C255

Bethesda, MD 20892
A free video on mental illness is available.

Office of Education
American Psychiatric Association
1400 K St. NW
Washington, DC 20005

For a copy of "The Constitutional Rights of Mental Patients," write your congressional representative at:

United States Capitol
Washington, DC 20515
202-224-3121

Osteoporosis

611. Osteoporosis, literally "porous bone," is a major cause of fractures in the spine, hip, wrist, and other bones as we age. The condition develops over a period of years; falling hormone levels, too little calcium in the diet, and a lifetime of inactivity all play a role. Osteoporosis is thought of as a disease of aging women, but 20 percent of Americans with the condition are men.

612. Osteoporosis isn't easy to diagnose in its early stages. Three or four methods of testing are available, however, including CT scans (computerized tomography). The kind of test depends on the area of the body to be examined, available equipment, and insurance coverage.

Many doctors feel that routine testing to

predict a woman's chance of having osteo-porosis-related bone fractures isn't war-ranted. However, a woman who is at high risk for osteoporosis may want to ask her doctor about a bone density measurement.

613. Caucasian and Asian women are most at risk for developing osteoporosis. At greatest risk in these two groups are women with early menopause or with a family history of osteoporosis. Risk also increases for women with fair skin and small frames. If several of the following risk factors apply to you, ask your doctor about tests to measure bone mass.

- Being over 65
- Being postmenopausal
- Having had your ovaries removed
- Using corticosteroids
- Smoking heavily
- Using alcohol heavily
- Eating a low-calcium diet
- Using diuretics
- Drinking coffee
- Being diabetic

614. Men are not immune to osteoporosis. While they are less likely than women to have the condition simply because of their greater bone mass, and because they have no biological equivalent to menopause, men may face osteoporosis in their later years. Here are the risk factors.

- Decrease in male hormones (called hy-pogonadism), which can reduce bone mass
- Use of steroids. These hormones are sometimes used to treat certain diseases and can lead to breakdown of bone.
- Alcohol abuse. Alcohol has been found to reduce circulating levels of testosterone. It weakens bones, even in relatively young or middle-aged men.

615. Diet and exercise can help prevent osteo-porosis. Foods high in calcium, like cheese, yogurt, milk, broccoli, and sardines, should be a regular part of the diet. Women who are nearing or who have passed menopause may need 1,000 to 1,500 mg of calcium a day. If your diet alone doesn't provide enough cal-cium, use a supplement.

It's also important to get enough vitamin D—200 IU daily—because it is needed for calcium absorption. Fifteen minutes of mid-day sunshine should do it. Food sources high in vitamin D include fortified milk and cere-als, egg yolks, saltwater fish, and liver.

Weight-bearing exercises such as walking, jogging, and stair climbing affect the mineral content of bones and can help reduce the chance of getting osteoporosis. Lifting weights has also been shown to slow bone loss. For more information, see *Strong Women Stay Young,* by Miriam Nelson (Ban-tam Books, 1997).

616. Getting enough calcium can also increase your kissability as you age. Thinning lips are commonly associated with aging. What really happens is that the whole face may change if bone mass is lost to osteoporosis. As a result, lips may invert or turn inward, and appear thinner. So get plenty of calcium in your diet and have full, kissable lips.

617. The goal in treating osteoporosis is to stop further bone loss and to prevent disabling falls. Many doctors prescribe hormones such as estrogen to slow the rate of bone loss; research is being done on the efficacy of combinations of calcium, vitamin D, and estrogen.

Bone loss is more rapid during the first five years following menopause; studies have found that dietary calcium has little effect at that time. As a result, some experts on osteoporosis feel that estrogen is the drug of choice for preventing bone loss in postmenopausal women or women with impaired ovarian function.

618. Being good to your bones doesn't have to mean eating five cartons of yogurt every day.

Many products, such as fortified orange juice, contain calcium-based food additives. Turn yourself into a label-reader to spot unsuspected sources of calcium. Some surprising sources are:

• Sardines, 3 medium (*not* the boneless variety): 370 mg
  • Cheese pizza, 1 slice: 220 mg
  • Macaroni and cheese, 1 cup: 200 mg
  • Oatmeal, 1 packet: 160 mg
  • Tomato soup, 1 cup: 160 mg
  • Baked beans, 1 cup: 140 mg

619. Research on osteoporosis continues apace. Clinical studies have shown that calcitonin, a thyroid hormone that inhibits the breakdown of bone, reduces back pain from compression fractures. However, the hormone has not yet been proved to prevent fractures.

Researchers are also investigating several nonhormonal therapies. One of the most promising is a drug used to treat Paget's disease (a condition characterized by abnormal bone growth). In another study, women who had suffered spinal fractures took etidronate, which seemed to slow the loss of bone reabsorption and, when combined with calcium, helped to build bone mass.

Sodium fluoride, another experimental treatment for osteoporosis-related spinal fractures, increases bone mass but does not prevent fractures. A new slow-releasing form of fluoride and calcium can reduce spinal fractures and build bone in elderly women.

620. For more information on osteoporosis, contact:

National Institute of Arthritis and
Musculoskeletal and Skin Diseases
Clearinghouse
Box AMS
Bethesda, MD 20892
301-495-4484

National Osteoporosis Foundation
2100 M St. NW, Suite 602
Washington, DC 20037
202-223-2226

National Women's Health Network
1325 G St. NW
Washington, DC 20005
202-347-1140

This is a clearinghouse for information on women's health issues; it also publishes a newsletter.

Pancreatitis

621. Pancreatitis is an inflammation of the pancreas. The pancreas is a digestive organ that produces enzymes and hormones to aid in digestion. Although the cause of about one-third of all cases is not known, many attacks are associated with gallstones, alcohol abuse, and malnutrition.

Certain drugs, including immunosuppressants, steroids, and sulfa drugs, may also make a person more prone to attacks. Symptoms are moderate to severe abdominal pain that may spread to the chest, back, and sides. If the cause is not drug-related, the best prevention is to avoid excessive alcohol use.

Panic Attacks
SEE ALSO ANXIETY DISORDERS

622. To the uninitiated, panic attacks and an anxiety disorder may seem to be the same. But the two are different.

People suffering from an anxiety disorder have a constant, general feeling of distress. Panic attacks are sudden, extreme episodes in which victims are often convinced that they're going to lose control, or even to die. During a panic attack, the heart races or

pounds. There can be chest pains, dizziness, nausea, flushing, chills, distortions of sight and sound, and a sense that something unimaginably horrible is about to occur. The sensations can last for an hour.

Young adults are more subject to panic attacks than older ones, but they can appear at any age. They are associated with depression and with abuse of medications and alcohol. According to one theory, they happen because the body's "alarm system" triggers unnecessarily, although scientists don't know why.

Various treatments are available, including relaxation techniques, medication, and specific forms of psychotherapy. Improvement usually comes in six to eight weeks.

Parkinson's Disease

623. Parkinson's disease is a progressive disorder of the central nervous system. It affects more than 1 million Americans, usually beginning between the ages of 45 and 65. It is named after James Parkinson, an English doctor and paleontologist who first described the condition in 1817.

Parkinson's disease occurs when nerve cells in the brain stop producing dopamine, a substance that serves as a messenger between nerve cells. Its symptoms include stiff limbs and joints, tremors, speech impediments, and difficulty in movement. Late in the course of the disease, some patients develop depression, dementia, and eventually Alzheimer's disease. Conversely, some

Alzheimer's patients develop symptoms of Parkinson's disease.

Medications such as levodopa (L-dopa) can improve diminished or reduced motor symptoms.

624. The treatment of Parkinson's has evolved dramatically over the last few decades. There are now a variety of medicines available, each aimed at a specific symptom of the disease (for instance, tremor amelioration). Scientists have implanted embryonic tissues containing dopamine cells into Parkinson's patients in an effort to modify disability; most patients showed some improvement.

Other experimental surgery is also offering improvement, though it's too early to judge its long-term effectiveness. In August 1997 the FDA approved an implantable tremor control device which reduced shaking in more than half the Parkinson's patients in clinical trials.

625. Many notables, including photographers Edward Weston and Margaret Bourke-White, struggled with Parkinson's as they aged.

Bourke-White's descriptions are particularly pungent: "To know what Parkinsonism is you must know . . . the bewilderment of finding yourself prisoner in your own clothes closet, unable to back out of it. You must experience the awkwardness of trying to turn around in your own kitchen—eleven cautious little steps when one swift pivot used to do the job. . . .

" . . . I often thought with thankfulness that if I had to be saddled with some kind of ailment, I was fortunate that it was something where my own efforts could help. I was amazed to see what the human body will do for you if you insist. Having to plug away at some exercise and finding I could make small advances gave me the feeling I was still captain of my ship—an attitude which is very important to me."

626. Self-care techniques, in addition to drugs, can improve the quality of life for Parkinson's patients. They include:

- Developing a daily activities chart and working to accomplish them
- Remaining physically active and as fit as possible
- Learning to pace activities to avoid fatigue
- Eating a balanced, high-fiber diet that keeps weight at about what it was at age 25
- Recognizing that depression and feelings of frustration are part of the disease
- Being open with others about the disease, when appropriate
- Carrying extra medication with you at all times
- Seeking out Parkinson's support groups

627. For information on Parkinson's disease, contact:

Parkinson's Disease Foundation
Columbia University Medical Center
650 W. 168th St.
New York, NY 10032
212-923-4700

National Parkinson Foundation
1501 N. 9th Ave.
Bob Hope Rd.
Miami, FL 33136
800-327-4545

National Institute of Neurological
Disorders and Stroke
Building 31, Room 8A06
Bethesda, MD 20892
800-352-9424

National Institutes of Health Neurological
Institute
P.O. Box 5801
Bethesda, MD 20824

Peptic Ulcers

628. Age is not a risk factor for peptic ulcers, but plenty of older adults are sufferers. Peptic ulcers occur when the body's normal defense against digestive acids is compromised, and sores result in the lining of the stomach or small intestine.

Recent research shows that most ulcers develop as a result of bacterial infection. The bacteria produce substances that weaken the stomach's protective mucus and make the stomach more vulnerable. Anti-inflammatory drugs such as aspirin, ibuprofen, and naproxen can also make the stomach susceptible to the effects of acid.

629. Ulcers don't always cause symptoms, especially in older adults. When they do, the most common is a gnawing or burning pain in the abdomen between the breastbone and navel. Aging adults often have vague discomfort in the stomach region, vomiting, and loss of appetite and weight. Bleeding may occur in the stomach and duodenum, but people are not always aware they have a bleeding ulcer because blood may not be obvious in the stool.

Ulcers are diagnosed with X rays or endoscopy. The presence of bacteria may be determined by a blood test, breath test, or tissue test. According to a National Institutes of Health study, the most effective ulcer treatment is a two-week, triple-therapy program designed to kill bacteria, reduce acid production, and protect the stomach lining.

Periodontal Disease

630. Periodontal disease—infections of the gums and jawbones—often doesn't show up until ages 40 to 50. That's because the condition doesn't have obvious symptoms until it is fairly far advanced. Still, it is a common cause of tooth loss after age 35.

With the disease, gums become inflamed and bleed. Pockets of infection may form between the teeth and gums, causing receding gums and loss of supporting bone. Early signs are red, swollen, bleeding gums.

Treatment of periodontal disease includes controlling infection by scraping tartar off teeth. Dentists also plane the tooth root until it's smooth to get rid of rough spots where germs gather; this also allows gums to heal closer to the teeth. Sometimes an antibacterial mouth rinse or antibiotic is prescribed. Sometimes gum surgery is necessary. Prevention of periodontal disease includes brushing and flossing daily.

Prostate Conditions

631. The prostate enlarges during most of a man's life. An enlarged prostate doesn't usually cause blockage of urine flow until late in life. Men often begin to notice symptoms after age 50; by age 80, some 90 percent of all men have symptoms of the condition called benign prostatic hyperplasia (BPH).

The most common symptoms are a hesitant, interrupted, weak urine stream; urgency and leaking; and more frequent urination, especially at night. Sometimes there are no symptoms until urination stops completely.

If BPH is found in its early stages, there seem to be fewer complications. Diagnosis can be made by means of a rectal exam to provide an idea of the size and condition of the gland, and by ultrasound, X rays, and cystoscopy. There is also a test to measure urine flow.

632. Treatment of BPH can range from a watchful attitude to surgery. Forms of surgery include:

• Transurethral surgery, which needs no external incision. This procedure is used in 90 percent of all operations.

• Open surgery, which requires an incision and is done when the gland is greatly enlarged or when there are complicating factors

• Laser surgery and microwave surgery, which are being explored to vaporize obstructing tissue

633. Even after treatment for BPH, it's important to have an exam once a year and to have any symptoms checked out. Sometimes scar tissue resulting from surgery may require a further procedure to stretch the urethra. That's done with an outpatient procedure called balloon urethroplasty. It widens the urethra with the help of a tiny balloon.

Other processes are also under investigation. One involves shrinking the prostate by using heat. In Europe, researchers are studying the use of tiny springlike devices called stents to push back prostatic tissue. New medications are still being developed.

 Prostate cancer is the most common form of cancer in men over 65.

And men as prominent as retired General Norman Schwarzkopf and Sidney Poitier have talked candidly about their battles with the disease. Its cause is unknown, but doctors think it is linked to male hormones and genetic factors, as well as to diet and environmental conditions.

The chances of having prostate cancer increase with age, and in its early stages it has no symptoms. Because of this, the American Cancer Society recommends that men over 40—especially African American men and men with a family history of the disease—have a rectal examination each year. Men over 50 should also have an annual blood test to check for prostate cancer.

635. Doctors treat slow-growing prostate cancer in its early stages by "watchful waiting." That means doing nothing except having regular checkups to monitor the disease.

For men with fast-growing cancers (or prostate cancer that has spread to other organs), treatment can include surgery and radiation and/or hormone therapy. There is a risk of impotence with all three methods, and surgery can also cause incontinence, although recent advancements in the procedure reserve more nerves needed for urination and an erection.

The short-term effects of radiation are similar to all such treatments for cancer: fatigue, diarrhea, and bladder irritation. Hormone therapy includes taking drugs to block the production of male hormones; sometimes surgery is required as well.

636. For more information about prostate function and health, contact:

American Prostate Society
1340 Charwood Rd.
Hanover, MD 21076
410-859-3735

American Prostate Association
P.O. Box 4206
Silver Spring, MD 20914
301-384-9405

American Foundation for Urologic Disease
300 W. Pratt St., Suite 401
Baltimore, MD 21201
410-727-2908
800-242-2383

Agency for Health Care Policy and Research
Publications Clearinghouse
P.O. Box 8547
Silver Spring, MD 20907
800-358-9295
Ask for "Treating Your Enlarged Prostate."

National Kidney and Urologic Diseases
Information Clearinghouse
P.O. Box NKUDIC
9000 Rockville Pike
Bethesda, MD 20892
301-468-6345

Seborrheic Ketoses

637. Warts they are not, although that's much easier to say than "seborrheic ketoses." These skin growths look like a dab of brownish black candle wax dropped on the skin, and almost everyone will eventually develop at least a few of them.

Seborrheic ketoses often appear on the hands and face. They are noncancerous growths of the outer layer of the skin. There may be just one, or there could be a cluster;

they may vary in size from a tiny dot to larger than a half dollar.

Forget salves, ointments, or medication to prevent or cure them. Seborrheic ketoses must be removed by a doctor, who will freeze them with liquid nitrogen and then scrape them from the surface of the skin; or they can be zapped with an electric current.

Shingles

638. Herpes zoster, commonly called shingles, is a viral infection left over from childhood. It is caused by the chicken pox virus lying dormant in the body's nerve cells for years. In adulthood, the virus—which is not related to herpes simplex—migrates along the path of a nerve to the skin surface, where it forms a blistering rash. The chest and torso are most commonly affected. If a facial nerve is involved, there may be eye problems. Even if there are few or no severe symptoms, long-lasting pain may occur.

Don't hesitate to see your doctor for relief. A prescription antiviral drug used to treat herpes simplex has proved effective for many cases of shingles. Less severe outbreaks are helped by soaking in oatmeal or cornstarch baths. In older adults, shingles often get better on their own.

Skin Cancer

639. The sun is usually the culprit in skin cancer. People with pale skin, light hair, and blue or green eyes are most at risk for skin cancer. Over a half million new cases of the disease are diagnosed each year.

There are three kinds of skin cancer.

• Basal cell carcinoma is the most common and looks like a pearly dome with prominent blood vessels. The cure rate is about 95 percent.

• Squamous cell carcinoma spreads far less than other skin cancers and has a similar cure rate to basal cell. It appears as a scaly red bump or as an ulcer that doesn't heal.

• Melanoma is the scary one. Such cancers that have not invaded the full skin layer can have a survival rate of 95 percent after five years. But those that have spread have only a 40 percent survival rate after five years. Melanomas are partially raised growths with irregular borders, asymmetrical shape, and colors that change.

640. Sunblocking products are your best defense. Dermatologists often recommend sunscreens with an SPF (that's "sun protection factor") of 15. Apply sunscreen a half hour before going out to give the skin time to absorb it, and don't forget to use a lip protector with a high SPF. Don't rub the product into your skin; stroke it on using a one-directional movement. If you're a woman, apply sunscreen to your face over your moisturizer, but under your makeup. Or you can purchase moisturizers with built-in sun-screen.

641. Check yourself for skin cancers. If you see moles or spots that suddenly change in color, size, or shape, have them examined by your doctor as soon as possible. The American Cancer Society recommends examining the face, hands, and body, looking for the "ABCD" early-warning signs:

A: asymmetrical shape
B: border irregularity
C: color variations within the mole or mark
D: diameter larger than a pencil eraser

642. Treating skin cancer usually involves surgery, radiation therapy, or chemotherapy—or a combination of all of these.

• Curettage means cutting away cancer cells. In many cases, a biopsy, done for testing, completely removes them.
• Electrosurgery involves running a current through the area. It is often used for large tumors or hard-to-reach areas. It leaves a small, flat, white scar.
• Cryosurgery uses liquid nitrogen to freeze and kill cells.
• Laser surgery burns away cells.
• Radiation, generally used only for advanced cases of melanoma, forestalls cell growth. Changes in skin color or texture may develop after the treatment.
• Topical chemotherapy is often used for actinic keratosis, skin lesions that can turn into squamous cell cancers. A cream or lotion is applied to the skin daily for several weeks. Inflammation is common, but there is usually no scarring.

Skin Conditions

643. Saving your skin from dryness, thinning, and wrinkling comes down to two words: lubrication and protection. Use lotions and creams to lubricate skin directly and a humidifier to add moisture to the air. Avoid long, hot baths. Shower instead, limiting soap use and capturing the wetness by applying a moisturizing product on damp skin.

Protection means keeping the skin away from the sun and from tanning salons. Tanning is the skin's response to damage from ultraviolet rays, and that fact ought to tell you something. An accumulation of exposure to the sun can cause cancer, but even moderate exposure can age skin prematurely. (See item 640 on sunblocks above.)

 If you do get sunburned, here's a home remedy that helps.

Many people find a lukewarm bath with a cup of milk added to the water will soothe a sunburn right after it occurs.

A number of readily available topical analgesics with ingredients like benzocaine, lidocaine, camphor, phenol, and menthol can ease the pain of a mild burn temporarily. Aspirin, taken as soon as possible after exposure, lessens the pain; so do cold compresses and products containing aloe. When burned skin begins to peel, moisturizers with cocoa butter and petrolatum can help relieve the dryness. If you have a severe sunburn or if your skin is blistered, see a doctor.

645. Perfumes and aftershave lotions can make skin more vulnerable to the effects of the sun. Some medications also increase sun sensitivity. These can result in rashes, sunburn, or more serious consequences such as cataracts, blood vessel damage, skin cancer, allergic reactions, and reduced immunity.

Some of the medications that can cause such photosensitivity are antihistamines, coal-tar derivatives (dandruff shampoos), nonsteroidal anti-inflammatory drugs (ibuprofen), phenothiazines (tranquilizers and antinausea drugs), psoralens, sulfonamides (sulfa drugs), antidiabetics, diuretics, and some antidepressants.

646. Retin-A (tretinoin), in prescription strength, works to make skin look smoother, clearer, and younger. It lessens roughness and superficial wrinkling and lightens age spots and freckles, although it may take six months or more to see any effects. When treated with Retin-A, the lower levels of the skin thicken, and new blood vessels form under the upper layer of skin, which thins. The result is younger, fresher skin. You should be aware though that the long-term effects of Retin-A have not yet been studied. Also, using the product makes your skin more susceptible to sunburn, and most users experience some skin inflammation that lasts up to three months. For more information, ask your doctor, or write:

Johnson & Johnson
P.O. Box 300
Route 202 S.
Raritan, NJ 08869

647. More information about skin care and the sun is available from:

American Academy of Dermatology
930 Mecham Rd.
Schaumburg, IL 60168

Food and Drug Administration
HFI-40
Rockville, MD 20857

National Cancer Institute
9000 Rockville Pike
Bethesda, MD 20892

National Institute on Aging
Box HYPO
Building 31, Room 5C35
Bethesda, MD 20892

Sleep Disorders

648. Older adults spend about an hour more in bed each night than do younger Americans. Younger people report sleeping about seven and a half hours nightly. Babies sleep as much as sixteen hours a day; children, about nine. Historians say our adult progenitors of a century ago slept for about nine hours every night.

As we age, we sleep less soundly and

wake more often. We dream throughout the night, not just toward morning. We are also more likely to develop a condition called advanced sleep onset—that is, falling asleep much earlier than wanted and awakening at 4:00 A.M. or earlier, unable to go back to sleep.

649. Insomnia can take several forms. It can mean taking more than thirty to forty-five minutes to fall asleep. It can mean waking up many times each night, or waking up early and being unable to get back to sleep.

Insomnia is generally a symptom of a problem—worry or anxiety—but a poor sleep pattern, left unresolved, can become a problem itself. If sleep disturbance lasts for more than a few weeks or interferes with activities, it may be time to do some investigating.

650. Some experts believe the treatment for insomnia is to stay awake longer. If you don't feel sleepy, don't go to bed. And, some experts advise, if you do feel sleepy, try staying up for a few hours anyway. Experiment with different bedtimes until you find the one best suited to your body's natural cycle, whether it's 8:00 P.M. or 2:00 A.M.

Sleeping pills are not recommended for long-term use. In fact, using them for more than a few nights in a row greatly reduces their efficacy—there may even be a boomerang effect, with the pills themselves causing insomnia.

And for now, forget melatonin as a sleep aid. Despite brisk sales for this brain hormone, it has not been studied enough to be proved safe for long-term use. Though there's evidence that it can help you sleep, researchers would like to know more about proper dosage and possible side effects.

651. Other common sleeping problems:

• Twitches, leg cramps, and movements called restless legs. These may increase with age and are more common in men. If they strike, get up and walk around.

• Bruxism, or grinding the teeth during sleep. Dental repairs sometimes cause the problem; other times they help it. Try a little self-help first: Clench the teeth firmly for five seconds and then relax for five seconds. Repeat several times a day for several weeks.

• Menopause-induced insomnia. Hormonal changes can produce hot flashes and sweating, muscle aches, anxiety, and agitation. Relaxation techniques and herbal teas may help.

652. Sleep apnea is a common nocturnal disorder, but one that only your partner may know about for sure. Apnea means "no breath," and victims may stop breathing for as long as two minutes, sometimes hundreds of times a night, and all without knowing it.

Good clues to sleep apnea—other than your partner's grumbles—are daytime sleepiness, coupled with loud snoring at night. A doctor must make the diagnosis. A range of treatments is available, including devices, medication, and surgery.

653. There are two types of sleep apnea. "Central" sleep apnea occurs when the respiratory muscles don't function properly; this form becomes more common as we age, affecting one in four over 60. For most, the problem is mild.

"Obstructive" sleep apnea, sometimes called upper-airway apnea, occurs when the airway is blocked. The muscles of the soft palate at the base of the tongue relax and sag, blocking airflow. Breathing is labored, and punctuated by pauses. The snoring sleeper appears to awaken but doesn't remember it in the morning. Each time breathing stops, the level of oxygen in the bloodstream falls, so the heart works harder to circulate blood. Blood pressure rises and may stay elevated after breathing restarts.

Obstructive sleep apnea often strikes overweight men. Female hormones and a different throat anatomy often protect women until menopause. After that, women may develop obstructive sleep apnea as often as men.

654. Lavender oil, once used to perfume the baths of ancient Romans, may help you get to sleep.

It has been employed in folk remedies for at least a thousand years, and may help overcome insomnia in older adults, according to a small study conducted by David Stretch of the Greenwood Institute at the University of Leicester in England. Previous pharmacological studies have also shown lavender oil to have a light sedative effect. Add a few drops of the oil to a bath before bedtime or purchase an herbal pillow—available at health food stores—stuffed with lavender.

655. For more information on sleep apnea and copies of the newsletter *Awake*, contact:

American Sleep Apnea Association
P.O. Box 66
Belmont, MA 02178

656. If you have trouble sleeping, take time to establish a positive sleep-time program.

• Go to bed only when sleepy.
• Get up about the same time every day.
• Establish a relaxing pre-sleep ritual, such as a warm bath followed by fragrant lotion and silk pajamas.
• Don't go to bed too hungry or too full.
• Exercise regularly, especially in the late afternoon, but don't exercise just before bedtime.
• Avoid caffeine and alcohol before bedtime.
• Don't nap. If you do, keep it to a midafternoon snooze of no more than thirty to forty-five minutes.
• Don't use your bed for reading and TV watching—use it for sex and sleep only, so it becomes associated with sleep in your subconscious.
• Don't make a habit of sleeping pills.

657. A sleep center is a laboratory that diagnoses problems by monitoring muscle activity, heart rhythms, breathing, and other functions. Many hospitals and health centers have sleep disorder clinics or sleep problem groups for the general public.

For additional information about sleep, contact:

American Sleep Disorders Association
604 2nd St. SW
Rochester, MN 55902

Better Sleep Council
P.O. Box 19534
Alexandria, VA 22320
Ask for "Sleep Better, Live Better Guide."

National Sleep Foundation
122 S. Robertson Blvd.
Los Angeles, CA 90048

Wakefulness-Sleep Education and
Research Foundation
4820 Rancho Dr.
Del Mar, CA 92014
Ask for "101 Questions About Sleep and Dreams."

Smoking and Health

658. Perhaps the title here should be "Smoking and *Un*health." Yes, cigarette smoking causes cancer. Tobacco smoke contains at least forty-three carcinogenic substances, causing many kinds of cancer besides the lung variety, such as cancer of the mouth, larynx, esophagus, kidney, bladder, pancreas, and cervix. Tobacco use accounts for one in three deaths from cancer in the United States, including 90 percent of all lung cancers among men and 70 percent among women.

There is no such thing as a "safe" cigarette. Smokeless tobacco (chewing tobacco) is not safe either. In fact, it is associated with cancer of the mouth. Pipe and cigar smokers who do not inhale are less likely to develop lung cancer than cigarette smokers, but they are at risk for cancer of the mouth, throat, larynx, and esophagus. Menthol cigarettes are not safer than others, and may even be more dangerous.

 659. It's never too late to quit.

That's because minutes after smoking your last cigarette, the body begins a series of regenerating changes, even if you're over 90. Within twenty minutes, blood pressure drops to normal. After eight hours, the carbon monoxide level in the blood is normal. After forty-eight hours, nerve endings start regrowing, and the ability to smell and taste is enhanced. After one year, coughing, sinus congestion, fatigue, and shortness of breath decrease. After five years, the lung cancer death rate decreases by almost half. And after fifteen years, the risk of coronary heart disease is that of a nonsmoker.

Don't worry about weight gain if you quit smoking. The average weight gain after quitting is only five pounds.

660. Here are eight more reasons to quit smoking.

• Your circulation will improve immediately.

• Your risk of smoking-induced heart disease is reduced by half.

• Many drugs will work better; sometimes dosage can be reduced.

• Your breathing capacity may improve.

• Sleeping problems may improve.

• You'll save money in both the cost of cigarettes and smoking-related doctor's visits.

• You have several chances to succeed, since research shows it usually takes a few tries to quit.

• You'll protect the ones you love. Secondhand tobacco smoke—smoke inhaled by nonsmokers around the smoker—has many harmful effects, especially for the spouses and children of smokers and especially those who have asthma or heart disease.

661. Over 30 million Americans have been able to quit smoking. Recent surveys suggest that quitting is a growing trend. There are many ways to stop, and no one method works for everyone. Many people can stop on their own, but others need help. Some studies have found that mature people who take part in programs to stop smoking have a higher rate of success than younger people do.

662. Withdrawal symptoms vary. Withdrawal symptoms reported by some people who quit smoking include anxiety, restlessness, drowsiness, difficulty concentrating, and digestive problems. Others have no symptoms at all. Nicotine chewing gums and patches, now available without a prescription, can help reduce withdrawal symptoms, although the gum and patches aren't recommended for those with heart disease. Many doctors also recommend joining a support group or using self-help materials. For instance, the American Lung Association has produced a book entitled *7 Steps to a Smoke-Free Life* (John Wiley, 1998).

663. For more information on the health risks associated with smoking and secondhand smoke, as well as material on how to quit, contact:

Office on Smoking and Health
Centers for Disease Control
4770 Buford Highway NW
Mail Stop K-12
Atlanta, GA 30341
404-488-5705

Stress

664. The older we get, the better able we are to deal with stress. In particular, studies of women have shown that while several age groups express dissatisfaction with personal relationships, older women experience less stress about it.

Stress can produce changes in the body and has been associated with ailments as diverse as angina, asthma, diarrhea, migraine, impotence, ulcers, and a dozen other health problems. It's immediately noticeable in tight necks and scalps (some believe the latter can lead to thinning hair), tension headaches, anxiety, and drinking to excess.

665. Stress can be diminished in a number of ways.

• Learn the relaxation techniques of yoga (especially breathing), meditation, or biofeedback.

• Get some exercise, and raise your endorphin levels.

• Change your thinking patterns to focus on the positive.

• Take the time to enjoy yourself with a movie or rented video, a good book, or a day trip.

• Adopt a pet from your local animal shelter.

• Express and discuss deep inner questions with a friend or in a journal.

• Seek out new friends, people different from those you've known all your life.

• Examine the situations and events that cause you stress, and see if it's possible to eliminate any of them.

• Learn to enjoy some downtime.

• Learn something new every day.

666. Look on feelings of isolation as a spiritual opportunity.

Beginning in her 50s and continuing into her 80s, poet and novelist May Sarton explored living alone, publishing journals frequently on the subject. Her first was *Plant Dreaming Deep* in 1968. Other titles include *Journal of a Solitude, At Seventy,* and *After the Stroke.*

Stroke

SEE ALSO DIABETES; HEART DISEASE; HIGH BLOOD PRESSURE

667. Stroke is the third biggest cause of death in the United States. It ranks after heart disease and cancer. It is of concern to all aging adults, but particularly people over 70. But there's good news about stroke, too. As a result of better monitoring and control of risk factors such as high blood pressure, the rate of death from stroke is decreasing. Life after stroke is also better, with 70 percent of victims remaining independent and 10 percent recovering fully.

There are three events that cause strokes: (1) a blood clot forms in an artery that supplies blood to the brain; (2) a blood clot travels from another part of the body into the brain and obstructs arteries there; or (3) an artery bursts and there's bleeding in the brain.

668. The body often gives warnings that a stroke could happen. They're called TIAs, short for "transient ischemic attacks." Symptoms of a TIA include brief episodes of weakness or numbness in a hand or other limb or a sudden lack of coordination. A TIA will pass and leave no permanent damage, but it does deliver a warning to see a doctor immediately. Here are some specifics to watch for.

• Sudden weakness or numbness of the face, arm, or leg

• Sudden dimness or loss of vision, particularly in one eye

- Sudden difficulty speaking or under-standing speech
- Sudden severe headache with no known cause
- Unexplained dizziness, unsteadiness, or sudden falls, especially with any of the above signs

669. Preventing a stroke centers on controlling the risk factors. Those are high blood pressure, heart disease, diabetes, cholesterol levels, and cigarette smoking. About 40 percent of all strokes are related to high blood pressure, and having diabetes doubles your chance of a stroke.

By the same token, careful control of blood sugar may lessen the severity of brain damage if you do have a stroke. Taking an aspirin a day for its blood-thinning properties is known to help ward off heart disease and may help with strokes, too. In fact, doctors often recommend aspirin after a TIA. The risk factors for stroke also respond to good diet, weight loss, and exercise.

670. The treatment for stroke, and the outlook for life after it, depend on a number of factors. Namely, the kind of stroke, its location, and its extent. Difficulty moving the eyes, coma, and severe weakness or paralysis are all indications of a large stroke and a less favorable future. In the first thirty days after a stroke, the death rate is between 20 percent and 30 percent.

In the first hours after a stroke, controlling blood pressure is the doctor's biggest concern. There is also new research that shows that brain cells uninjured in the stroke can be preserved if a patient is given "clot-busting" drugs immediately. There is also likely to be testing—CT scans or MRIs, for example—to figure out what is going on in the brain and where. Later, the doctor will be concerned about preventing more clots or correcting the damage from hemorrhaging. Both can involve drugs; and the latter, surgery.

671. The body begins to repair itself shortly after a stroke. Many people make marked progress in speech, vision, and movement in the first three weeks after the stroke. The greatest progress in mobility occurs generally in the first six months. Speaking, balance, and self-care skills can take perhaps as long as two years. There are a number of rehabilitation programs, often available through hospitals.

The emotional and social sides of stroke also present a challenge for victims and their families. More than half of all stroke victims become depressed, and they may isolate themselves even after physical disabilities have improved. Support groups and a grieving process for what has been lost can help.

672. For more information about stroke and its aftermath, contact:

Courage Stroke Network
3915 Golden Valley Rd.
Golden Valley, MN 55422
612-588-0811

National Institute of Neurological
Disorders and Stroke
31 Center Dr., MSC 2540
Bethesda, MD 20892
800-352-9424

National Stroke Association
300 E. Hampden Ave.
Englewood, CO 80110
303-762-9922

American Heart Association Stroke
Connection
800-553-6321

Teeth and Dentures

SEE ALSO JAW PAIN; PERIODONTAL
DISEASE; TEMPORAL ARTERITIS

673. Too often, mature adults feel they no longer need dental checkups. Wrong. Mouth bacteria and tooth decay are equal-opportunity attackers.

Bacteria in the mouth thrive on sugars, whatever your age, producing decay-causing acids that dissolve minerals on tooth surfaces and form a sticky, colorless film on the teeth called dental plaque. With age, tooth decay can attack the roots of teeth if the roots are exposed by gum disease or receding gums.

674. Here's a quick review of good teeth- and gum-cleaning methodology, along with some tips.

• With a soft-bristle brush and using fluoride toothpaste, brush teeth on all sides, holding the brush at a forty-five-degree angle.

• Brush carefully along the gum line.

• Lightly brush your tongue to remove plaque and food debris.

• Floss. If you don't know how, ask your dentist for a demonstration. If flossing results in bleeding gums, pain, or irritation, see your dentist.

• Use an antibacterial mouth rinse.

• If arthritis makes it hard to hold a toothbrush, try attaching a sponge or Styrofoam ball to the toothbrush handle with a wide elastic band to make the brush easier to grip.

• If shoulder movement is limited, lengthening the handle with a piece of wood (a wooden spoon would work) or plastic helps. So do electric toothbrushes.

675. When it comes to paying for them, you may think dental crowns are fit only for royalty. But once you have them, you'll know they're worth the coin of the realm.

Crowns are a kind of jacket that fits over a damaged tooth. They can save teeth that are badly decayed or wobbly due to gum disease, and also remodel stained, chipped, or misshapen teeth.

Porcelain crowns are usually good for front teeth, because they look like natural ones. Gold is often recommended for back teeth, since it's stronger than porcelain or plastic. A tip for those about to be crowned: Bring a portable cassette player with earphones and listen to your favorite music or book on tape during tedious grinding.

676. Dentures may seem awkward at first. Choose soft, nonsticky food when first learning to eat with dentures, and cut it into small pieces, chewing slowly and using both sides of the mouth.

Whether dentures are partial or full, keep them clean and free of food that can cause stains, bad breath, and gum irritation. Brush dentures daily with a special denture care product. Soak them overnight while you sleep, and rinse your mouth with a warm saltwater solution in the morning, after meals, and at bedtime.

677. Unlike partial or full dentures, which are taken out and put back in daily, a fixed bridge is permanently cemented to the remaining teeth. It can be expensive, but has many advantages:

- It's locked in place, and you can't lose it.
- It doesn't require special pastes or adhesives.
- It doesn't come out at night.
- You can eat anything.
- It's more attractive, since appearance isn't affected by clasps, often visible with partial dentures.

678. Dental implants are anchors that hold replacement teeth permanently in place. There are several different types of implants, but the most popular are metal screws made of titanium and surgically placed into the jaw-bones. Because bone heals slowly, the installation of implants can often take up to a year or more, much longer than the installation of bridges or dentures.

For information on implants and other toothy subjects, contact:

Clinical Center
National Institutes of Health
Bethesda, MD 20892
301-496-2563

National Institute of Dental Research
Building 31, Room 2C35
31 Center Dr., MSC 2290
Bethesda, MD 20892
Ask for "Fluoride to Protect the Teeth of Adults," "What You Need to Know About Periodontal (Gum) Disease," "Dry Mouth (Xerostomia)," and "Chemotherapy and Oral Health."

National Oral Health Information
Clearinghouse
1 NOHIC Way
Bethesda, MD 20892
301-402-7364

American Dental Association
211 E. Chicago Ave.
Chicago, IL 60611
800-621-8099
ADA sponsors the national Senior Smile Week each year.

Temporal Arteritis

679. This common condition can cause difficulty in chewing in older adults. Temporal arteritis causes the arteries of the temple area of the forehead to swell, reducing the blood flow to the muscle used in chewing.

It can begin with a severe headache, pain when chewing, and tenderness in the temples; it may be followed in a few weeks by a sudden loss of vision. Other symptoms include shaking, weight loss, and low-grade fever. While the cause of temporal arteritis is unknown, it's thought to be a disorder of the immune system. Early treatment with medication can help prevent vision loss.

Tuberculosis

680. Tuberculosis (TB) is an ancient disease— traces of it have been found in prehistoric man. Once on the wane in the United States, it is now making a comeback.

About a third of the new TB cases occur in those over 65. Many of these victims were originally infected more than fifty years ago and still carry the organism, which lay dormant until body changes triggered it.

Symptoms of TB are often vague but include recurrent coughing, feeling tired and weak, and unexplained loss of appetite and weight. A person who is bedridden or weakened by HIV or other infections has an increased chance of developing tuberclosis.

Once identified with a skin test and chest X ray, TB usually responds to drugs over a period of six to nine months.

Urinary Tract Infections, Cystitis

681. Urinary tract infections plague about 10 percent of older people, most of them women. An increasing number of men get them as they age and prostate difficulties increase. The most common type of urinary tract infection is called cystitis, and its most common symptom is frequent and urgent urination, sometimes with pain.

A course of oral antibiotics usually alleviates the condition, and a heating pad or warm bath can help with discomfort in the interim.

682. To ward off urinary tract infections, drink plenty of water—at least six glasses per day. Experts also suggest:

• Drink cranberry juice or take vitamin C supplements, because they make the urine acidic and inhibit the growth of some bacteria.
• Urinate when you feel the need; don't delay.
• Wipe from front to back to prevent bacteria from entering the vagina or urethra.
• Take showers instead of baths.
• Empty the bladder shortly before and soon after sexual intercourse.
• Don't use feminine hygiene sprays and douches. They are unnecessary and destroy "good" bacteria.

Varicose and Spider Veins

683. A group of women doctors in Minneapolis made a spider-vein pact in medical school. Later in life when the need arose, they would make a party out of getting together and zapping each other's spider veins.

Varicose and spider veins occur in men and women of any age. They most frequently affect women of childbearing age and older, and women with a family history of them. Varicose veins usually form on the legs and thighs as a result of poor blood circulation, causing veins to become enlarged. The veins become visible and cause aching legs, particularly when standing. Spider veins appear on the surface of the skin on the thighs, ankles, and feet and sometimes the face. They look like the short, fine clusters of a web and usually don't hurt.

684. The causes of varicose and spider veins are not completely understood. They may be the result of poor circulation, or weakness in the vein walls that causes pooling of blood. Less commonly, varicose veins are caused by a disease like phlebitis.

Varicose veins are often treated by removing the "bad" veins with outpatient surgery or sclerotherapy. The surgery, often called stripping, is done under local anesthesia by passing a flexible device through the vein and removing it through an incision near the groin. With sclerotherapy, a fine needle is used to inject a solution directly into the vein. The vein then turns into scar tissue that fades from view.

Sclerotherapy is used for spider veins, and that's the method the Minneapolis doctors have planned for themselves. Laser or electrocautery treatments are sometimes employed, especially for the face, but the latter method can cause scarring and changes in skin color.

685. The cost of vein removal varies. Many insurance plans don't cover it, since it can be considered elective or cosmetic surgery.

Treatment isn't always necessary. Discomfort can often be reduced by wearing support hosiery and maintaining normal weight. Regular exercise helps, too, because it empties veins of pooling blood. A balanced diet is always important. Here are a few other tips.

- Avoid standing too long in one place.
- Don't sit too long either.
- Crossing the legs or sitting on the legs or feet blocks blood flow.
- Elevate your legs. Get them above your heart, and gravity will help blood get out of the ankles and legs.
- Elevate your feet when you sleep.
- Flex your feet. Rotate them and periodically pump them up and down.
- If you are taking hormones for menopause, ask your doctor their effect on varicose veins.

686. The removal of varicose veins is sometimes the subject of consumer fraud. Be wary of promises that include phrases like "major breakthrough," "permanent results," "unique treatment," "painless," or "absolutely safe." Consult a doctor you trust.

Weight, Obesity

687. It's the news you've been waiting for all your dieting life. Studies show that people in their 60s who are slightly overweight have a better chance of living to their 80s and 90s than their underweight counterparts.

Still (and you knew there would be a "still," right?), too much weight is bad for your health. If you're more than 20 percent to 30 percent over your ideal weight, medically you're considered overweight and statistically at a higher risk for several serious medical conditions. If you plan to diet, consult your doctor or a nutritionist first. Chapter 6 on nutrition and exercise can also help. Do avoid fad diets.

688. Hypertension, gallstones, kidney stones, adult diabetes, and some kinds of cancer are all associated with obesity. Being overweight increases your risk for high blood cholesterol and high blood pressure, two major risk factors for coronary heart disease.

Sudden weight gain or loss can signal metabolic disorders. See your doctor if you have excessive weight gain or weight loss—if you have a weight loss of more than 5 percent of your body weight in less than six months, if your appetite declines, or if you suffer a weight loss due to severe vomiting or diarrhea.

 689. **Better a pear than an apple, when it comes to shape.**

That is, as you age, the location of excess weight may be just as important as how much you weigh. The way in which bodies store fat is categorized as two distinct body types: pear-shaped and apple-shaped.

The pear-shaped body type, more common to women than men, carries fat below the waist in the buttocks, hips, and thighs. This type of fat distribution is harmless. On the other hand, men and women who have an apple-shaped body, carrying fat in the abdomen above the waist, are at greater risk for metabolic problems and possibly heart disease.

690. If you are overweight, even moderate weight loss—that's 5 percent to 10 percent— can substantially reduce blood pressure. You may also be able to reduce your LDL (bad cholesterol) and triglycerides and increase your HDL (good cholesterol).

In addition, weight loss may reduce your blood pressure without your having to decrease your sodium intake. Weight loss is recommended for all overweight people who have high blood pressure. Even if weight loss does not reduce your blood pressure to normal, it may help you cut back on blood pressure medications.

Chapter 8:

Dying and Death

D eath happens. Theologians, philosophers, and psychologists work hard to help us see that it is a natural part of life, its last great adventure. While the adventure may not seem to

have a happy ending since the desire is to continue living, it is still what Gail Sheehy calls in *New Passages* "the greatest adult mystery of all"—as inevitable as sunset and as potentially remarkable.

Death often occurs earlier to men than to women. The average age of widowhood in the United States is 56, and half of all women over 65 are widows. That is because women generally survive men by seven or eight years and also because women still tend to marry men older than themselves. What all this means is that many older women spend a period of time caring for an ailing partner and then must cope with loss, learn to live alone, and eventually plan for their own deaths. The pop philosopher who proclaimed that "old age isn't for wimps" must have had these remarkably strong women in mind.

This chapter is designed to help with these situations—impending death and the loss it-

self—whether you are male or female. We leave it to you to define the good death. This chapter offers the practical—a definition of death, how to cope with grief, how to plan a low-cost funeral. We hope it will also evoke some sweet memories of the celebration of life that death can be.

Experiencing and Surviving Loss

691. Defining death is not as easy as it seems. Because of advances in medical technology, death can mean different things to different people. A respirator, for example, can keep a brain-dead person breathing for months, even though there is no hope of the patient regaining consciousness. The medical profession has responded to the challenge of machines by defining death according to four specific criteria:

- Inability to receive or respond to signals
- Absence of spontaneous breathing
- Absence of reflexes
- An electroencephalogram (EEG, or brain wave test) with no activity

692. Dr. Elisabeth Kübler-Ross, a noted expert in the field of dying and death, has heavily influenced modern thinking on the subject. Kübler-Ross believes it is unwise to rob a dying patient of the belief that he or she may recover. People should be told they are seriously ill, she says, but should not be made to feel the situation is hopeless. At the same time, she adds, every patient has a right to honest, open answers. Much of her writing emphasizes sitting with patients and talking until they are ready to discuss the approach of death themselves.

693. The terminally ill, and the people who love them, often go through the same, predictable stages. Kübler-Ross identified these stages after years of observing and treating the dying during her years of psychiatric practice. Some people go back and forth among stages, or experience several at once. Others skip one or more stages completely. The stages are:

- Denial. This temporary reaction makes the person doubt the news given by the doctor. He or she often seeks a second opinion.
- Anger. The patient becomes angry and resents healthy people—often family members and medical staff.

- Bargaining. A person makes a heroic attempt to live for a particular reason or event—a wedding or a college graduation. This phase may take a great deal of physical effort.
- Depression. There are often two phases: One is in direct reaction to the news, and the other is an eventual withdrawal, a kind of preparation for the loss of life.
- Acceptance. It means just that. Extreme fatigue and a great need for sleep are symptoms of this stage.

694. With sudden death, there is no chance to say good-bye. Kübler-Ross says even after the shock of a sudden death, the family must go through the same stages of grief as with a prolonged passing. They may take longer, however, than those experienced by a family that was able to prepare for the death.

The medical profession often does not handle the family well after a sudden death, Kübler-Ross says. There is a tendency to want to sedate upset members or to hustle them out of the hospital once the news of the death is delivered. She urges medical professionals to take time with family members when there is a sudden death, and to allow them to view the body in some fashion if they wish shortly after the death. This can help them later to accept the death.

695. About four weeks after a sudden death, family members may want to talk again with those who were present at the death. In fact, Kübler-Ross urges medical professionals to seek out families for follow-up at that point, when family members will be ready to ask the questions that shock and denial made impossible earlier. They may want to know if the dying person was conscious, said anything near the end, opened his or her eyes one last time, or had someone to hold his hand during the final passage.

The questions and the answers can help family members work through their grief, Kübler-Ross says.

696. The loss of a spouse or life partner can result in grief that is especially profound. Many people report that they feel numbness and shock at first, and it serves to propel them through the many details of the funeral. There is crying, of course, and there can be relief that the dying process is over—and guilt for that relief, and over whatever emotional issues were left unresolved. Frequently, there is anger at the dead for dying in the first place or at the people who cared for the patient.

697. Disbelief about the death—a feeling the loved one should still be sitting in his or her chair—and a refusal to accept it are also a part of the package. The feeling can last for many months and may be accompanied by an unwillingness to get on with life and to accept the death. A classic example is Queen Victoria, who insisted her dead consort's clothes be laid out for him every day for many years. In a fictional vein, the Pulitzer Prize–winning playwright Marsha Norman wrote in an early play of a widow who could not deflate a beach ball because her dead husband's breath was caught inside. A surprisingly large number of people report being visited by the deceased, who come to reassure them that they are happy in the afterlife.

698. Grief should not be ignored or repressed.

Some people think it is unbecoming and improper for survivors to show grief over a death. Often, family members are sensitive to special circumstances that a death creates for young children, but don't realize how distressing such loss is for older adults.

"A misconception about aging is that the older you get, the less it hurts when someone dies," says Dr. Ralph L. Klicker of the Thanos Institute. "Just the opposite is true. The elderly experience so many losses that death of a loved one can be devastating."

699. The physical and emotional toll of caring for the terminally ill often leads to deteriorated health of the caretaker. Studies of elderly couples have shown that a surviving spouse runs a great risk of dying within a year or two after his or her partner. The stress of caring for the sick spouse, coupled with the loneliness and challenge of adjusting to a new life, leaves the survivor vulnerable to infection and disease.

Some people report feeling panicky or childlike in the face of the secondary losses that accompany a death. Husbands lose not only wives, they lose cooks and laundresses and social directors. Wives lose not only husbands but also home handymen and car mechanics. If the couple socialized primarily with other couples, isolation may follow the loss of one-half of a pair.

700. Recovery from grief is painful and takes time. The permanence of death is felt gradually. The AARP's Widowed Person's Service has found that the period of intense grief can last from a few months to a year or more. Don't let anyone rush you through the grieving process—it is different for everyone.

Counselors recommend following a light schedule at this time—don't take on any new responsibilities if you don't have to, and try to avoid making drastic changes, such as moving to a new home. Allow yourself time to cry and to regain your perspective. Support groups for widows and widowers can be helpful.

701. Grieving people can become clinically depressed and in need of professional help. That diagnosis is made when someone who is grieving shows no sign of overcoming the feeling, or when there is a severe depression, above and beyond normal sadness and grief, that lasts more than a few months after a death. The following may be signs of such depression.

- Lack of interest in any activities
- Inability to relate to other people, including close family members and children
- Weight loss
- Inability to sleep
- Neglect of personal hygiene

702. Holidays may not be the same, but they can still bring some joy.

Many people report that their *dread* of spending a holiday without their spouse was worse than the actual holiday itself. In a publication of the National Funeral Directors Association, Victor Parachin, a grief counselor in Claremont, California, recommends:

- Hold a family conference about how to handle a holiday after a death.
- Keep expectations low on everything, from the number of presents given at Christmas or Hanukkah to the amount you cook at Thanksgiving. Retreat when you need to. Cry if you need to.
- Do something symbolic to honor the person you've lost. Light a special candle. Give everyone gifts of your spouse's favorite candy. Contribute to his or her favorite charity.
- Touch base with the religious or philosophical basis of the holiday. Volunteer to help others on that day.

703. Recovering from grief is an active process. Here are some tips to help you find comfort.

- Get a pet. A dog can provide companionship and protection, and cats can be very affectionate.
- Ask a friend or relative to call you every morning. The call will get you going and alleviate the feeling of waking up alone.
- Make concrete plans for special days when you know you'll feel nostalgic.
- Set a festive table for yourself, even if you're eating alone.
- Rearrange your furniture. Slipcover the sofa. Change the location of the bed.
- Entertain at home. Invite friends for a small snack, or dessert and coffee—don't try to re-create dinners you had as part of a married couple.

• Check out Chapter 2 for suggestions on how to use your time.

704. One of the first steps to recovery is saying good-bye. In the AARP booklet "On Being Alone," Ruth Jean Loewinsohn suggests an exercise:

Divide a sheet of paper in half, and on one side write down the things you admired, respected, or liked about your spouse or partner. Don't list more than ten items. On the other half of the paper write down the things you disliked or didn't respect. Be truthful. Even though you may not like the negative feelings, try to put down ten items.

Let yourself feel any emotions that occur while making these lists.

Now put the paper in your pocket or purse. When you begin to extol your late spouse's virtues, take the paper out and reread it. It will remind you that your spouse was a real person with both virtues and faults.

705. "Either that wallpaper goes, or I do." These were the last words of Irish writer Oscar Wilde, a great wit to the end. Humphrey Bogart is reported to have quipped on his deathbed, "I should have never switched from Scotch to martinis."

706. For more information about handling a spouse's death, contact:

Widowed Person's Service
AARP
601 E St. NW
Washington, DC 20049
202-434-2277

National Council on the Aging
409 3rd St. SW
Washington, DC 20024
202-479-1200
800-424-9046

Thanos Institute
P.O. Box 1928
Buffalo, NY 14238
800-742-8257
Offers a pamphlet on dealing with grief within the family.

Planning for Your Own Death

707. Planning for death can take as much brainpower as running a business or managing a household. The stories of managing well with what you've got are legion—from Toni Morrison's descriptions in *Song of Solomon* of poor African Americans in the South paying a few pennies every two weeks for burial insurance, to the Minnesota grande dame who knew that death was near, and before she slipped into unconsciousness, wrote a check for her funeral expenses so the money would be available before her checking account was frozen in probate.

Advance planning means you decide how you want things to go at your death. Don't try to do such planning until you feel you're ready, however. Older adults often report that while they couldn't face these decisions for a long time, there did come a day when they were ready to do so.

708. If you are diagnosed with a terminal illness, you have many rights. For example:

• You may demand that no one in your family be told of the prognosis.

• You may refuse treatment even if you will die without it.

• You may demand and receive adequate medication for pain control even if it will shorten your life.

If a crisis puts you in the hands of paramedics or sends you to an emergency room, your medical directives should be readily available, as should someone designated as your medical advocate. Otherwise, standard emergency procedures will be followed.

709. If you don't want to be kept alive by tubes, transfusions, and respirators, make a "living will."

A properly executed living will states that you do not wish to be kept alive by certain artificial methods. Doctors are then free to stop treatment and allow their patients to die—according to the person's instructions—without fear of liability.

About a quarter of all Americans have living wills, according to the American Medical Association, and the number is growing rapidly. Many states have their own version. You should be able to get a living will form through your local hospital.

710. Another legal document that you may want to consider grants "power of attorney" to another person, for health care purposes. This person will become your health care agent, or proxy. He or she will be able to make decisions for you if you can't speak for yourself. These decisions aren't limited to the ending of life; they also cover many treatment situations that often can't be foreseen.

Be sure the person who holds your health care proxy understands your wishes. A discussion with your doctor, or a review of death and dying handbooks, can help you understand the issues.

711. Here are some subjects to discuss—and to get in writing—with your potential proxyholder:

• Whether or not life-sustaining procedures be started if you're not able to survive without them

• The ending of life-sustaining procedures, including feeding and water

• The kinds of pain treatment that are acceptable

• The length of time you wish treatment to continue

• Whether blood transfusions or blood products be used

• If you have incurable cancer, whether chemotherapy and radiation be withheld

• Whether your agent can donate your organs and, if so, under what circumstances

• Whether you prefer to die at home, in a hospice, or in a nursing home

• Whether, if experimental treatment is available, you wish to be considered for it

712. For someone dying over a period of weeks or months, a stay in a hospital or nursing home may be the best choice. In that case, family members can ask to modify institution rules to make the patient's time there easier.

Family can arrange, for example, to have visiting hours extended. Close relatives may be able to spend the night near the dying person. If family members aren't available, the terminally ill can be comforted by regular visits from a member of the clergy or other counselors provided by the facility. Sometimes pets and other comforts are allowed.

Many counselors urge that wherever the dying process occurs, terminally ill people not be treated as if they're already dead. If you are terminally ill, ask your friends and family to continue including you in life's activities as much as possible.

713. Hospices help make the end of a terminally ill person's life as comfortable as possible. Hospice workers can provide painkillers such as morphine in doses higher than what is normally recommended, and they provide emotional support in the form of counseling—often of a spiritual nature—to patients and their families. Hospices operate under the philosophy that death is a natural part of life and can even be a chance for personal growth.

714. Hospices try to respect the wishes of terminally ill people who want to die at home but who fear being a burden on their family. Hospice care works in one of two ways: The patient can move into a hospice building, or hospice workers can visit the patient in his or her own home. They can also help family members care for the terminally ill at home, by training them in basic medical procedures.

715. The original concept of "hospice" comes from the Middle Ages. The word itself means "doors open to travelers." A hospice was a place of care, often attached to a religious order, for travelers, the young, or the poor.

The modern hospice movement began in England in the late 1960s, led by Dr. Cicely Saunders. The first American hospice opened in New Haven, Connecticut, in 1974. The National Hospice Organization now estimates that a fifth of the people who die in the United States each year do so in a hospice program. In 1996, according to the organization, there were some three thousand hospices working with 450,000 patients.

716. The cost of hospice care is often covered by Medicare, Medicaid, and other insurance. In fact, hospice care is emerging as a cost-efficient way of treating the dying, much less expensive than traditional hospital costs for, say, a terminally ill cancer patient. As a result, the number of for-profit hospices is growing. While hospices have usually been nonprofit organizations, sometimes attached to hospitals, there were 367 for-profit ones in 1996, up from 74 three years earlier.

717. For more information about hospices, contact:

National Hospice Organization
1901 N. Moore St., Suite 901
Arlington, VA 22209
703-243-5900

718. The right of the terminally ill to choose their own time of death is the stuff of headlines in the 1990s. Assisted suicide remains illegal in all states but Oregon, where a 1994 law permitting it is currently being challenged in court. Still, many choose such an end to their lives implicitly when they issue "do not resuscitate" orders to their doctors, or through more active means that exist in a gray area outside the law.

719. Tough thinking should be applied to such decisions:

• Such a decision must be made by the patient himself and no one else.
• Such a decision should never be made in the throes of depression or despair.
• Pain treatment should be examined and perhaps adjusted if a terminally ill patient is contemplating suicide.

For more information, contact:

Hemlock Society USA
P.O. Box 101810
Denver, CO 80250-1810
800-247-7421

American Association of Suicidology
4201 Connecticut Ave. NW, Suite 310
Washington, DC 20008
202-237-2280

720. After you die, your organs and tissues can enhance the lives of others.

Young people are preferred donors for major organs, but people over 60 can donate corneas, middle-ear tissue, bones, and skin.

If you like the idea of making an organ donation, sign a donor card—in many states it's part of your driver's license. Be sure to tell your family members of your wishes, since they may also have to give permission after you die. You should also alert caregivers at hospitals and nursing homes to your wishes.

You can also bequeath your body to a medical school for use in teaching or study. They can return your ashes to your family after study is complete. If you're interested, call a local medical school and ask about signing up.

721. Your funeral is your last party, and you *can* plan for it. Most libraries have several dealing-with-death handbooks with checklists to help guide your thinking about everything from the kind of service you want to saving money on funeral costs.

One we liked is *Dealing Creatively with Death,* by Ernest Morgan (Zinn Communications, 1994). It discusses everything from "Living with Dying" to sample burial services of several kinds. It includes a to-do checklist for your survivors, and also the suggestion that you make a file of final arrangements that includes all your thinking and planning.

722. Among the plans that should be included in a final arrangements file are:

- A description of the funeral or memorial service you would like to have
- A list of people to notify of your death, their phone numbers and addresses
- The names, phone numbers, and addresses of your lawyer and executor
- Copies of your will, and information on financial affairs such as bank statements, investment account statements, and insurance and Social Security records, plus a list of debts and any other financial encumbrances

723. Morgan's book includes less obvious items that your survivors may need to be reminded of:

- Child care during the funeral, and security at your house or apartment while the family is away
- An obituary for the newspaper. You may want to write your own.
- Plans for food and housecleaning during the pre- and post-funeral times
- Housing for out-of-town mourners
- Disposition of any flowers that may be sent
- Notification of utilities, landlord, newspaper delivery person, and the post office

724. The average cost of a funeral, not including the burial site, was $4,782 in 1997. The information comes from a survey of members by the National Funeral Directors Association.

It is possible to prepay for funeral services if you want to plan ahead. Some people buy a burial insurance policy or a separate life insurance policy for the costs of a funeral.

Funeral directors also often sell what they call "pre-need" plans, and such programs allow you to comparison shop. You work with a funeral director and make decisions about your funeral just as if you were planning someone else's. You eventually sign a contract for the services, which should guarantee prices. Many states require that anyone selling such plans be licensed. The Federal Trade Commission requires that you be provided with detailed price lists and an itemized bill when signing a contract.

725. Prepaying funeral expenses can be done in one lump sum or in installments. The disadvantage of installments is that you may need the service before payments are complete.

Whichever way you pay, there are several funding mechanisms. Your payment may be put into an annuity, a special joint savings account, or a bank trust, so that your payment earns interest. The disposition of any extra money above the cost of the funeral and the accounting for it should be decided in advance.

726. There are some disadvantages to prepaying funeral expenses. If your heirs are not aware of such arrangements, they could pay a second time before they find out about the prepaid plan. If you move, or die away from

home, there can be extra transportation and embalming costs you had not planned for. In addition, you may not be able to change your mind about arrangements once they have been made.

There can also be tax considerations, because money in a trust or annuity is taxable. You will need to determine who pays those taxes and when. Some people solve these problems by establishing a savings account with joint ownership with their executor, containing enough money for the services they think they will need.

727. Cemetery sites are generally purchased from the cemetery itself, not the funeral director.

Such purchases come with many of the same caveats as prepaid funerals. Purchases are generally for the burial plot itself, and may or may not include long-term upkeep, or "perpetual care," as the industry often calls it.

If you move and wish to dispose of a cemetery site, you may have to sell it yourself if there is no provision for the cemetery to buy it back from you.

728. There are ways to save money on funerals, if you think ahead.

Cremation, for example, is generally cheaper than embalming and burial if you or your heirs make many of the arrangements without a funeral director. With a funeral director and a traditional ceremony, the costs are often about the same.

Some people save money by buying memorial stones in advance and having them carved with what they want to say, saving a space for the final date. Other people make

or have made a wooden box suitable for a coffin, and use it for storage or other purposes until it is needed.

729. Memorial societies are nonprofit, cooperative organizations run by their members to help reduce the costs of funerals.

They generally do not offer the services themselves or collect fees for them, but they do comparison shopping to keep prices low, and steer members' survivors to the low-cost providers they have found. The funeral arrangements often involve cremation rather than burial, because of the lower cost.

These societies grew out of the Farm Grange associations in the Northwest early in the century. They claim they save their members 50 percent to 75 percent on the cost of a funeral. They generally do not accept prepayment for funerals and only charge members a nominal membership fee.

730. Funeral arrangements offered through memorial societies can be genuinely spartan.

And the limited number of societies can mean that you might have to belong to a society far from where you live.

For more information on memorial societies, contact:

Continental Association of Funeral and Memorial Societies
6900 Lost Lake Rd.
Egg Harbor, WI 54209
414-868-3136

731. For further information on death and dying, contact:

National Cancer Institute
Cancer Information Service
9000 Rockville Pike
Bethesda, MD 20892
800-422-6237

Choice in Dying
200 Varick St.
New York, NY 10014
212-366-5540
800-989-9455
*Provides information on refusal or
removal of life-sustaining treatments.*

Center for Health Law and Ethics
Institute of Public Law
University of New Mexico School of Law
1117 Stanford NE
Albuquerque, NM 87131

Organ Donation: The Living Bank
P.O. Box 6725
Houston, TX 77265
800-528-2971

Part

*Money Matters
Matter*

Chapter 9:

What Goes Out Must Come In:
Social Security, Pensions, and Investments

So how are you going to pay for it? Life over 55, that is? You've probably thought hard about what you'd like to do with your time in retirement. You may have wondered what your health will be like as you age, tried to predict, and then decided not to worry about it yet. With any luck, you're already squirreling away savings for retirement, either through a savings plan at work, your personal savings account, or both.

Whatever you're doing, you're probably not counting on Social Security benefits to support you. Only about 35 percent of Americans expect Social Security to provide the majority of their retirement income, according to a 1996 *USA Today* story. Most people anticipate that the major portion of their retirement income will come from money they've earned and put away themselves. The majority expect most of their retirement money to come either out of the 401(k) savings retirement funds they have at work or from their investments in stocks, bonds, and mutual funds.

Already, people are relying increasingly on their own savings. According to a recent study by the U.S. Department of Treasury, on average, households with retirement income over $20,000 a year receive only 20 percent of that from Social Security and 25 percent from employer pensions. The largest single portion of the average retirement income—39 percent—comes from personal savings and investments.

What that means is that your biggest job in retirement—and in the years just before—will be and is managing your money. This chapter and the following two will help you do that. In this chapter we'll talk about the income side of your personal balance sheet—what you're likely to get from Social Security and pensions and how, where, and with whom to save. In subsequent chapters, you'll find information about spending and estate planning.

The Home Stretch

732. If you're 55 and have been working outside the home, chances are you've already begun to save for retirement. However, there's no time like the present to stop and assess whether you'll have what you need if you retire at the standard 62 to 65 years old. In fact, if you're 55, you have only seven to ten years left to assemble the assets you need for freedom when the nine-to-five grind is over.

When reviewing your present situation, assume a life expectancy of 90 years. If you and your spouse are of different ages, use the number of years until the younger of you reaches the age of 90.

733. When assessing your retirement needs, ask yourself these questions and consider the implications of each answer:

• How long, realistically, before you need your retirement money?

• How stable are your current earnings? How much debt do you have? What are your prospects for future earnings and investment income?

• How do you feel about risk? Can you accept higher short-term risk for higher returns, or are you uncomfortable with risk in general?

• Once you retire, how will your assets and income keep up with inflation?

• How will you meet escalating health care costs?

• Can you afford to lead the kind of retirement life you envision?

• Will you outlive your money?

734. Here are some additional thinking points, based on national trends, that can affect retirement savings.

• We live longer, so we have to stretch our retirement saving farther than we might have originally planned.

• We tend to retire early, so there are fewer years to save and more years to spend.

• The Social Security system faces increasing pressure to meet the needs of the growing number of retirees, but the situation isn't as bad as some have led the public to believe. (See Social Security items below.)

• Rather than offering the traditional pension plan, many American corporations are shifting the responsibility of saving for retirement to individuals through the use of 401(k) plans, to which employees make contributions.

• The average worker changes jobs more than six times during a work life, reducing the likelihood of a significant pension from one employer.

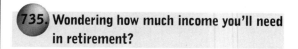 **735. Wondering how much income you'll need in retirement?**

A good rule of thumb is to assume it will be 60 to 80 percent of what you expect your final annual salary to be. If you make $50,000 a year now, for example, and you estimate that you'll need 75

percent of that for retirement, you'll need $37,500 annually.

The precise amount you'll need depends on a number of variables:

• Housing. If you own a house, paying off your mortgage early means a reduction in housing expenses. If you rent, your housing costs won't change much.

• Social Security taxes. Unless you plan to work part-time, you won't be paying them.

• Savings. If you're saving now for a goal such as a child's education, chances are you won't have that expense in retirement.

• Travel. You may wish to travel more, and such plans should be reflected in your retirement expenses.

• Medical costs. In retirement, you may need additional medical insurance over and above Medicare.

736. Find out what you'll receive from Social Security. The amount of your monthly Social Security payment is figured by taking into account the date you started working, the date you plan to retire, and your salary along the way. If you're 55 now and earned $50,000 in 1997, you can probably expect almost $16,000 annually from Social Security if you started working at 22 and retire at 65. For a more specific calculation, call the Social Security Administration at 800-772-1213. (Be warned: The phone line is busiest early in the week and early in the month, but it is open 24 hours a day.)

You also need to estimate what you're likely to receive from employer pensions, if you have them. Haul out your paperwork from your pension plans, look up the customer service telephone numbers, and call and ask. Below you will also find a discussion of the ins and outs of various kinds of pension plans.

737. Now you can calculate what you need in savings. Your retirement savings should cover the total amount of any gap between your projected expenses and what you will receive in Social Security and pension benefits.

While it would be grand to have enough banked that we could live off the interest generated by our investments, not touching the principal during retirement, that's simply not realistic for most people. Most financial experts say that you can plan to spend 4 to 5 percent of the principal of your savings each year as you calculate your retirement income and expenses.

738. Here are the most basic basics about saving for retirement:

• Save regularly. Start now, if you haven't already. Don't wait until you have "extra" income, because such a day may never come. Make savings a part of your basic budget. Payroll deductions are a good way to enforce savings.

• Don't park a large amount of money in a bank savings account over a long period of time. Such accounts don't pay enough interest. Be alert for high-interest products—read about them below.

• Whatever method you use for savings, you should reinvest the earnings on your investments, rather than taking them as a check. Reinvestment can have a significant impact on your savings.

• Take advantage of tax-deferred savings programs. Plans such as 401(k)s and IRAs should be the bedrock of your savings strategy. They allow you to defer income taxes until you withdraw the funds at retirement— a time when your tax rate will be lower. See items 754–763 for more information.

739. Most workingwomen have a greater need for retirement planning than men, because they will have to do more with less. Statistically, women earn less money than men throughout their working lives, so they have less available for retirement savings and investments. In addition, many pension plans are based on the amount of earnings throughout a worker's life, a fact that means women who take time out to raise children will have fewer retirement funds. Some women who return to the workforce choose to work only part-time, so their eligibility for retirement benefits is reduced again.

Yet women generally live about seven years longer than men, so their smaller retirement savings will have to go further than men's. In addition, many women will find themselves as the primary caregiver for spouses or parents, adding more stress to finances.

740. For more information geared toward women and savings, contact:

Worker Equity
American Association of Retired Persons
601 E St. NW
Washington, DC 20049

741. Both men and women should be wary of forced early retirement. Traditionally, the decision to retire before age 60 has been a personal one. Increasingly, this decision is thrust on employees when companies merge, restructure, downsize, or otherwise reduce their workforce.

Additional benefits are usually offered as inducements for early retirement. They are often onetime offers that the employee must decide on relatively quickly. The incentives may include enhanced pension benefits, a retiree health insurance plan, and lump-sum cash payments.

While the package may sound good, you should think carefully about the salary and benefits you'd be giving up. If your company has a pension plan, money in it often grows substantially in the last years of work, so you may be giving up more than you get if you accept an early retirement package. For example, any such package should include medical benefits, but these days fewer and fewer do.

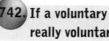 **742. If a voluntary retirement plan isn't really voluntary, you do have recourse.**

If a request for early retirement is coupled with the threat of imminent layoffs, subtle coercion, or a short window of eligibility for accepting the proposal, then it probably isn't voluntary.

If you decide to remain in your job, your employment rights are protected by the federal Age Discrimination in Employment Act of 1967 (ADEA). It covers most workers or applicants for work 40 and over and was amended to prohibit discrimination in early retirement incentives adopted after 1990.

743. If you believe you are being forced into retirement, contact:

Equal Employment Opportunity
Commission
1801 L St. NW
Washington, DC 20507
202-634-6036
800-872-3362

744. For more information and helpful booklets on planning retirement, contact:

American Association of Retired Persons
601 E St. NW
Washington, DC 20049
Ask for "Look Before You Leap: A Guide to Early Retirement Incentive Programs" (D13390), "The Age Discrimination in Employment Act" (D12386), "Planning Your Retirement" (D12322), "Working Options: How to Plan Your Job Search," (D12403), "A Guide to Understanding Your Pension Plan" (D13533).

A Financial Team

745. Now is a good time to assemble a financial team to help you with your planning. You're going to be facing decisions about your life savings, and expert advice can help. The idea is to get advice that fits your needs and is objective, but that also allows you to have control of your own financial decisions. You'll benefit from such a team when you retire, so go ahead and get it ready now.

The first member of the team should probably be an accountant. You may also want to consult a financial planner, and if you have complicated financial affairs or have a large net worth, you may need the help of a lawyer as well.

746. For personal business matters, look for an accountant who handles families and individuals. Your accountant should help with your taxes, evaluate your insurance coverage, guide your estate planning, question you about how you spend your money, and come up with ideas on how to save money. He or she should be able to advise you on financial statements for bank loans and help evaluate, for example, a stockbroker's advice. Accountants' fees are tax deductible.

There are two types of accountants: certified public accountants (CPAs) and public accountants (PAs). CPAs have taken and passed a special exam; PAs may have taken many courses and have considerable experience, but they haven't passed a qualifying exam.

747. Don't let a phony "financial planner" take advantage of you. The term "financial planner" isn't well defined. It may be used loosely by accountants, stockbrokers, insurance agents, and others. In many states, almost anyone can call himself a financial planner. And the incompetent and the less scrupulous often prey on retirees who have their life savings at stake. One way to find a path through the thicket is to ask about certification and to insist that whoever you hire have certification from a nationally recognized organization. (See below.)

748. The following require that those they certify as financial planners take extensive courses and pass examinations.

National Association of Personal Financial
Advisers (NAPFA)
1130 Lake Cook Rd., Suite 150
Buffalo Grove, IL 60089

International Association for Financial
Planning (IAFP)
2 Concourse Pkwy., Suite 800
Atlanta, GA 30328
404-395-1605

Institute of Certified Financial Planners
(ICFP)
2 Denver Highlands
10065 E. Harvard Ave., Suite 320
Denver, CO 80231
800-282-7526

Chartered Financial Consultants (CFC)
270 Bryn Mawr Ave.
Bryn Mawr, PA 19010

749. A good financial planner will review your total financial picture and suggest how your money can work better for you. He or she will want to look at historical financial documents including tax returns, investment statements, retirement and estate planning reports, wills, and insurance policies.

The financial planner will help you determine your net worth, and will take a look at your debts, making suggestions about consolidation, paying them off, and refinancing. He or she will point out changes that need to be made in your finances and then help you develop a financial plan based on your personal goals and ability to tolerate risk. The financial planner will also review your files with you and refer you to other specialists, such as lawyers, if you need them.

750. If you think a financial planner could be useful, shop around and interview several. Here are some questions to ask.

- What credentials do you have?
- Are you registered with the federal Securities and Exchange Commission (SEC) or any other agency?
- How do you prepare a financial plan?
- How many people do you work with?
- Will I work with you, or do you refer me to others?
- Will you provide me with references?
- May I see a copy of one of the reports you have prepared for a client with a similar background?

751. Financial planners can be paid in one of two ways. They can charge you a fee for their service, or they can receive commissions on the investment products they sell you. Some planners receive a blend of both.

Fee-only planners base their charges on the financial data they gather and adapt to your needs and on the assistance they give you in using their advice. Hourly or flat fees are common—the planner should be able to estimate how much his or her services will cost. Payment is required whether or not you take the advice.

752. Commission-only planners derive their income by selling you a financial product. For example, if you buy insurance on the advice of a financial planner, the planner receives a commission from the insurance company for persuading you to buy that insurance. Until you develop an informed and trusting relationship with your planner, exercise caution in following the advice of someone who works only on commission.

Also be wary of financial planners who push certain investments for all their clients. That's almost always a tip-off that they're earning a commission from selling that investment and that they might be more interested in collecting their fee than in the investment's suitability for you.

753. Even if you use a financial planner, it's a good idea to keep an eye on your own investments. A subscription to the *Wall Street Journal,* for example, will keep you up to date on financial affairs in general and provide a lot of good reading, too. Consumer magazines and newsletters, available at most public libraries, are good at explaining personal finance and helping you evaluate products. Some helpful periodicals are *Money, Kiplinger's Personal Finance, Consumer Reports,* and *Sylvia Porter's Retirement Newsletter.*

Tax-Deferred Retirement Savings

754. Employer-sponsored retirement savings plans allow you to put away money before you pay taxes on it. A contribution reduces your taxable income during your working life. Often, your company will also contribute to your nest egg. Some plans also allow you to put away after-tax dollars once you've hit a ceiling in pretax contributions.

You don't pay taxes on your savings until you retire and start to withdraw the money, and that's usually at a lower rate than during your working years.

Participation in a tax-deferred plan requires you to decide how your savings will be invested. Often, your employer will offer a limited selection of stock funds, bond funds, and annuities, and the employee is responsible for choosing from that selection.

755. Such retirement plans are often called by the numbers and letters used for them in the tax code.

• 401(k) plans are available through for-profit companies.

• 403(b) plans are available through tax-exempt organizations, such as schools and health care facilities. They often permit "catch-up" savings as you near retirement if you haven't taken full advantage of them previously.

- 457 plans are available for state, county, and municipal workers.

If you're still working and don't know about these programs, find out if such a plan is offered by your employer, and contribute the maximum amount allowed.

756. The best known of the above retirement savings plans is the 401(k). In early July 1997 the *Wall Street Journal* published a front-page story about what one source called "the 401(k) millionaires." It detailed a growing number of Americans in their 50s who had invested their retirement savings plans in the stock market and who are now finding themselves millionaires. One fund group, T. Rowe Price Associates, Inc., for example, reported it had 120 such millionaires among its 700,000 individual accounts in 1995. Eighteen months later there were 308 among 870,000 accounts.

757. Your company may also offer a profit-sharing plan for retirement. Under such a plan, the company president decides once a year how much will be contributed to the retirement savings of its employees, and the contribution is divvied up among all employees. Again, the money in the plan is not taxed until it is withdrawn. It is portable when an employee leaves the company.

758. ESOPs—that is, employee stock ownership plans—give workers stock in the company they work for. ESOPs are often touted as a way to increase employee productivity. But in fact, they tie a worker's retirement fortunes to the fortunes of the company and have the effect of putting all an employee's nest eggs in one basket. By law, employers have to allow workers to diversify their holdings by selling stock beginning at age 55 if they want to, and many financial experts recommend doing just that.

759. An individual retirement account (IRA) is an excellent retirement savings vehicle not necessarily tied to your employer. Again, taxes are deferred until you withdraw the money you've put into it.

An IRA permits workers under age 70½ to contribute up to $2,000 per tax year. Contributions are tax deductible depending on your income level—in 1997, $40,000 and under for a married couple—and whether you and your spouse are covered by an employer's retirement plan.

Again, you must decide how and where to invest your IRA, thereby determining its earnings. In addition, there are heavy penalties for withdrawing money before you reach retirement; IRAs cannot be used as collateral for loans.

760. A "rollover IRA" is designed to receive the retirement savings of people who leave a job or retire. A rollover IRA protects the tax-deferred savings coming out of an employer-sponsored retirement plan by providing another tax-safe vehicle for those monies.

Without a rollover IRA, the new retiree or job-changing worker faces a mandatory 20 percent deduction from the sum for federal income tax, and, if you're under age 59½, a 10 percent IRS penalty for early withdrawal.

761. There are two new kinds of IRAs—one for college tuition and another for retirement.

With an education IRA, parents can save $500 per year per child. Those dollars aren't tax deductible, but they do avoid federal taxation when withdrawn to pay for college—a possible boon to baby boomer parents who waited until their 30s and 40s to have children.

Under what is called a Roth IRA—named for the chairman of the Senate Finance Committee when it was conceived—you can invest after-tax dollars in an IRA account that can be withdrawn tax free when the account has been open at least five years and the owner is at least 59½ or disabled or has died. An owner can also withdraw up to $10,000 tax free to buy a first house. If education money is needed, the owner of a Roth IRA can withdraw funds early without the 10 percent penalty usually charged, but he or she will have to pay income tax on the earnings.

762. There are two kinds of Keogh plans: profit-sharing and money-purchase. Keogh plans are individual retirement plans for people who are self-employed. They enable you to set aside pretax dollars for your retirement. The profit-sharing ones are the more flexible, especially if you can't count on regular profits each year. With a profit-sharing

Keogh, you can contribute a specified percentage of net profits up to a maximum dollar amount each year. You can change the amount yearly and can make smaller or no contributions in years you have few profits.

With money-purchase plans you have to determine a percentage of income that you will contribute each year—at least 3 percent of your income—and keep to it year after year. There is a hefty penalty if you do not.

As with IRAs, you can't touch your Keogh money until you reach retirement age, and there is a penalty for early withdrawal. Keoghs can be opened at banks, brokerage houses, and other financial institutions.

763. "Simplified employee pensions" are usually called SEP-IRAs because they are basically large-caliber IRAs. They can be established by anyone who is self-employed, or by a small company for its employees. It can all be done with very little paperwork at a bank or brokerage house.

This plan allows tax-deductible, tax-deferred contributions of up to 13 percent of earned income, a maximum of $30,000 per participant per year in 1996. You have until your income tax deadline every year—even if it's extended—to set up the account and make the contribution.

For more information about SEPs, contact:

Investor Information
Vanguard Group
Vanguard Financial Center
P.O. Box 2600
Valley Forge, PA 19482
800-662-7447

Ask for "An Employer's Guide to Understanding SEPs."

Pension Rights Center
916 16th St. NW, Suite 704
Washington, DC 20006
202-296-3776

764. Annuities are insurance products that allow you to set aside an unlimited amount of after-tax money. The interest on an annuity grows, and is not taxable until money is withdrawn. With some products, called variable annuities, you decide how the money is invested, choosing among stock funds, bond funds, and the like offered by the insurance company.

Annuities also offer a variety of withdrawal options when you retire, including those that will guarantee you a stream of income for the rest of your life, much the way pensions do. Many variable annuities offer a death benefit if the owner dies before beginning to withdraw payments. The death benefit often returns the principal of the annuity to the heirs no matter what the stock market has done to its value.

765. In recent years, variable annuities have become very popular with people over 55—but be careful! They look like a way to defer taxes on retirement nest eggs. But they are expensive products and the tax benefits may not be that great, especially for high-net-worth individuals.

Charges and fees associated with annuities can be so high that they offset some of the tax-deferred growth of your investment. Here are some other problems.

• Many annuity funds have high up-front commissions or formidable surrender penalties, lowering their returns. Typical costs include a 1 percent annual management fee, as well as maintenance charges and other fees.
• Withdrawal penalties ranging from 1 percent to 10 percent can be levied.
• Annuities are tax-deferred, not tax free, and the IRS imposes penalties if you withdraw before age 59$\frac{1}{2}$.

766. Any money withdrawn from an annuity is taxable, and will be taxed at your present tax rate. If you're well-to-do, that rate may be higher than the 28 percent capital gains tax rate you'd be paying had you put your nest egg in a stock-based mutual fund. In fact, wealthy retirees typically have a combined tax rate of 40 percent.

For more information about annuities, contact:

National Association of Life Underwriters
1922 F St. NW
Washington, DC 20006
202-331-6031

767. Companies that want to sell you investment products often offer good information on financial planning for retirement. You can contact them, and other, more objective sources:

T. Rowe Price
Investment Services

100 E. Pratt St.
Baltimore, MD 21298
800-541-5790
Offers worksheets and workbooks.

Fidelity Investments
82 Devonshire St.
Boston, MA 02109
800-544-8888
Ask for its "Retirement Planning Guide."

American Association of Retired Persons
601 E St. NW
Washington, DC 20049
202-434-2277
Publishes dozens of free financial planning booklets.

Internal Revenue Service
800-829-1040
The IRS has many pamphlets and brochures.

Your Investments

768. There are thousands of investment vehicles, sold by everyone from insurance agents and banks to stockbrokers and financial advisers. As you think about investments for your last decade before retirement and beyond, ask yourself again about the risk you are willing to take and about possible major expenses (children still facing college? elderly parents needing support?). Many financial advisers recommend that you review your investments annually, looking at each investment's performance over the previous three years and comparing it with others in its class.

769. If you're investing money for the first time, here are some money-saving tips:

• Don't rely on telephone or mail solicitation to purchase an investment product.
• If you are contacted by a bank, brokerage house, or other financial institution about investing, spend time talking with managers. Be sure you understand what they are selling. Don't rely solely on verbal explanations. Get information in writing.
• Get advice from other sources, such as your accountant or tax adviser, before you act.
• Shop around. See what other banks, investment houses, or brokers in your area are offering.

770. There are four tests to apply to any investment before making it.

The Wall Street Journal Lifetime Guide to Money (Hyperion, 1997) makes the following recommendations.

1. It should be easy to understand.
2. Its chances of making money should be good.
3. If you need to sell in a hurry, there should be a good market for it.
4. It should be relatively inexpensive to hold and sell as well as to buy.

Stocks and Stock Funds

771. Here's another rule of thumb for people in their 50s: Subtract your age from 100 and put that percentage of your investments into stocks and stock funds. In fact, that rule generally makes for a rather conservative portfolio, some experts say. If you weren't good at saving and investing in your 30s and 40s and still need to accumulate substantial funds for retirement, you will likely need to put a higher percentage of your current investments into stocks. That's because over the long haul—even with the big fluctuations that the stock market can show from year to year—stocks earn an average of about 10 percent a year (government bonds earn about 5 percent, and Treasury bills earn about 3 percent). So if you need to amass dollars, the stock market is the fastest way.

772. The current advice is to invest in the stock market DURING retirement, too. That wasn't always true. In the past, the advice was to invest in stocks for growth during the earning years and then switch to bonds and other safe, conservative, fixed-income investments in retirement and live off the income.

These days, with our longer life spans—and at least a quarter of a lifetime spent in retirement—and inflation at about 3 percent, financial experts are recommending that retirees keep as much as 50 percent of their assets in stocks or stock funds. Some recommend going as high as 70 percent, while others say an older adult's investment in stocks should not fall below 30 percent.

773. Stocks aren't everything, nor should they be. A wise investor has a diversified portfolio, including stocks and bonds and the equivalent of cash in money market funds or certificates of deposit.

Once you've decided on asset allocation among stocks, bonds, and cash, there should be some diversification within each category. Investments in stocks or stock funds, for example, might include some large companies and some small ones, and some foreign companies in addition to domestic ones.

774. If you've decided to try stocks and stock funds, here is some basic information. Buying a share of a stock in a company means becoming part owner of that company. If your company prospers, your shares of stock grow in value. The reverse is also true, of course.

775. You need to balance RISK against POTENTIAL. Historically, stocks have been very good investments, because they grow with inflation. The least risky stocks are usually those issued by solid, well-established companies. The chances of making a great deal of money come with investments in new companies where there is potential for great growth.

776. If you want to be sure of investing in socially responsible companies, here are some books to guide you.

• Jack Brill, *Investing from the Heart: The Guide to Socially Responsible Investments and*

Money Management (Crown Publishing Group, 1993)

• Gary D. Moore, *The Christian's Guide to Wise Investing* (Zondervan, 1994)

• Ritchie P. Lowry, *Good Money: Profitable Social Investing in the '90s* (W. W. Norton & Co., 1991)

• James Melton and Matthew Keenan, *The Socially Responsive Portfolio: Balancing Politics and Profits in Institutional Money Management* (Irwin Professional, 1993)

777. Before making an investment in stocks and stock mutual funds—or any other financial products—you must decide who will sell them to you. You can use a brokerage firm and its salespeople, also known as stockbrokers; the firm's account executives or registered representatives can also sell. You can also use your bank or insurance company, depending on the kind of product you decide to buy. There are small brokerages and large ones, discount brokerages as well as full-service ones.

778. Here are some tips to help you choose well.

• Don't rush. Resist salespeople who urge you to open an account immediately.

• Talk with salespeople at several firms. If possible, meet them face-to-face in their offices and ask about their investing experience, professional background, and education.

• Find out about the disciplinary history of any brokerage firm and sales representative by calling 800-289-9999. It is a toll-free

hotline operated by the National Association of Securities Dealers, Inc. State securities regulators can also tell you if a sales representative is licensed to do business in your state.

• Understand how the sales representative is paid. Ask for a copy of the firm's commission schedule and what fees or charges you will be required to pay when opening, maintaining, and closing an account.

• Ask if the brokerage firm is a member of the Securities Investor Protection Corporation (SIPCO). For further information, contact SIPCO at 805 15th St. NW, Suite 800, Washington, DC 20005.

779. A small local brokerage firm may have fewer services, but a keener knowledge of local-company stocks. Again, shop around. Talk to the firm's manager, and outline your goals and needs. Ask for references from three or four people who have been clients for several years—and call them. Brokers who seem to have "millionaire clients" may not be best for you, since they might not be sufficiently aware of opportunities for smaller investors.

When you do select a stockbroker, try that person out for a few months. If the broker follows your orders and you do fairly well, give him or her a few more months.

780. Discount brokers are for those who do their homework. If you do a lot of research on your own before buying stocks, and only need the broker to buy or sell orders on your behalf, you may be better off with a discount broker. He or she will charge a fraction of what a full-service broker does.

Before selecting a discount broker, call

and ask for descriptive literature about the firm. Examine it, and note the differences in services offered; figure out which rates are best for you.

If you want someone who'll take a personal interest in you and your situation and who will supply analytical reports, stick with a full-service firm.

781. Discount brokers advertise in the financial pages of many newspapers. Here are some national discount brokerages.

Accutrade: 800-228-3011
Fidelity Investments: 800-544-7272
Kennedy, Cabot & Co.: 800-252-0090
Muriel Siebert & Co.: 800-872-0711
OLDE Discount Stockbrokers: 800-872-6533
Quick & Reilly: 800-222-0437
T. Rowe Price Discount Brokerage: 800-225-7720
Charles Schwab & Co.: 800-648-5300
Waterhouse Securities: 800-934-4478

782. Brokerage firms generate a lot of research about companies, stocks, bonds, mutual funds, and other financial instruments. The information is a sales tool for them, especially with their big institutional investors. Brokers are generally glad to send individual investors such information, if asked.

Good information on companies and financial products is also available from the SEC. If you're Internet-literate, the SEC maintains a service called EDGAR that offers electronic copies of documents that companies must file (*http://www.edgar-online.com*). Or contact:

U.S. Securities and Exchange Commission
Office of Consumer Affairs
450 5th St. NW
Washington, DC 20549
202-942-7040

783. If you suspect a problem with your broker or with your account, talk promptly to the sales representative's manager or the firm's compliance officer. Some brokers attempt to "churn" accounts, especially those of older adults. That is, they generate excessive buys and sells, because the transactions boost their commissions.

If you begin to worry about your account or question the actions of your broker, keep written records of all conversations and ask for written explanations. You may want to consult an attorney knowledgeable about securities laws. Your local bar association can help you locate one.

784. The National Futures Association has developed an Investor's Bill of Rights.

It helps consumers know what they should expect in a securities transaction. Some of your rights include:

- Honesty in advertising
- Full and accurate information
- Disclosure of risks
- Explanation of obligations and costs
- Time to consider what you're getting into
- Responsible advice
- Best-effort management
- Complete and truthful accounting

- Access to your funds
- Recourse, if necessary

785. For a complete copy of the Investor's Bill of Rights, contact:

National Futures Association
200 W. Madison St., Suite 1600
Chicago, IL 60606
800-621-3570

786. The average American buys stocks through a mutual fund, not directly from a company or a broker.

A mutual fund is a group of people with investment goals similar to your own who, instead of investing on their own, put their money in a pooled fund and hire a professional manager to invest on their behalf. The combined holdings are known as the fund's portfolio.

Mutual funds are not actually started by a group of friends who want to invest. They are products created and sold by various financial institutions. They're a good way to invest for people who don't want to check the stock market every day or who want to diversify but don't have the resources to do so on their own.

When you buy a mutual fund, you purchase shares. The number of shares you buy is determined by the share price of the fund, the net asset value (NAV), plus any sales charge—called a load—if one applies. "No load" funds have no sales charge.

787. Mutual funds earn money in two ways:

- Through a distribution of the profits. Distributions include interest from the fund's bonds, and dividends from the stocks, as well as capital gains—the profit earned from selling securities for more than what was paid.

- Through share appreciation. Some mutual funds are designed for little or no share price fluctuation, while others can fluctuate significantly daily. As the value of the securities in a fund increases, a fund's share price increases—that is, the value of your investment rises.

788. There are three major kinds of mutual funds.

Each kind has its own risks and rewards.

- Money market funds. These are relatively low risk, compared with other funds. They are limited by law to certain high-quality, short-term investments. Many investors think of them as a place to park cash that may be needed soon.

- Bond funds. These are sometimes called fixed-income funds. They carry a greater risk than money market funds but could pay higher yields. There are many different types of bonds, and these funds can vary dramatically in risk and reward.

- Stock funds. These are also called equity funds. They are generally the riskiest of the funds, but they can also offer the highest returns. There are many kinds of stock funds. Growth funds, for example, focus on stocks that may not pay a regular dividend but have the potential for large capital gains. Some funds specialize in a particular industry segment, such as technology stocks.

789. When you buy an investment product, you are likely to encounter unfamiliar and confusing terms.

Always insist that your investment salesperson give you a simple explanation of anything you don't understand. Some terms you'll probably hear:

Front-end loads or *asset-based sales charges:* sales commissions—the way the brokerage, bank, or other intermediary makes its money
Back-end loads: fees charged when you sell; also called contingency deferred sales charges
12b-1 fees: fees charged by some funds to cover advertising and marketing costs
Management fees: fees that pay the mutual fund's investment adviser (the person who recommends which investments the fund should buy or sell); also called investment advisory fees or account maintenance fees.

790. Revenue from a mutual fund is taxable, unless it's in a tax-deferred account such as an IRA. At the end of each year, the mutual fund company will let you know what you earned. Keep your account statement so you can figure out your taxes.

If you invest in a tax-exempt fund (such as a municipal bond fund), some or all of your dividends will be exempt from federal, and sometimes state and local, income tax. You will, however, owe taxes on any capital gains.

791. As with all investments, there are some drawbacks to mutual funds.

• They are not guaranteed or insured by any bank or government agency.

• Mutual funds always carry risks, some types more than others. A higher rate of return typically involves a higher risk of loss.

• Past performance isn't always a reliable indicator of future performance. Beware of dazzling claims.

• All mutual funds have fees that lower your investment returns.

• You can buy some mutual funds by contacting the fund directly. If you buy through a broker, bank, financial planner, or insurance agent, you generally pay an extra sales charge.

792. For information on mutual funds, contact:

Fidelity Investments
82 Devonshire St.
Boston, MA 02109
800-544-8888
Ask for "Getting Started with Mutual Funds: A Fidelity Common Sense Guide."

U.S. Securities and Exchange Commission
Washington, DC 20549
Ask for "Invest Wisely: An Introduction to Mutual Funds."

Bonds and Bond Funds

793. Bonds have been out of favor as long-term investments during the 1990s because the stock market has risen very high very rapidly—and paid higher returns. Bonds are issued by companies or governments as a kind of IOU to the buyer when the company or government needs to raise money. This loan—in the form of a bond—is paid off by a specific time, at a specific rate of interest. Bonds are also referred to as fixed-income securities.

Bonds are a good way to diversify an investment portfolio. They can be helpful if you have a specific savings goal for, say, five years in the future when the bond matures. Tax-free municipal bonds are a great way for those living in high-tax states such as New York, California, and Massachusetts to get a tax break.

794. Besides the fact that they haven't earned as well as stocks in recent years, bonds have another downside. Companies and governments sometimes default on their interest payments, and bond owners not only lose that income, but the price of the bonds falls.

Bonds often get caught by rising interest rates, too. Their prices move opposite to interest rates. That is, if interest rates are high, bond prices are low—and that affects the bond owner's ability to sell the bond before its maturity date if he or she needs the money invested in the bond.

There's another reason that bonds can be hard for small investors to sell before their maturity date. The bond market is dominated by big institutional investors who think in hundreds of thousands of dollars, not tens of thousands. So to sell a small batch of bonds, an individual investor usually has to take a lower price.

795. And then there's the fact that all but Treasury bonds can be "called." That means they can be paid off at face value before they mature, sometimes leaving the investor with his or her money before it was wanted. If interest rates are low, finding a new bond to replace the one that was called can be expensive, and chances are, it won't pay as much interest.

For simplicity's sake, it may be that Treasury bonds—or U.S. savings bonds (see items 812–814)—are the best bond investment. They can't be called, and there's no danger of default on interest payments, as with corporate and municipal bonds.

796. Bonds can be bought individually, or they can be bought through a bond fund. If you would like to add bonds to your investment portfolio, it often takes a smaller chunk of money to buy into a bond *fund* than to buy a single bond. Many bond funds also let investors write checks against the fund.

However, if you do buy an individual bond, you know what your return will be and when you will get your full investment back. An individual bond can also be a better choice if you think you might have to sell before maturity, or if you have a major investment coming up and need to match a maturity date with that event.

Riskier Investments

797. Some financial planners recommend gold as a protection against inflation, and to safeguard long-term purchasing power. An example they cite is that the price of the average American house in 1975 was $39,000, and by 1986 that same house cost $92,000. The rise in price was mostly due to the decline in the value of the dollar. However, the same amount of gold could have bought that house in both 1975 and 1986.

Gold offers instant liquidity, is as easy to buy as stocks, bonds, or CDs, and is available through brokerage firms, banks, and coin dealers across the United States. You can take direct possession and enjoy the security of having the gold in your own home or safe-deposit box. But be careful: There are many opportunities for fraud in the buying and selling of gold.

798. Gold prices float freely in accordance with supply and demand. The price of gold responds very quickly to political and economic events, rising freely, for example, when inflation scares the country.

Like your house and other real estate, gold is a "hard asset." Many financial advisers think a house is enough of a hard asset in most portfolios and recommend against buying gold. It may be an appropriate investment if hard assets give you psychological comfort or if you have a large portfolio.

799. Diamonds are probably not your best investment friend. If you've been a diamond dealer your entire life, investing in them or in other precious gems may be a good idea. If not, avoid any investment until you get several price quotes, and make sure any stone you buy has a recent certificate of quality from the Gemological Institute of America.

When you buy a diamond in a piece of jewelry, get a written receipt specifying cut, clarity, carat, and quality of the gem. If you have questions, or need more information, contact:

Jewelers Vigilance Committee
401 E. 34th St., Suite NI3A
New York, NY 10016

Jewelers of America
1185 Ave. of the Americas, 30th Floor
New York, NY 10036
Jewelers of America has several free, helpful pamphlets on buying gold, silver, and gems.

Gemological Institute of America
800-421-7250

800. If you're interested in buying rare coins for investment, learn about them first. Talk with a numismatist—an expert in coins—who has carefully studied various aspects of coins, including rarity, grading, market availability, and price trends.

If you receive solicitations about investing in coins, keep these points in mind:

• Apply the same common sense to coins as you would any investment claims.
• Make sure you know the dealer's reputation.
• Don't be taken in by promises.
• Get a second opinion from another source.
• Comparison shop.
• Take possession of any coins you buy,

store them in a safe-deposit box, and make sure they are insured.

801. For more information about investing in rare coins, contact:

American Numismatic Association
818 N. Cascade Ave.
Colorado Springs, CO 80903

Professional Numismatists Guild
P.O. Box 430
Van Nuys, CA 91408

Federal Trade Commission
Rare Coins
6th St. and Pennsylvania Ave. NW
Washington, DC 20580

802. If you've ever tried to sell Grandmother's heirlooms, you know that cashing out of antiques and collectibles is no walk in the park. It takes a thorough knowledge of antiques and their market, coupled with patience—and then you never know if you did as well as you might have.

The best advice about such items is to buy and own furniture, art, and other collectibles that you like and want to have around without much regard to their value as investments. Collections of limited-edition plates, ceramic village scenes, medallions, guns or military gear, and other items are fun to make and display. But fluctuations in the market for them make it almost impossible to know the exact value of any collection.

Cash Investments

The riskiest action you can take may be to keep all your money in safe but low-yielding investments.

That's because the effect of inflation and longevity can whittle away your savings.

Among the investments that may not earn enough to keep up with inflation are cash, passbook savings, certificates of deposit, cash-value life insurance, conservative money market funds, fixed annuities, U.S. Treasury bills, and U.S. government bonds.

804. But some of those investments can come in handy in an emergency. Most financial advisers suggest that you have three to six months' worth of "run your household" money in easy-to-access places. That's in case the roof gives out or the car dies. In addition, such a cushion allows you to take more risks with other assets, since you know you have the basics covered.

Bank savings accounts, certificates of deposit, money market funds, U.S. savings bonds, and Treasury bills are all good places to put such funds. Money stored there earns only a little interest but is readily available in an emergency.

805. A passbook savings account at a bank was once the only safe way to keep money. After all, such an account is insured by the government up to $100,000. The accounts are very liquid—you have access to your money all the time. And it takes very little money to open one and maintain it.

While keeping your money in passbook savings is better than putting it under the mattress, it's not much better. Interest rates on the accounts may be less than inflation, so you lose a bit of buying power every year. Interest paid by a bank is fully taxable. No checks can be written on a savings account. Some banks charge fees on savings accounts that eat away at any earnings, because the banks want to discourage such accounts.

806. You may need a NOW account rather than a savings account. NOW stands for "negotiable order of withdrawal," and such an account allows you to keep your money safe, earn a little interest if you maintain a minimum balance, and still have check-writing privileges.

NOW accounts usually pay interest similar to bank savings accounts. They are risk-free, as with a passbook savings account, and they permit unlimited check-writing, as with a checking account. There are no fees if you keep a minimum balance.

If you don't keep a minimum balance, a NOW account can be loaded with fees. In addition, the method that some banks use to compute interest can also minimize interest earnings. Ask carefully about fees and restrictions before you sign up.

807. A certificate of deposit (CD) is a special kind of bank deposit that generally earns more interest than a savings account. When you buy a CD from your bank, you agree to keep the money in the bank for a certain amount of time, usually six months to five years. The amount of interest paid on your CD depends on how long you agree to keep your money in the bank.

The bank must give you your money back when you ask for it, but if you withdraw a CD before it matures, you generally pay a penalty. If something happens to the bank and it can't pay, your deposit is generally insured by the U.S. government up to $100,000.

808. Money market funds keep your cash available while often earning more interest than savings and NOW accounts. Many people who once used passbook savings have switched to money market accounts, although they are not insured like the savings accounts.

The minimum balance is usually about $1,000, and transfer and withdrawal are easy. The amount of interest earned fluctuates based on what the fund has earned by investing the pool of money assembled from you and other investors. The rate often hovers near the amount paid on a six-month U.S. Treasury bill.

The amount paid in one bank's fund may vary from the amount paid by other banks, so shop around. The income from money market funds is taxable. If you are in a high tax bracket, check into money market funds that invest in tax-free municipal securities.

809. Along with certificates of deposit, U.S. government-backed securities are among the safest investments available. The federal government doesn't pay top interest rates, but the rate usually beats CDs and sometimes money markets. You're also compensated in reduced risk. Interest is paid on indicated dates, and at maturity, you'll get your initial investment back plus interest.

The money you earn on Treasury securities is subject to federal income tax but not state and local taxes. You can purchase Treasury offerings from a broker or bank for a fee, or you can buy them yourself directly from the government through an auction bidding process when they are issued. To find out more, contact:

Bureau of the Public Debt
Securities Transactions Branch
U.S. Treasury
Washington, DC 20226
800-366-3144

810. Treasury bills—"T-bills," in the industry—can be bought for as short a time as thirteen weeks or for as long as fifty-two weeks. The minimum investment is $10,000, and additional bills can be bought in smaller amounts.

T-bills are favorites with banks, corporations, and millionaires with extra cash, because they are a vehicle for storing large amounts of money for short periods of time. If quick cash is needed for an emergency, T-bills can be sold on the open market.

811. Treasury notes are for longer-term investing—say, two to ten years. Two- to three-year notes require a minimum investment of $5,000. Five- to ten-year notes can be had for a minimum of $1,000.

Treasury bonds are long-term securities that go from ten to thirty years. Sometimes they win, sometimes they lose, compared with investments in other securities. When interest rates go up, those who are holding these long-term bonds with lower interest rates are usually hurt. But the opposite can be true, too.

For more details about treasury notes and bonds, or other offerings, contact:

Federal Reserve Bank of Philadelphia
Public Information/Publications
P.O. Box 66
Philadelphia, PA 19105
215-574-6675: general information
215-574-6580: current offerings
202-874-4000: Bureau of the Public Debt and Public Information Center

812. U.S. savings bonds aren't just for kids anymore.

For a long time these low-cost bonds, sold through banks, paid very low rates. Now the rates have risen, and you can get bonds that pay just a bit less than Treasury securities.

The payout is now close to that of the interest you would earn on a CD. The interest is exempt from state and local taxes. No commission is charged, and you can invest as little as $50. Savings bonds are not traded on the open market like Treasury bonds.

The downside of savings bonds is that they can't be redeemed until six months after buying, and they can't be sold or used as collateral for loans. You also can't buy more than $30,000 worth in one year. It is also difficult to know their value at any given moment, and often a trip to the bank is required in order to find out.

Stolen or lost bonds are replaceable at no cost. Simply go to your issuing bank and fill out Form PD 1048, then wait for your replacement. Or write to the Bureau of the Public Debt, Parkersburg, WV 26106.

813. The two types of savings bonds are EE and HH. EE bonds are the most common and are available in denominations of from $50 to $10,000. They are sold at a discount of 50 percent. If you buy a $500 bond, for example, you put down $250, keep the bond until maturity, then collect $500.

Federal taxes are paid on EE bonds only when the bonds are cashed in. Financial planners sometimes consider EE bonds a sort of IRA.

HH bonds can be bought only by exchanging matured EE bonds for them; in that case the income earned from the EE bonds is still tax-deferred. HH bonds mature in ten years. Like other bonds, and unlike EEs, they pay interest twice a year and are taxable when that interest is paid.

814. For more information on savings bonds, contact:

Office of Public Affairs
U.S. Savings Bonds Division
Department of the Treasury
1111 18th St. NW, Suite 403
Washington, DC 20226
Ask for Table PD 3600, a listing of the current market value of issued savings bonds.

Consumer Information Center
P.O. Box 100
Pueblo, CO 81009
Ask for "The Savings Bonds Question and Answer Book."

800-USA-BONDS
This number gives current rate information on U.S. savings bonds.

Now That You're Retired, Where's the Money Coming From?

815. So the day has finally come—no more nine-to-five grind—you're retired. The next phase of your financial life begins, and it's time to start spending some of the cash you've put away.

Your postretirement finances are likely to be almost as complicated as your preretirement ones—at least in the first year, until you get the hang of things. Chances are, you'll have several sources of income in retirement: Social Security; your company's pension plan; and whatever savings you've put away yourself. Plus you'll be eligible for Medicare. Perhaps you want to keep working in some fashion, starting a new career or pursuing an old one part-time. Maybe it's time to sell your house and get the cash out of your largest hard asset. Perhaps your spouse has not yet retired, and you need to figure your retirement finances in relation to his or her continued earning.

Social Security

816. Afraid to count on Social Security as a source of income, after all the media reports about its troubles? Don't be. During the late 1990s Washington was concerned about Social Security reform, but the program isn't going to run out of money tomorrow. There will probably be some changes to account for the fact that there will be more people claiming Social Security in the coming years (that is, the baby boomers) and living longer, to boot. But an August 1997 issue of *Fortune* magazine advised in a headline, "Don't Panic. Social Security Will Be There for You."

817. The most likely change to Social Security is that the rich will pay more and get less when they retire. Currently, Social Security taxes—6.2 percent—are paid on the first $65,400 of income during the working years. Look for that ceiling to go up, and for the wealthy to be able to draw fewer dollars when they retire.

Taxes on Social Security income are also likely to go up in the future. In 1997 Social Security recipients with incomes over $34,000 for an individual, and $44,000 for a couple, paid taxes on up to 85 percent of their Social Security income. Lawmakers are likely to want to tax more of that income in the future.

818. The retirement age will be going up—maybe even to age 69. If you were born before 1938, you will be eligible for full Social Security benefits at age 65. However, beginning in the year 2000, the age at which full benefits are payable starts to gradually increase for people born in 1938 or later. It increases until it reaches 67 for those born in 1960 and later. For example, if you were born in 1940, your full retirement benefits are due at age 65½. If you were born in 1950, your full retirement is age 66.

819. You don't get back every dollar you pay into Social Security. Here's how your dollar gets divided up.

- 68 cents goes to a trust fund that pays monthly benefits to retirees and their families, and to about 8 million widows, widowers, and children of workers who have died.
- 19 cents goes to a trust fund that pays for Medicare.
- 12 cents goes to a trust fund that pays benefits to people with disabilities and their families.
- 1 cent goes to administrative costs for all the trusts described above.

820. Ninety-two percent of older Americans receive Social Security benefits. In 1996 the average payment was $745 a month for a single person and $1,256 for a couple.

The Social Security Administration has more than thirteen hundred offices in cities and towns across America. The SSA and the Health Care Financing Administration (the Medicare people) produce many publications and fact sheets designed to explain these complex programs. Here are some free booklets that you can pick up at an office, or receive by calling 800-772-1213.

"Retirement" (Publication 05-10035)
"Disability" (05-10029)
"Survivors" (05-10084)
"Medicare" (05-10043)
"SSI" (05-11000)
"Benefits for Children with Disabilities" (05-10026)

821. Don't fall for official-sounding agencies offering to send you Social Security information for a fee. It's all free from the government itself, and you can get it yourself by calling.

Another warning: In order to prevent your Social Security number from being used fraudulently, be careful of whom you give the number out to. In addition to its official uses by the Social Security Administration, the number is often used by banks, insurance companies, and many other business and government agencies for record-keeping and identification purposes. You can legally refuse to provide your Social Security number to anyone, especially a credit card company.

822. These days, you can elect to receive Social Security benefits as early as age 62. Taking your benefit before your full retirement age has both advantages and disadvantages. The advantage is that you can collect benefits for a longer period of time. The disadvantage is that your benefit is thereby permanently reduced. If you start receiving your benefits early, they are reduced five-ninths of 1 percent for each month before your full retire-

ment age. For example, if your full retirement age is 65 and you sign up for Social Security when you're 64, you will receive 93$\frac{1}{3}$ percent of your full benefit. At 62, you would get 80 percent.

823. Signing up for your retirement benefits means you have certain rights and responsibilities. When you start receiving Social Security, you are obligated to let the agency know when something happens that might affect those benefits. Let them know if:

- You move
- You get married or divorced
- You change your name
- Your income or earnings change
- You become a parent
- You are imprisoned
- You leave the United States
- A Social Security beneficiary dies or becomes unable to manage his or her funds

Once you start receiving benefits, you will be sent a booklet that explains your rights and responsibilities.

824. Continuing to work full-time beyond retirement age—and delaying Social Security benefits—can increase the benefits you eventually get.

Your extra income usually increases your average earnings, and the higher your average earnings, the higher your Social Security benefit will be. In addition, a special credit is given to people who delay retirement. This credit, which is a percentage added to your Social Security bene-fit, varies depending on your date of birth. For people turning 65 in 1995, the rate was 4.5 percent per year. The rate gradually increases in future years, until it reaches 8 percent per year for those who turn 65 in 2008 or later.

825. Once you begin receiving Social Security payments, the law limits the amount of money you can earn at a job and still keep those benefits. This provision only affects people under the age of 70. Limits on earnings go up annually, often by about $1,000 a year. Here are the figures that applied in 1997.

• If you are under age 65, you can earn up to $8,640 and still collect all your Social Security benefits. For every $2 you earn over that amount, $1 will be withheld from your Social Security benefits.

• If you are aged 65 through 69, you can earn up to $13,500 and still collect all your benefits. For every $3 you earn over that, $1 will be withheld from your Social Security.

826. A surrogate can be appointed to take care of Social Security benefits for a recipient unable to handle his or her own financial affairs. The surrogate, called a representative payee, is usually a relative, friend, or other interested party. All benefits are paid to the representative's name on behalf of the beneficiary.

A representative payee's responsibilities include:

• Using benefits for the personal care and well-being of the beneficiary. Excess funds must be saved for the beneficiary.

• Keeping the Social Security Administration informed of any events that affect the beneficiary's eligibility

• Filing a periodic accounting report with the government to show how you spent or saved the benefits you were paid

For more information, call or visit any Social Security office and ask for "A Guide for Representative Payees," Publication No. 05-10076.

827. Social Security benefits are not just for the worker who has retired. They extend to his or her survivors, including spouse, divorced spouse, children, and dependent parents.

Frequently, because women often earn less than men, a spouse's survivor's benefits are greater than benefits a woman accrued for herself in her own working life. Social Security rules allow a person to receive the larger of the two payments, but not both.

In fact, the value of the survivor's insurance under Social Security is often more than that of a commercial life insurance policy. For more information, contact Social Security at 800-772-1213.

828. Get Social Security benefits from—or give them to—a former spouse. Survivor's benefits are available to divorced widows and widowers, even if the former spouse has remarried. Qualified ex-spouses will be eligible for benefits if:

• They are at least 60 years old, or 50 if disabled, and were married for at least ten years

• They are of any age, and caring for a child who is eligible for benefits from the parent

• They are not eligible for an equal amount of, or more, benefits on their own

• They are not currently married, unless the marriage took place after age 60 (or 50 if disabled) and aren't receiving equal or higher survivor's benefits from a remarriage

If an ex-spouse does receive benefits, this will *not* affect the amount of benefits payable to other survivors. Even if you've had several spouses, each may receive benefits without its affecting the benefits your present spouse receives.

829. By January 1, 1999, everybody receiving Social Security benefits will have their checks deposited directly into their bank accounts. The direct-deposit system is being phased in gradually: People who retire after May 1, 1997, will automatically be signed up, and those who retired prior to that will be able to elect the service if they wish.

The idea of direct deposit is safety: If benefits go directly to the bank, there's less chance a check will be stolen or misplaced. The service should also make funds available more quickly.

Pensions

830. Pension plans are going the way of the dinosaurs. While about 60 percent of all large companies still have them, the trend these days is for employers to ignore the expensive pensions that once benefited workers who

stayed with the company for their entire careers. Instead, such employers offer sponsored retirement savings plans, such as 401(k)s. Even companies that have maintained pension plans have cut the amount contributed and made it harder to qualify.

But that's not necessarily bad news for workers who make frequent job changes. Retirement savings plans move with you when you leave an employer; pensions do not—although you can still collect from a former employer's pension plan when you retire.

831. For some, employer pension plans may provide a significant portion of their retirement income. A pension is money put into a fund or trust by your employer in your behalf during your working career. The money is invested and is later used to pay benefits to retired employees who meet certain requirements. Many pensions are paid out in the form of an annuity—that is, equal payments over a lifetime, often calculated on salary and number of years of service. Other plans allow employees to take a lump sum at the time of retirement or a combination of annuity and lump sum.

The Employment Benefit Research Institute estimates that a person who works for three different employers for ten years each over a thirty-year period can expect roughly two-thirds the pension benefits of another employee earning a similar salary but who worked for a single employer over the same period.

832. Military and civil service pension plans are very valuable. The benefits of military pensions are often more generous than those of others. First of all, they allow soldiers and sailors to retire after twenty years of active uniformed service, regardless of their age. They also pay survivor's benefits to the mother of the retiree's children, and to spouses, if they were married to the military retiree for at least one year. Unlike standard pension plans, which are tax exempt, military pension benefits can be taxed by the IRS and sometimes by the state.

Civil service employees are also well rewarded when it comes to pension benefits. Longtime federal employees, for example, can expect to receive about 60 percent of their final salaries in pension benefits. However, special regulations to qualify for a pension often apply.

833. In 1997 a federal audit found that thousands of Americans don't receive correct pension payments.

That's because of errors made by their former employers, who had little incentive to get things right as they tried to comply with complex pension laws. About a third of those underpaid were shortchanged by at least $1,000.

It is advisable to take personal responsibility for your pension payment. Before you retire, ask in writing for a copy of the pension plan, any explanatory employee booklets, and a written calculation of your individual benefits. You might want to have a financial planner or pension consultant review the information, especially if you have elected a lump-sum payment.

To answer questions about the fairness of your pension, contact the federal Pension and

Welfare Benefits Administration. The address and phone number are below (item 847).

834. Although you accrue retirement benefits while participating in a pension plan, you don't have a right to them unless you are "vested." Being *vested* means having the right to collect benefits.

A worker can participate in a pension plan within six months after turning 21, and after working one thousand hours during a year's time. Vesting, however, takes much longer. In most cases, you must work five years for the same company to receive pension benefits. A less common type of vesting allows workers to become partially vested after three years, and gradually more so after four, five, and six years. With such a plan, full vesting occurs after seven years of service.

Not all work time may count toward vesting. Breaks in service of longer than five years, or not working enough hours in a calendar year, can cause you to lose credit toward vesting. Military service, age, and other changes may also affect vesting.

835. A company usually has one of two types of traditional pension plans. A defined benefit plan—the most common type—gives you a specific amount of money when you retire, calculated by a formula based on your income and years of service. An integrated benefit plan takes Social Security payments into consideration when calculating your pension benefits.

The amount of integrated pension benefits depends on the formula used by the employer; it isn't unusual for a monthly pension check to be reduced by as much as half. The integration formula used to determine your original pension benefit isn't affected by any changes in Social Security, such as cost-of-living increases.

836. There are several ways of calculating pension payments under a defined benefit plan. Probably the most generous are the *final average pay* method and the *highest average pay* method. They are what they sound like: Benefits, adjusted for years of service, are calculated on (1) an average of your earnings over the last three to five years before retirement; or (2) the years of your highest earnings, which may not necessarily be the same as your salary at retirement.

The *career average pay* method takes into account the salary you received during *all* your years at a company—including the low-paying first years. This calculation generally results in lower benefits.

With the *cash balance* plan, the company invests, say, 5 percent of your salary annually; when you retire, you receive either a lump sum or the equivalent amount paid in installments.

837. You'll probably be eligible for a full pension at age 65, although some plans allow you to collect full benefits earlier. If you keep working for the same employer past 65, your pension will be deferred and will likely be larger when you do receive it. If you keep working under the plan past age 70, the law requires that you start receiving pension payments by April 1 of the year after you reach age 70.

When you're ready to apply for your pen-

sion benefits, write to the person in charge of your plan. You should receive a reply within ninety days. It can take an additional ninety days to determine your eligibility. If your plan manager states that you are not eligible for pension benefits, he or she must give you a written explanation as to why. Procedures for appealing your claim should be included with the papers that describe your plan.

838. Pension benefits can be paid out in different ways. They usually come as monthly checks, received over the lifetimes of the retiree and his or her spouse.

Some plans, however, offer benefits over a defined number of years, or as payment in a onetime lump sum. (If the total value of your pension is $3,500 or less, your plan can require that you take it as a lump-sum payment.)

Lump-sum payments often have tax consequences, unlike other payment mechanisms, which are tax exempt. Unless the money is put directly into an individual retirement account (IRA) or another employer's plan within sixty days, 20 percent will be withheld automatically for federal taxes.

If you're younger than $59\frac{1}{2}$ when you receive the lump sum, you'll also have to pay a 10 percent tax penalty, although there are some exceptions to this rule.

839. So how do you know whether to take your pension as a lump sum or paid out over time?

Experience shows that when employees are given the lump-sum option, they take the money and run. And employers like that just fine, because they get to take that liability off their books right away. To know for sure if a lump sum is the right choice, you would need to know how long you will live. But here are some other considerations that might help you decide.

• If you take a lump-sum payment, you'll have to manage the money yourself, attempting to ensure sufficient funds for your lifetime as well as an inheritance for your family.

• You must consider how the amount of the lump sum will be calculated, what the tax implications are, what the current interest rates are, and what the interest payments will be.

• If your pension plan has a generous cost-of-living escalator on regular pension payments, you may receive more in the long run than with a lump-sum payment.

840. Most pension plans have a joint and survivor annuity. That means that a pension is payable over the lifetimes of both spouses, not just the lifetime of the retiree. A person selecting this option will receive a lower amount each month during his or her lifetime, but at the retiree's death, the spouse continues to receive a portion of the pension benefit for life.

There are drawbacks to this plan. One is that it reduces the worker's monthly benefits to pay for later benefits to the surviving spouse. And, in cases of divorce, the courts treat a pension as an asset of the marriage that can be divided as part of a divorce settlement. This option also allows courts to award survivor's benefits to the divorcing spouse.

841. Excellent sources of information on pension rights after divorce are: *Your Pension Rights at Divorce: What a Woman Needs to Know* ($14.95) and *Protecting Your Pension Money* ($6.00). Both are published by Pension Publications, 918 16th St. NW, Suite 704, Washington, DC 20006.

842. While you're attempting to decide on survivor benefits, your insurance agent may recommend a "pension maximization" plan. *The Wall Street Journal Lifetime Guide to Money* (Hyperion, 1997) advises just saying no to such a suggestion.

The idea behind pension maximization is that you would cover yourself only via your pension—keeping monthly payments as high as possible—and then buy an insurance product to cover your spouse's needs after your death. The problem is that the cost of insurance when you reach retirement age is so high that it's hard to afford enough to do what survivor pension benefits would.

843. If you go back to work after your pension has started, you may lose your benefits—but you may not. In some cases, pension plans are legally permitted to end your benefits if you return to work after you have begun receiving them. Plans differ, and the rules usually depend on the age at which you go back to work, whether one or more employers pay into your plan, and how many hours you work each month.

The rules about pensions and work are more stringent for people under 65. If you are over 65 and your payments stop because you go back to work, payments must start up again when you stop working.

844. Here are some guidelines pertaining to pensions and work.

- If you are over age 65 and work fewer than forty hours a month, you can generally work anywhere and still receive your full pension.
- If you are over 65, you can work more than forty hours a month without losing your benefits if only one employer pays into your pension plan.
- If you are over 65 and more than one employer pays into your plan, you can work and continue to receive your full pension, with one exception: You may not work at a job generally done by other plan members in the local area.

845. By law, your pension plan administrator is required to provide you with a clear description of your plan, free of charge. The description will detail the plan's rules, including eligibility requirements and information about applying for benefits.

If you write and ask for information, the plan administrator is required to respond within thirty days. And as long as you're writing, ask for an individual benefits statement that shows your accrued benefit. It will help you estimate what will be paid out when you retire.

846. A pension plan is secure only if the company is. Companies in serious financial trou-

ble can close down their pension plans as long as they notify workers about what's going on and protect assets already in the pension program. If that happens, some benefits may be paid by the Pension Benefit Guarantee Corporation (PBGC). However, only pension plans that are insured by the PBGC are protected. Not all plans are.

Plan rules can also change. Some companies have started limiting pension payments to 50 percent of salary, no matter how long an employee has worked for the company. The 50 percent cap generally applies only to the salary earned in the years *after* this new plan rule takes effect.

To contact the PBGC, call or write:

Pension Benefit Guaranty Corporation
1200 K St. NW
Washington, DC 20005
202-326-4000

847. There are several places to go for help if you think there's a problem with your pension plan. The mission of the U.S. Department of Labor's Pension and Welfare Benefits Administration (PWBA) is to protect the pension, health, and other benefits of participants and beneficiaries of private-sector employee benefit plans.

The PWBA sets rules for benefit plans to help keep assets secure. It investigates misuse of plan money and assists plan participants in understanding their rights as well as their obligations. The PWBA can also provide individualized assistance through the pension maze.

Contact the PWBA at:

U.S. Department of Labor
Pension and Welfare Benefits
 Administration
Division of Public Information
200 Constitution Ave. NW, Room N-5666
Washington, DC 20210
202-219-8771

848. The federal Employee Retirement Income Security Act (ERISA) protects pensions and welfare plans from financial mismanagement and misuse of assets. If you think your pension money is being mismanaged, call the Department of Labor regional office nearest you:

Atlanta: 404-347-4090
Boston: 617-424-4950
Chicago: 312-353-0900
Cincinnati: 606-578-4680
Dallas: 214-767-6831
Detroit: 313-226-7450
Kansas City: 816-426-5131
Los Angeles: 818-583-7862
Miami: 305-651-6464
New York: 212-399-5191
Philadelphia: 215-596-1134
St. Louis: 314-539-2691
San Francisco: 415-744-6700
Seattle: 206-553-4244
Washington, DC: 202-254-7013

849. Other sources of information and help:

Employee Plans Technical and Actuarial
Division

Internal Revenue Service
1111 Constitution Ave. NW, Room 6526
Washington, DC 20224
202-622-6074, 202-622-6075

American Association of Retired Persons
Work Force Programs Department
601 E St. NW
Washington, DC 20049

Veteran's Benefits

850. If you or your spouse served in the military, you may be eligible for many benefits through the Veterans' Administration (VA). That includes pensions and medical assistance. Eligibility for most VA benefits is based on discharge from full-time service as a member of the Army, Navy, Air Force, Marines, or Coast Guard, or as a commissioned officer in the Public Health Service, the Environmental Services Administration, or the National Oceanic and Atmospheric Administration.

Certain benefits and medical care require wartime service. The Veterans' Administration recognizes the following war periods: World War I, World War II, Korean conflict, Vietnam era, and Persian Gulf War.

851. When filing a claim with the VA for the first time, you must submit a copy of your service discharge form. That is, form DD214. It verifies your dates of service and type of discharge. If you do not have the form, you must provide your full name, military service number, branch of service, and dates of service.

There are many sources of information about veteran's benefits. Veterans' Administration counselors can help, as can state governments which have offices devoted to administering veteran programs and helping veterans in filing claims.

The booklet "Federal Benefits for Veterans and Dependents" (VA Pamphlet 80-95-1) is available by writing to the U.S. Department of Veterans Affairs, Washington, DC 20420. The Veterans' Administration home page on the Internet is *http://www.va.gov/*. The benefits number is 800-827-1000.

Medicare

852. Medicare is our country's health insurance program, designed primarily for older Americans. It can make a big difference to the cost of your life after 65.

To be eligible for Medicare benefits, you must be 65 or older (although certain disabled people under 65 are eligible, too). The program provides basic protection against the cost of health care, but it doesn't cover *all* your medical expenses, nor does it cover the cost of most long-term care.

Medicare and Medicaid are two different things. In general, Medicare is for older Americans, and Medicaid is for low-income Americans of any age.

853. There are two parts to Medicare:

• Hospital insurance (also called *Part A*). This is free once you reach age 65; it is financed by the portion of the payroll tax that also pays for Social Security.

• Medical insurance (also called *Part B*). This requires enrollment, and the payment of monthly premiums ($42.50 per month in 1996). About 95 percent of those eligible choose to enroll.

854. Medicare's PART A helps to cover much of the expenses incurred by a hospital stay. Part A—hospital insurance—helps cover the cost of inpatient care in a hospital or skilled nursing facility, or for care from a home health agency or hospice.

If you are admitted to a hospital, you must first pay the annual $760 deductible. After that, Medicare will pay for a semiprivate room, meals, regular nursing services, lab tests, X rays, and the costs for the operating room, intensive care, the recovery room, drugs, and all other medically necessary services and supplies.

In a skilled nursing facility, services covered under Medicare include a semiprivate room, meals, regular nursing services, rehabilitation services, drugs, medical supplies, and medical appliances.

855. If you opt for Medicare's PART B—the voluntary medical insurance—it will cover doctor's fees, after a $100 annual deductible. It also covers outpatient hospital care, clinical laboratory tests, medical services, medical supplies, and durable medical equipment.

Doctor's services are covered whether you are treated in a physician's office, in a hospital, or in an outpatient facility. Covered services include surgical services and diagnostic tests, X rays that are part of the treatment, medical supplies furnished in a doctor's of-

fice, and drugs that can't be self-adminis-
tered.

856. Some doctors "accept assignment" from Medicare.

That means they agree to accept the rate that
Medicare pays for a procedure, without charging
the patient anything in excess of that. Doctors
who do not "accept assignment" are not permitted to charge more than 15 percent above the
Medicare amount.

In either case, your doctor's office will submit
the Medicare paperwork for you after your visit.
Most will also file the paperwork for "medigap" insurance ("medigap" is an additional insurance
that can be purchased to cover whatever
Medicare won't—see Chapter 10 for more on this).

857. Terminally ill Medicare beneficiaries can choose hospice care instead of regular Medicare benefits for traditional management of their illness.

A Medicare-approved hospice generally
provides most of its services in the patient's
home. There is no deductible payment for
these benefits. Covered services include
physician services, nursing care, medical appliances and supplies, drugs for pain and
symptom relief, short-term inpatient care,
medical social services, physical therapy, oc-
cupational therapy, speech/language therapy, pathology services, and dietary and
other counseling.

Copayments are required for prescription
drugs for pain relief and symptom management at a cost of up to, but not more than,
$5 for each prescription.

858. Medicare covers the total cost of both flu and pneumonia shots.

You don't have to pay any coinsurance or meet a
deductible. Both types of shots are a very good
idea, since flu and pneumonia together are the
sixth leading cause of death in the United
States, and the elderly are especially vulnerable. The Public Health Service recommends that
everyone 65 and older get a pneumonia shot—
one may protect you for a lifetime.

859. While Medicare is like money in the bank for a large portion of your medical expenses, there are many things it *doesn't* cover.

Items
not covered include custodial care, eyeglasses, hearing aids and examinations to
prescribe or fit them, phone calls made from
your hospital room, TV in your hospital
room, and most over-the-counter and prescription medicines.

The exception to the last is prescription
drugs for pain relief and symptom management, which are partially covered. Patients
can be charged 5 percent of reasonable cost,
but not more than $5 for each prescription.

Medicare also doesn't pay for cosmetic
surgery, most immunizations, dental care,
routine foot care, and routine physical
checkups. Although some personal care services—for instance, bathing assistance and
eating assistance—can be covered as part of
any skilled care that is given, they are never
covered alone, except under the hospice
benefit.

As a result of these "gaps" in Medicare
coverage, many people buy an additional insurance, called "medigap," to fill in the holes.

860. Other extra costs that Medicare doesn't cover:

• All charges for care outside the United States and its territories, except in certain instances in Canada and Mexico

• All charges for services of naturopaths, Christian Science practitioners, immediate relatives, or charges imposed by members of your household who might be involved in caring for you

• All charges for the first three pints of whole blood, or units of packed cells, used in each year in connection with covered services, unless the three pints are replaced by donation to a blood bank

861. To be eligible for Medicare once you have turned 65, you must have worked for ten years, or be married to an eligible person. Actually, it is possible to receive Part A benefits even if you have *not* worked for ten years. It's called premium hospital insurance, and it costs $187 a month (in 1997). To be eligible, you have to have worked for between thirty and forty quarters (a quarter is any three-month period) in a job covered by Medicare.

You should apply for Medicare three months before your 65th birthday by contacting your local Social Security office. Usually very little needs to be done. If you have already applied for, or are already receiving, Social Security benefits when you turn 65, you'll automatically get a Medicare card in the mail. The Medicare card will show that you are eligible for both Part A (Medicare hospital insurance) and Part B (medical insurance) benefits.

862. You can sign up for Medicare's voluntary PART B during the general enrollment period each year. It runs from January 1 through March 31. But in order to sign up for Part B, you have to already have Part A. Part B coverage will begin July 1 of the year you enroll. There may be a late enrollment surcharge of 10 percent for each twelve-month period during which you could have had Part B, but did not choose to enroll.

863. Medicare beneficiaries can choose how they receive hospital, doctor, and other health care services covered by the program. In other words, you can choose between traditional fee-for-service care or managed care. This choice can affect the amount of money you pay for these services. Most people use the traditional fee-for-service system, visiting a hospital or doctor of their choice and paying any cost beyond the amount Medicare pays.

864. More and more people are turning to health maintenance organizations (HMOs). These are also known as *managed care plans* or *prepaid* or *coordinated care plans.* HMOs offer comprehensive medical services provided by a network of health care providers. Medicare coverage is the same under both systems. The differences include how the benefits are delivered, how and when payment is made, and the amount of out-of-pocket expenses you incur.

865. Be alert for Medicare fraud and abuse. If you believe that a doctor, hospital, or other provider of health care services performed unnecessary or inappropriate services, or that they billed Medicare for services you did not receive, report this information immediately to the Medicare carrier or intermediary that handles your claims.

It's generally against the law for a doctor or supplier of medical equipment to fail to charge you the Medicare deductible and coinsurance amounts. These amounts *can* be waived, but only after careful consideration of a particular patient's financial hardship. If a doctor or supplier offers to waive payments without considering your individual circumstances, or when you haven't asked to have the payments waived, immediately report the offer to the Medicare carrier or intermediary.

866. To obtain help, and for more information about Medicare, contact:

Health Care Financing Administration
6325 Security Blvd.
Baltimore, MD 21207

Group Health Association of America
1129 20th St. NW, Suite 600
Washington, DC 20036

Health Insurance Association of America
1025 Connecticut Ave. NW
Washington, DC 20036

Medicare Beneficiaries Defense Fund
1460 Broadway, 8th Floor
New York, NY 10036

There's Income in Your House

867. If you own your home, it's probably the most valuable thing you own.
If you bought a tract house in the 1950s for $10,000 or $15,000, it's probably worth ten to twenty times as much now. And even if you're still paying off a mortgage, chances are you built up significant equity in the house.

As you think about your financial picture just before and just after retirement, you might consider selling your house and doing something else with the cash. If you can't bear the thought of moving, there are ways to convert the value of the home to cash, continue to live there, and fix up the place at the same time.

868. There's a onetime, capital gains tax break for homeowners over 55 who sell their dwellings.
For that age bracket, there's no tax on the first $125,000 of capital gains for an individual or a couple selling a house. Another factor to consider is that after you die, the value of your house may make your estate so valuable that your survivors will have to pay estate taxes. An accountant or tax attorney will be able to give you more details on the full ramifications of selling your house.

869. For more information about selling your house, contact:

Consumer Information Center
Department 568Z
Pueblo, CO 81009

Ask for "A Home of Your Own: Helpful Advice."

U.S. Department of Housing and Urban Development
451 7th St. SW, Room 5100
Washington, DC 20410
800-424-8590

American Association of Homes and Services for the Aging
901 E St. NW, Suite 500
Washington, DC 20004

Federal Trade Commission
Public Reference, Room 130
Washington, DC 20580

870. Don't rush into a home equity loan, in spite of what those pushy television commercials say.

There can be better options.

Home equity loans are made by banks and other lenders against the value of your house—that is, the equity you have in it after making years of mortgage payments. Such loans usually work much like a mortgage, with fixed interest rates and payments to make every month. The interest on what you borrow, up to a loan of $100,000, is tax deductible.

871. A home equity loan will reduce the value of your home. That's something to keep in mind if you think you might sell your house later on. Another drawback is that if you are unable to make the monthly payments, you could lose the house.

If you decide on a home equity loan, compare the offerings from at least four banking institutions. Look at the annual percentage rate, points (up-front fees), closing costs, and other fees, and, if you get a variable-interest-rate loan, the index for any rate changes.

872. A line of credit against your house can mean having cash for an emergency or for big repairs on the dwelling itself. Arranged through a bank or other lender with the value of your house to guarantee it, it is rather like credit card debt in that you pay interest only if you use the money. Often, the line of credit is attached to a checking account, and you write a check when you need to use your line of credit. Interest rates can vary over time.

Lines of credit are often easier to set up when you have a regular salary, so if they interest you, get one in order before you retire.

873. Reverse mortgages enable older homeowners to convert the value of a home into cash—without having to sell the house *or* make regular loan payments. A reverse mortgage (RM) is also called a home equity conversion (HEC), and as of 1997, they were available in all states but Alaska, South Dakota, and Texas.

A reverse mortgage is a loan, offered by private, public, and federally insured lenders, that provides money to a homeowner either in monthly payments or as a line of credit when requested by the borrower. Neither the loan nor the interest on it has to be repaid until the borrower sells, moves from the home, or dies. As a result, reverse mortgages can provide monthly cash for as long as the homeowner-borrower lives.

Generally, the older the borrower and the greater the property's value, the larger the amount that can be borrowed.

874. However, reverse mortgages are usually considered to be a last-resort source of cash from a house. They can be more expensive than a conventional mortgage, with higher interest rates and up-front fees. And it is always possible to lose the house, or for monthly funds to be cut off. Reverse mortgages can also be hard to find, with not every lender offering them. Before committing yourself, be sure to check with a lawyer or accountant who understands the process.

875. If you live to the end of a reverse mortgage, you may have to sell your house in order to pay off the debt. When the house is sold under these conditions, the homeowner or heirs keep any profit above the loan debt, but the house is not available to pass on to heirs. Should the homeowner die before the end of the loan term, the loan must still be repaid, usually by sale of the house.

876. To qualify for a reverse mortgage, a borrower must usually be aged 62 or over. He or she must also own and occupy a single-family, one-unit home with little or no mortgage balance, and maintain the home as a primary residence during the term of the reverse mortgage. Any mortgage balance will be paid off with the reverse mortgage. There are no asset limitations to joining in this program.

877. There are several types of reverse mortgages. *Fixed-term* RMs are uninsured mortgages that provide cash payments to a borrower for a predetermined length of time, generally from three to ten years, as selected by the borrower. Repayment is required at the end of the loan term. Minimum ages for eligible borrowers range from 65 to 70. Fixed-term RMs are available in several states.

Self-insured RMs provide monthly payments for as long as the borrower lives, even if both spouses who own the home together have to move from the property. The ages of eligibility for this type range from 60 to 70. This plan also includes an immediate or deferred annuity, purchased with loan proceeds, that provides monthly income for life. However, proceeds from the annuity are taxable and can affect eligibility for benefits from public programs such as Supplemental Security Income (SSI) and Medicaid.

There are also *federally insured* RMs available through the Federal Housing Administration (FHA), banks, and other lending institutions. These are insured through the FHA. For this national plan, borrowers must be aged 62 or over, own and occupy a single-family, one-unit home with little or no mortgage balance, and maintain the home as a principal residence for the duration of the reverse mortgage.

878. For more information on reverse mortgages, contact AARP. It provides a booklet that lists lenders state by state, along with their names and phone numbers. Ask for publication D13253 ("Reverse Mortgage

Lenders List"). AARP has many other excellent books and fact sheets on the subject. Ask for "Home-Made Money: Consumer's Guide to Home Equity Conversion" (D12894), "Relocation Tax Guide" (D13400), and "Reverse Angle" (a bulletin providing updates on reverse mortgages). Their number is 800-424-3410.

879. Sale-leasebacks are another way to get cash out of your house. Businesses do it with their real estate all the time. With a sale-leaseback plan, the homeowner sells the house to an investor, who then immediately rents it back to the seller on a long-term—often lifetime—lease.

The lease contract spells out the rights and responsibilities of each party. Typically, the new owner takes over expenses such as taxes, repairs, and insurance. The seller receives a down payment, plus regular monthly payments, through a land contract or deed of trust.

A sale-leaseback transaction can be drawn up by a knowledgeable real estate attorney and doesn't generally involve a lending institution. Since there are significant tax implications from this transaction, consult your financial adviser for details.

880. For more information on sale-leasebacks, contact:

National Center for Home Equity
Conversion
7373 147th St.
Apple Valley, MN 55124
612-953-4474

881. If you don't want to sell your house or take a loan against it, maybe you can turn it into a moneymaker. You may think that "rooms for rent" went out decades ago, but with high rents and the growing number of single people, renting a room in a house is making a comeback. There may also be the possibility of converting part of your house into a rental apartment.

Think about the kind of renter you'd like to share your home with. Perhaps a young adult will shovel the walks and walk the dog in exchange for a portion of the rent. Many older adults with a room to rent advertise for someone nearer their own age, who can then become a companion.

882. Before going much further, check your local zoning ordinances. Make sure you can legally convert one or more rooms into rental property. Also check with your area agency on aging, because in some places, retired people get a special dispensation to earn rental money from their homes.

Think logically about your house: Is it suitable for sharing with a roomer or an apartment dweller? Is there an outside entrance that could be turned into a private entrance? Will it be necessary to add a small kitchen or an additional bathroom? You may have to put some money into adapting the house—make sure you'll make at least that much back on the rent. Rental income will also have tax implications for you, so you should have a discussion about it with an accountant.

Frauds, Swindles, and Scams

883. The riskiest investment of all is a fraud, swindle, or scam. There are scam artists everywhere, and older adults can be particularly vulnerable to them. As an 80-year-old Narrowsburg, New York, woman said in a June 1997 story in the *New York Times* about a telemarketing scam, "I've been a widow for nineteen years. It's very lonely. They were nice on the phone. They became my friends." The scam cost her thousands.

884. **Here are some of the most common financial scams.**

• Investment frauds offering precious stones, metals, coins, or real estate. The con artist may pay false profits initially to dupe the victim and gain credibility.

• Bank audit scams involving a con artist pretending to be an investigator checking out a theft from your bank. If you reveal your account number, the con artist drains the account and disappears.

• Insurance fraud aimed at those shopping for coverage to supplement Medicare. People often buy policies that don't meet their needs.

• False billing scams, with the con artist claiming you ordered a product but haven't paid for it. They often threaten that your credit will be ruined if you don't pay.

885. Mail and phone solicitors may actually be scammers trying to get your credit card and bank account numbers. Giving out your private, important numbers increases the chance that money will be taken from you. Other swindles include sweepstakes offering free prizes—often worthless junk—as a ploy to sell an overpriced product, and sympathy scams, which play on the emotions of the bereaved. The con artist gleans the names of victims from the newspaper obituaries and then claims that the deceased family member ordered a product or service shortly before their death.

886. Home fix-it scams usually involve the offer of inexpensive repairs. They require you to pay up front for "supplies," and once payment is received, the "repairman" disappears. A variation on this trick is the repairman who charges a high rate for shoddy, inferior work and materials.

887. Telephone investment fraud is on the upswing. The operation is usually housed in what's known as a boiler room—a big room filled with high-pressure salespeople who call hundreds of prospects around the country. They may get to you because you responded to a newspaper ad or a direct-mail card for investment information. Or they may simply take your name out of the phone directory.

The subject matter of the scams is often coins, gems, art, oil and gas leases, interests in oil wells, application services for cellular telephone licenses, gold, silver, and chromium, and nuclear metals used in high-tech or defense industries. There are also many frauds tied to investments based on new, high-tech products. The con artist hopes to make it difficult for consumers to scrutinize their inflated claims of value.

888. Fraudulent telemarketers have found another way to steal your money: automatic debits from your checking account. While automatic debiting can be a legitimate payment method for your mortgage or other bills, consumers across the country are complaining about unauthorized debits from their checking accounts. If a caller asks for your checking account number, or any other information printed on your check, don't give it.

889. This new telemarketing ploy usually works this way: You get a postcard or a phone call saying you have won a free prize, or that you can qualify for a major credit card, regardless of past credit problems. If you indicate interest, the telemarketer immediately asks if you have a checking account, going on to explain the offer and making it sound too good to pass up. The goal is to persuade you to give out numbers that identify your account.

Once the fraudulent telemarketer has your checking account number, it is put on a "demand draft," which is processed much like a check. Unlike a check, however, the draft does not require your signature. When your bank receives the draft, the amount stated is taken out of your checking account and given to the telemarketer's bank. You may not know that your bank has paid the draft until you receive your next bank statement.

890. Anyone can be fooled. Con artists appeal to weaknesses such as financial worry,

greed, confusion, trust, being easily intimidated, and emotional vulnerability. Sometimes just being careful, suspicious, or skeptical is all that's necessary to avoid being swindled.

Don't sign anything unless you have read it carefully; better yet, have your lawyer read it. Swindlers often take advantage of the confusion and forgetfulness brought on by medication—they will contact you and demand payment for items you can't recall ordering. If you don't remember ordering something, don't pay for it until a third party (lawyer or family member) has checked it out. Don't give your credit card numbers or checking and saving accounts numbers over the phone, unless you have called a legitimate company to place an order. And be very careful about giving out your Social Security number.

If you are suspicious, call the police, the Better Business Bureau, or a local prosecutor's office. It's difficult to charge a slippery con artist with a crime, but certain acts can be used to obtain a civil injunction and restitution of your money.

891. Here are some additional tips.

• Remember, no legitimate salesperson will claim to offer a risk-free investment.

• Don't be pressured into buying immediately, no matter what the seller says.

• Invest only in business opportunities you know something about.

• Get all the information you can, in writing, about the investment, and then verify the data at the local library.

- Beware of testimonials from "satisfied customers." Anything can be faked.
- If it sounds too good to be true, it probably is.
- Just hang up.

892. For further information about protecting yourself from fraud, contact:

National Futures Association
Public Affairs and Education
200 W. Madison St., Suite 1600
Chicago, IL 60606
800-621-3570
Offers a direct, well-illustrated brochure on telephone swindlers.

Institute of Certified Financial Planners
10065 E. Harvard Ave., Suite 320
Denver, CO 80231
800-282-7526
Ask for "Avoiding Investment and Financial Scams: Seeking Full Disclosure Is the Key."

Chapter 10:

The Expense Side: Bargains, Credit, Insurance, and Taxes

If older adults are known for anything when it comes to spending money, it's the discount—everything from dollars off and free coffee at movie theaters and fast-food restaurants to special rates for hotels, air travel, and rental cars. Older people know how to save money on food (early bird specials), on public transportation, on admissions to cultural and sports events, and on a host of other living expenses.

American business has been and continues to be generous to the over-55 set. Business executives know that many of us have plenty of disposable income and that we also know how to conserve it. After all, the oldest of us lived through the Depression and learned the hard way how to be thrifty. Besides, everyone loves a bargain.

The next third of life is about spending what we've saved while also watching the bottom line to be sure we have enough to carry us through retirement. In this chapter you will find a short discussion of budgeting. There is information on managing credit and special help with paying the rent and making home repairs. It will also help you think through major expenses such as insurance and taxes.

Know What You Spend

893. Figuring out your expenses before and after retirement doesn't have to be an agonizing process. If you calculate what you spend before retirement, you'll be able to be fairly accurate about your needs after it.

To get a fix on your expenses now, add up all your income for the year and subtract taxes and the amount put into savings. The rest is what you spent. Horrifying, isn't it?

894. To find out exactly how much you spend and on what, carry a pad and pencil with you for the next few months. Every time you spend money for any purpose, write down the item and its cost in your notebook. After a few months, you'll be able to analyze your spending habits and you'll know where every penny is going—and it may surprise you! The practice will also instill the habit of reconsidering each purchase before you make it.

895. There are fixed expenses and there are flexible expenses. The most common fixed expenses are rent or mortgage payments, property taxes, maintenance charges on a condominium, insurance premiums, and savings.

Flexible expenses include medical expenses, clothing, dry cleaning and laundry, furniture and appliances, housecleaning, home repairs and improvements, gifts and charitable contributions, travel and vacations, entertainment, sundries and grooming products, and postage.

Food is a fixed expense in that you need to spend money on it every month, but the amount you spend can be flexible.

896. It is the flexible expenses that will probably change most when you retire. Perhaps, for example, you'll spend more on travel and entertainment than during your working life, and less on going-to-work clothes and the dry cleaning to care for them.

The American Financial Services Association sells a printed monthly calendar/worksheet that lists fixed and variable expenses and provides good money-saving tips. Contact:

American Financial Services Association
1101 14th St. NW
Washington, DC 20005

Good Deals for Older Adults

897. Shop around for a bank that wants your business. About 70 percent of all commercial banks offer no-fee-checking to Americans 60 or 65 and older. Many institutions combine free checking with a package of other benefits, including:

• Special rates on certificates of deposit (CDs)
• No-fee or low-fee debit cards
• Overdraft checking privileges
• Special rates on loans
• Discounts on safe-deposit box rentals

898. Get free dental care by being part of a study on tooth implants. For information, contact:

Clinical Center
National Institutes of Health
Bethesda, MD 20892

Free dental care is also available from student dentists, supervised by a professor. For information, contact:

National Institute of Dental Research
Research Data and Management
Information Section
5333 W. Bard Ave., Room 539
Bethesda, MD 20814

899. Many physicians volunteer their services at free clinics. According to a recent American Medical Association survey, physicians average more than six hours a week of free or reduced-fee care. Most local medical societies keep lists of various regional and county programs, and of physicians who volunteer their services. Check under "Associations" in the yellow pages to find a local phone number for a medical society.

As for prescription drugs, many medications are available free of cost directly from drug manufacturers. Ask your doctor to contact the Pharmaceutical Manufacturers Association to see if you qualify for a free-drug program.

900. Under the federal Hill-Burton program, low-income patients can receive hospital care without cost. To see if you qualify, contact:

Hill-Burton Hotline
Health Resources and Services
Administration
5600 Fishers Lane, Room 11-19
Rockville, MD 20857
800-492-0359

901. The Legal Services Corporation gives legal help to low-income people in civil lawsuits. The program follows certain guidelines as to which cases it accepts and the financial eligibility of potential clients. To reach the free legal aid office nearest to you, look in the blue pages of your phone book.

A tax attorney's advice is yours at no charge from the Internal Revenue Service. The IRS provides tax attorneys who specialize in retirement and pension plan issues. Call 202-622-6074, Monday through Thursday, between 1:30 and 4:00 P.M., and ask for the Employee Plans Technical and Actuarial Division.

902. Many states have free hotlines to help older Americans with legal advice on Social Security and Medicare.

Services vary. Some will refer you to lawyers who offer assistance on a sliding fee scale, while some offer help at no charge. Call:

Arizona Legal Hotline for the Elderly:	800-231-5441
California Senior Legal Hotline:	800-222-1753
Florida Hotline for Older Floridians:	800-252-5997
Maine Legal Services for the Elderly:	800-750-5353
Michigan Senior Alliance, Inc.:	800-347-5297
New Mexico Lawyer Referral Services for the Elderly:	800-876-6657
Ohio Pro Senior, Inc.:	800-488-6070
Pennsylvania Legal Hotline for Older Americans:	800-262-5297
Texas Legal Hotline for Older Texans:	800-622-2520

If you live in a state other than those listed above, contact the ElderCare Locator, National Association of Area Agencies on Aging, 800-677-1116.

903. Write your own will—with a little help. Many county cooperative extension offices offer classes and give away forms to help you write your own will. Local law schools will often help, too. Many hold legal clinics staffed by law students, with review by qualified attorneys. To find out about these, call the main number of the nearest law school, and tell the switchboard attendant what you're looking for.

904. Veterans and their families are eligible for burial in national cemeteries, with Uncle Sam footing most of the bill. Burial benefits through the Veterans' Administration include a grave site, opening and closing of the grave, and perpetual care of the site. Headstone markers and their placement are also provided at the government's expense.

Spouses and the minor children of veterans may also be buried in a national cemetery. A surviving spouse of a veteran who then married a nonveteran, but whose remarriage was ended by death or divorce, is also eligible for a burial in a national cemetery. This provision covered Jacqueline Kennedy Onassis's burial at the side of President John F. Kennedy in Arlington National Cemetery. For a list of available cemeteries, call 800-697-6947.

905. Older adults who need to improve their homes may be eligible for a government grant. The U.S. Department of Housing and Urban Development (HUD) has a special program called the Home Investment Partnership Program. It awards grants of $1,000 or more to help seniors make repairs or improvements,

such as installing wheelchair ramps and guardrails in the bathroom. To locate the closest program, and to get application information, contact:

American Communities
P.O. Box 7189
Gaithersburg, MD 20898
800-998-9999

906. The government also offers interest-free home improvement loans. Under some circumstances, interest is charged, but at a very low rate. Often, these loans don't have to be repaid until the borrower moves to a new dwelling or dies.

Information on such loans is available through a state housing finance agency, local housing authority, or housing and community development office; check the blue pages of the phone book for their numbers.

907. Older homeowners may qualify for property tax deferral. These public programs allow older people to defer paying property taxes until they move to a new location or after their death. Each program has its own rules and regulations, though interest rates generally range from 6 percent to 8 percent. Variations of this program are available in about twenty states. Contact your state or local property tax collector's office for details.

908. If coming up with the rent is a struggle, you may be able to get help from the federal government. HUD has a voucher program for low-income city dwellers that limits the rent they must pay to a percentage of their income. To apply, locate your local HUD office in the blue pages of the phone book.

Help for rural renters is available through Rural Housing and Community Development Services. This agency offers payments for approved rents. Again, consult the blue pages of the phone book for a local office.

909. The federal Administration on Aging runs many free programs and offers much free information. Topics include housing, homemaking, nutrition, legal matters, transportation, and consumer affairs. Most programs are handled through a national network of state agencies on aging.

To find the service nearest you, call the ElderCare Locator Hotline, 800-677-1116, or write:

Administration on Aging
330 Independence Ave. SW
Washington, DC 20201

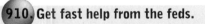 **910. Get fast help from the feds.**

If you have been frustrated trying to reach the right federal government department, or if you have a complicated question, you can talk to a real person at the Federal Information Center. It has a specially selected and trained staff.

Simply dial 800-688-9889 between the hours of 9:00 A.M. and 8:00 P.M. eastern standard time. Users of telecommunications for the deaf should call 800-329-2996. You'll first get a menu of subject-area options, or you can hit "0" and hold for that real person.

Those who are on-line can ask questions through the federal Website at *www.info.gov.*

Credit—Getting It, Keeping It

911. In our card-carrying society, credit is an arrow you want in your quiver as you plan for retirement and its expenses. For example, you may want to put a big purchase or repair on a credit card and then pay off the debt when one of your certificates of deposit matures. Or you may want to take out a loan and use the cash to cover your expenses, while your retirement savings continue to grow in tax-deferred splendor.

But you may find that when a salary ends—or a spouse dies—your credit status changes. You may even face age discrimination when you try to reestablish your credit. It's a good time to pay close attention. Creditors use various criteria to determine what loans they'll make and who they think is creditworthy. Under the law, a creditor may ask your age, but use of this information is restricted. The law says your age cannot be the basis for a decision to deny or decrease credit if you qualify otherwise.

912. When dealing with older adults, a potential lender cannot:

• Refuse to consider retirement income in rating a credit application
• Require you to reapply, change the

terms of your account, or close your account just because you retire or reach a certain age

• Deny you credit or close an account because credit-related insurance such as life, health, accident, and disability isn't available to people your age

913. If you become widowed or divorced, creditors may try to close your accounts, even though this is forbidden by federal law. They are, however, permitted to ask you to reapply for accounts, even if you have used them for years.

To avoid the problem, many widows continue to use credit cards in their deceased husband's names. This practice isn't recommended—you should go ahead and establish credit in your own name. And if you separate or divorce, make sure your name is removed from joint accounts. Otherwise, you can be liable for new charges your former spouse runs up.

914. To get credit in your own name, you must establish a credit history. Start small. The best way is to get one credit card, use it to make purchases, and then make payments regularly and/or pay off the balance.

Get one of the credit cards that most banks offer. Gasoline and department store credit cards are also easy to apply for. Read the small print or make a telephone call to make sure that your creditor reports to one of the national credit bureaus which track the performance of individuals with their lenders—this is how you will establish a track record of repaying credit.

915. As you age, the maximum amount of debt you should carry should remain the same. It should be about 10 percent to 15 percent of your gross income, excluding a mortgage. The available debt on credit cards should be no more than 30 percent to 40 percent of your income.

If a sudden illness or other major event should make it impossible to pay your bills on time, contact your creditors at once and work out a new payment plan.

916. Low-cost help on dealing with debt is available through the Consumer Credit Counseling Service, a nonprofit organization with more than 850 offices across all fifty states. Find the one nearest you by checking the telephone directory or by calling 800-388-2227. You can also contact:

National Foundation for Consumer Credit, Inc.
8611 2nd Ave., Suite 100
Silver Spring, MD 20910
301-589-5600

If you're having credit problems, or would simply like more information, contact:

Federal Trade Commission
6th St. and Pennsylvania Ave. NW
Washington, DC 20580
202-326-2222
Offers many free publications, including "Fix Your Own Credit Problems" and "Women and Credit History."

Bankcard Holders of America
560 Herndon Pkwy., Suite 120
Herndon, VA 22070

703-481-1110

800-553-8025

Offers a list of low-interest credit cards in addition to information on credit laws and general credit practice.

Insuring Your Risks

917. In your later years, your need for life insurance lessens and may even disappear entirely. Unless you have a younger spouse or dependent children or grandchildren, your need for a death benefit—money paid when you die—may have vanished.

If you want life insurance protection only, buy a *term life* policy. It covers you for a specified number of years (usually one to ten); if you die during that period, your beneficiaries collect the face amount of the policy. Generally such policies are renewable, but often only until age 70.

If you buy a *whole life, universal life,* or other policy that builds cash value in addition to insuring your life, you should plan to hold it for at least fifteen years. Canceling these policies after only a few years can double your costs.

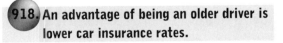

918. An advantage of being an older driver is lower car insurance rates.

You can save several hundred dollars a year by comparison shopping for automobile insurance. Call your state insurance department for a publication showing typical prices charged by dif-

ferent companies. Then call at least four of the lowest-priced licensed insurers to learn what they charge for the coverage you currently have.

If you do change agencies, make sure that your new policy is in effect before you drop your old one.

Property Insurance

919. It's a good idea to take out insurance on your dwelling and its contents. Many experts think that Americans are overinsured for small losses and underinsured for large ones—that is, premiums are wasted on $100 to $500 risks, and not enough is spent on devastating losses. Check to be sure the insurance on your house, condo, or apartment—and on its contents—has kept pace with inflation. Some possessions acquired thirty years ago are worth a lot more now.

920. The basic difference among residential policies is the number of "perils" covered. The more perils (for instance, fire or lightning), the more expensive the policy. There are general policies that cover many risks, but even the most inclusive don't usually cover earthquakes and floods. You must buy separate coverage for them.

When buying homeowners' insurance, many people follow the "80 percent rule" and insure that percentage of their property's total value. It's based on the premise that even if your entire house is lost, the foundation and land are not usually destroyed.

Most homeowners' policies cover injuries to others that occur on the property—personal liability—and loss of and damage to possessions, often including items such as credit cards and trees and shrubs.

921. Renter's insurance is as important as homeowner's insurance. Such policies primarily cover personal property and liability.

If you have substantial assets to protect, and if you can afford it, consider supplementing your auto and homeowner's/renter's coverage with an additional $1-million umbrella liability policy. Such a policy offers protection above the limits of your other policies. It pays out after your basic policy coverage is depleted, which can happen more quickly than we like to think is possible.

922. For more information about property insurance, contact:

National Consumers League
1701 K St. NW, Suite 1200
Washington, DC 20006
202-835-3323

National Insurance Consumer Helpline
800-942-4242

Insurance Information Institute
110 William St.
New York, NY 10038
212-669-9200

National Association of Insurance Commissioners
120 W. 12th St., Suite 1100
Kansas City, MO 64105
816-842-3600

Health Insurance

923. There are a number of health insurance options to consider as you age. While you continue to work, you'll probably be covered by the group insurance you have through your employer. If you work beyond age 65, it may be a good idea to retain your group coverage and put off signing up for Medicare, because Medicare is probably more expensive and doesn't cover as much. Compare the costs and benefits before you make this decision.

If you retire, you will be covered by Medicare (see Chapter 9) after you reach age 65. But you may want to buy "medigap" insurance to cover the expenses that Medicare doesn't. There is also long-term care insurance to consider—a tall order, since there is often no easy or simple way to determine what you'll need deep into retirement.

To make matters more complicated, new laws often change Medicare coverage. State laws, too, often change. You'll want to look to your area agency on aging, a lawyer, or a financial planner for guidance on such changes.

924. Medigap insurance is private health insurance designed to supplement Medicare's benefits. A medigap policy generally pays for Medicare-approved charges not paid by Medicare. It often includes deductibles, coinsurance charges, the cost of outpatient prescription drugs, the first three pints of blood used in surgery, and skilled nursing care.

925. The federal government has set minimum standards for medigap policies. Individual states regulate medigap, too. Most states limit the medigap insurance market to no more than ten standard policies.

Medigap insurers must use the same format, language, and definitions in describing the benefits of each of the ten approved medigap plans. They are also required to use a uniform outline of coverage to summarize benefits. The standardization of plans means that when you shop for a medigap policy, it is relatively easy to make comparisons among them.

The ten standard medigap plans are lettered A through J, with benefits becoming more comprehensive as you move through the alphabet.

926. If you decide to buy medigap insurance, shop carefully.

Some tips:

• Be aware that policies that supplement Medicare are not sold or serviced by either the state or federal government.

• Review your health care requirements and finances and then read the outline of coverage carefully. Don't end up buying more coverage than you really need.

• Check for "preexisting condition" exclusions.

• Pushy marketing can be a red flag. Don't buy if high-pressure tactics are used.

• If you decide to buy, complete the application carefully; don't believe an insurance agent who says your medical history isn't important.

• Don't pay cash; pay by check, money order, or bank draft, so you have a record of your purchase.

• Don't switch from one policy to another unless you're sure you'll get different benefits, better service, or a more affordable price.

If you have difficulties, contact your state insurance department, or call 800-638-6833 for the U.S. Department of Health and Human Services.

927. For further information about medigap policies and possibilities, write:

Health Care Financing Administration
6325 Security Blvd.
Baltimore, MD 21207

National Association of Insurance Commissioners
120 W. 12th St., Suite 1100
Kansas City, MO 64105

Both the Health Care Financing Administration and the National Association of Insurance Commissioners offer a helpful booklet, updated annually, called "Guide to Health Insurance for People with Medicare." In addition to specific medigap information, it also lists the toll-free hotlines for each state's insurance department and agency on aging.

Medicare Beneficiaries Defense Fund
1460 Broadway, 8th Floor
New York, NY 10036

928. Besides medigap, there are three other ways to supplement Medicare coverage:

• By joining a health maintenance organization (HMO)

• By arranging to keep any coverage that you had from your employer

• By qualifying for Medicaid benefits, or assistance to the low-income residents of your state

929. A Health Maintenance Organization (HMO) is a form of "managed care." The term "managed care" refers to an organization comprised of doctors, hospitals, and other providers who all operate on a fixed, preset fee. If you belong to such an organization, you pay a monthly premium which usually covers doctor visits and treatment; and usually, you can go only to doctors and hospitals within the provider network (some managed care providers also contract with independent physicians).

The idea is to keep the cost of health care low, both through the set-fee policy and by offering preventive care (which has been shown to be more economical in the long run than treating illness once it arises). However, managed care facilities have been criticized for undertreating patients and for shuffling them in and out as quickly as possible, since physicians usually make the same amount of money regardless of how much time they spend with each patient.

930. HMOs differ from traditional insurance in these ways:

• You choose a doctor and hospital, and sometimes a pharmacy for prescription medications, only from among the HMO's network of providers.

• If you need a specialist, the HMO will provide one.

• You pay a monthly premium, which covers you for preventive care and most routine illnesses.

• There are no deductibles or large coinsurance payments, although you may pay a small fee with each visit.

• You file no claim forms.

931. Point-of-service (POS) and preferred provider organizations (PPOs) are two more forms of managed care. They operate much like HMOs, except with these, you have the option of using doctors and hospitals from outside the network. If you do choose independently, you pay a deductible and then your costs are covered in the same way as with conventional insurance; premiums are usually higher than those of an HMO. Some PPOs impose restrictions, such as preexisting-condition exclusions.

932. You may want to consider joining a Medicare HMO. With this type of coverage, you are a member of an HMO—but instead of writing out a check each month to pay for it, the cost is picked up by Medicare. The care provided is only that which is covered by Medicare. Many offer at least partial coverage for prescription drugs, dental care, hearing aids, and eyeglasses. The benefits may vary by HMO, so read the fine print to determine which benefits are offered by each plan.

With a Medicare HMO, there is no need for medigap.

933. Find out what ninety thousand other people think of their health care plan. The U.S. Office of Personnel Management will send you a free, eight-page report in which ninety thousand federal workers rated their satisfaction with over 250 health plans nationwide. Contact them at:

U.S. Office of Personnel Management
Box 707, 1900 E St.
Washington, DC 20415

934. Medicaid supplements Medicare benefits—and not only for low-income older Americans.

In general, only the neediest qualify for Medicaid. But you can be deemed "medically needy" if you have unusually high health care expenses, and little or no assets, or other resources to turn to. Benefits vary from state to state, but in general, Medicaid covers hospitalization, physicians, and nursing home services. Nearly 70 percent of nursing home residents are paying for their care through Medicaid. As with Medicare, Medicaid HMOs are available.

935. Hospital indemnity insurance is targeted at the aging. It pays a cash amount for each day you're in the hospital for a specified number of days, and insurance for specific illnesses such as cancer. If this interests you, consider the policy carefully and be sure it does not duplicate the coverage you already have.

936. Worth particular attention is long-term care insurance to cover a catastrophic illness or disability. Such care can range from help with daily activities at home to skilled care in a nursing home.

Predicting who will need long-term care is difficult. A study reported in the *New England Journal of Medicine* in 1991 found that two out of three people who turned 65 in 1990 will never need nursing home care, but that women are more likely to need it than men, and that the older you get, the more likely you are to be cared for in a nursing home.

937. Long-term care can be expensive, and so can the insurance to cover it. In 1997, for example, long-term care insurance policies with inflation protection cost as much as $2,000 a year for people aged 65. Nursing home residency averaged about $38,000 a year in 1997. Skilled nursing care in your home comes to about $12,300 a year. Nationally, about a third of all out-of-pocket nursing home expenses are paid by individuals and their families, and more than two-thirds by Medicaid after recipients have depleted their other financial resources. Medicare generally does not cover such care.

938. In general, you should not consider such coverage if your primary income in retirement is Social Security. It's too expensive, especially when you consider the fact that you might never need it. And if you already have a certain illness or condition that predisposes you to need long-term care (such as Alzheimer's disease), you may not be able to buy it anyway, because insurance company underwriting standards will screen you out.

For a helpful booklet on the ramifications of long-term care insurance, "A Shopper's Guide to Long-Term Care Insurance," contact:

National Association of Insurance
Commissioners
120 W. 12th Street, Suite 1100
Kansas City, MO 64105
816-842-3600

939. Any sort of insurance that costs only "pennies a day" usually provides very little coverage. And insurers who promise to write policies "with no medical examination" usually end up offering you a pretty poor deal. For more information on low-cost insurance policies, contact the National Insurance Consumer Helpline at 800-942-4242.

Your Taxes

940. And now the bad news: You could end up in a higher tax bracket upon retirement. It could be the result of losing your deductions—house mortgage, dependent children—while continuing to earn. If you decide to become self-employed, you are required to pay a 15.3 percent federal self-

employment tax. And don't forget that Social Security income is taxable.

And then there are all those back-end taxes on retirement savings payable when you withdraw from 401(k)s and IRAs. If you meet the age requirements for withdrawals (after age $59\frac{1}{2}$), the monies are taxed as regular income. If you're in one of the higher tax brackets, your rate could be more than the capital gains rate of 28 percent, the rate applied to wins in the stock market.

941. Of course, many people will have lower income upon retirement, and therefore pay less at tax time. A general rule of retirement is to use taxable investments and bank accounts first; don't dip into your tax-deferred accounts unless it's absolutely necessary, since they will continue to grow as long as you leave them alone.

It's also worth saying again that retirement finances and taxes can be so complicated that it's worth getting the advice of an accountant or financial planner (*see Chapter 9*).

942. If you take your pension payment as a lump sum, you should roll the money over into a tax-deferred individual retirement account (IRA). That way, you'll avoid a big tax bite initially; you can pay the taxes gradually, as you draw money out of the account.

If you take that lump sum and need to start using it to live on, it's taxable immediately. But again, there's a way to ease the burden. It's a process called forward averaging, whereby taxes are paid over a period of five years. Your accountant will be able to tell you more about this.

943. Upon retirement, most people take their 401(k) savings as a lump sum. They, too, should roll the money over into a tax-deferred IRA. If they then begin withdrawing it as needed, they'll have to pay federal taxes of up to 39.6 percent on the previously untaxed dollars as they take the money out, and probably some state and local taxes.

Many people have several kinds of IRAs—some with money not yet taxed; some with money that has been. It would seem logical to withdraw the already-taxed funds first, right? Of course it doesn't work that easily. The IRS counts your IRAs as one big pot of money containing a percentage of pretax funds and a percentage posttax. When you withdraw from any IRA, you'll have to pay tax on a percentage reflected from the percentages in your overall IRA holdings.

944. Here's some good tax news that any older adult can take advantage of.

• People over 55 are allowed to sell their houses and then shelter amounts of up to $62,500 for a single person, and $125,000 for a couple, from capital gains taxes (this can only be done once).

• You can give each family member up to $10,000 per year without having to pay taxes on it (the recipient doesn't have to pay taxes, either). You can pay tuition or med-ical bills for a family member with the same benefits.

• If you are lucky enough to own art or fine collectibles that you want to dispose of, you can donate them to a nonprofit institution and take a tax deduction of the full market value.

945. If you retire before age $59^{1}/_{2}$, it is possible to withdraw from an IRA without paying a penalty.

Usually, a 10 percent fee is imposed. But the IRS allows early retirees to calculate "substantially equal" sums that will be needed for the duration of the retiree's life, and that of his or her spouse, and to begin withdrawing them monthly.

The amount can be determined by figuring the probable value of the IRA over time, accounting for its interest earnings, whatever its current value. The withdrawals must continue for five years, or until the owner of the IRA turns $59^{1}/_{2}$, whichever is longer. After that period, the sums can be refigured.

946. You must begin withdrawing from your retirement savings at age $70^{1}/_{2}$. If you want to keep as much money safe from taxes as possible, you'll use monthly calculations similar to the ones above.

The withdrawal sum will be based on IRS actuarial tables that predict your life expectancy, but the life span of a beneficiary can also be figured in, reducing the amount you withdraw each month.

947. Call the IRS at 800-829-1040 for help with your taxes. Services include:

• Tax counseling for people 60 and older. Volunteer tax counselors are often retired people associated with nonprofit organizations receiving grants from the IRS for their expenses. Ask about the service when you call.

• Walk-in service. Most IRS offices offer publications, forms, and in-person guidance.

• Hearing-impaired services. If you have a telecommunications device for the deaf (TDD), call 800-829-4059.

• Sight-impaired services. Limited braille tax materials are available at Regional Libraries for the Visually Impaired.

948. If you can't pay your taxes, the IRS's Problem Resolution Program (PRP) may help. It can assist with overdue returns and explain payment options, as well as help with other tax problems that can't be resolved through normal channels.

The PRP may also be able to help if you are suffering significant hardship, such as being unable to provide food, shelter, clothing, or medical care for you or your family, because of a tax problem.

But don't wait until the IRS comes to you. Seek out the PRP and let the IRS know you have a problem. Request Form 911, "Application for Taxpayer Assistance Order to Relieve Hardship," by calling 800-829-1040.

949. The IRS offers a number of booklets that may be of interest to older taxpayers. They include information about your tax status over age 50, retirement benefits, life insurance proceeds, and making a good profit from the sale of your home. The following are but a few of their offerings:

"Tax Information on Selling Your Home" (Publications 523 and 2119)
"Credit for the Elderly or Disabled" (524)
"Medical and Dental Expenses" (502)
"Equivalent Railroad Retirement Benefits" (915)
"Introduction to Estate and Gift Taxes" (448)

Order from the IRS at 800-829-3676. For a catalog of all the Internal Revenue Service publications, call 800-829-1040 and ask for catalog number 15315W.

Get a free publication designed to help older adults pay fewer taxes. It's called "Protecting Older Americans Against Overpayment of Income Taxes," and it details legitimate income tax deductions, exemptions, and tax credits. It's written in easy-to-understand language, with many examples and checklists. For a free copy, contact:

Special Committee on Aging
U.S. Senate
Washington, DC 20410
202-224-5364

950. Be wary of tax preparers who offer an immediate refund on your return. "Rapid refund" often means that you get a loan in anticipation of the refund and that loan usually carries a very high interest rate. Steer clear, too, of fraudulent tax preparers who claim to have a special relationship with the IRS.

Free tax help is available from the IRS, and it's easy to get, especially if you contact them before the crunch in March and April.

Chapter 11:

Estate Planning

I f you own anything at all, you have an estate, and you should plan for its disposition. Your estate includes, of course, real estate, but also other property such as furniture, art, jewelry, and cars, as well

as the value of investments, retirement plans, life insurance, and cash. Even if some of these assets are owned jointly, they are still part of your estate.

This final chapter can't advise you on who should benefit from your estate, but it can show you ways to make receiving your bequests easier for the next generation. That guidance means everything from how to get your financial records in order so your executor can find them, to setting up strategies to help lessen estate taxes.

951. Much of estate planning centers on avoiding estate and inheritance taxes. The federal estate tax is worth paying attention to. While spouses can pass assets to each other tax free, and the first $625,000 of an estate (rising gradually to $1 million after 2005) willed to others is not taxed, the tax beyond that is between 37 and 55 percent.

The government's philosophy is to make it

easy for you to acquire assets for retirement—and with the strength of the stock market in the late 1990s, amassing an estate worth over $600,000 has become a reality for many. But after those funds have been used during retirement, the government would like to take as much as possible of what's left after you die.

952. But many experts believe that taxes should *not* be your first consideration. As four estate planners noted in an October 1997 issue of *Fortune* magazine—an issue devoted to retirement planning—the first element of estate planning should be deciding who and/or what will benefit after your death from your life's accumulation of assets.

The choices can be hard ones—they may cause bad feelings among family members and friends. As those financial planners told *Fortune,* it's not what an heir himself is getting that usually upsets a person, it's what all the other heirs are getting. Siblings may be at odds with each other before a parent's death if one among several is chosen as the parent's executor.

953. The circumstances of modern life further complicate estate planning. A good example is aging baby boomers who started families late in their childbearing years. Estate planning for them can involve consideration of both infirm parents and minor children. And with an increasing number of divorces, remarriages, and unmarried couples living together permanently, there is often a galaxy of evaluations and decisions about who should benefit from which estate.

A concrete, explicit, and carefully thought-out estate plan—shared with family members in advance—can help avoid tangles of fact and emotions.

954. Good estate planning involves the four Ps. They're discussed at length later on in this chapter, but briefly, they are:

• People. Do you want your estate to provide for family members? The employees of a family business? A charity that benefits the needy, artists, or scholars?
• Property. What do you own, and what is it worth? Do you have a list of all your assets, including personal effects as well as cash and investments?
• Plans. How would you like to divide your property, and how can you minimize taxes as you do so?
• Planners. Whom do you need to advise

you, and how do you find such people? You should be especially interested in counselors who are knowledgeable about tax codes and their impact on any bequest you make.

955. Get started by getting organized. You'll want your heirs to have easy access to your financial records when they need them. Besides, assembling the documents with their addresses, phone numbers, and account numbers can help you plan and get a handle on what you have and what you want to pass on.

Your filing system need not be elaborate—just get all the files on the same subject together in the same place. The simplest method is to get cardboard boxes and label them "Financial Records," "Personal Records," "Health Records," and "Legal Records." As you find or receive documents, put them in the appropriate box. If you can, make individual file folders for specific topics within each of the four general categories.

956. Your "Financial Records" file should contain specifics on these topics:

• Sources of income such as Social Security, pensions, and investments, along with identification numbers
• Medicare and other insurance, including life, health, and property
• Bank accounts (checking, savings, and credit union)
• Location of safe-deposit boxes and keys to them
• Copies of tax returns

- Mortgages—account numbers and how and when payments are due
- Credit card and charge account names and numbers
- Other debts and creditors, account numbers, and payments
- Location of property records, including deeds and bills of sale
- Location of all valuable personal items such as jewelry or family heirlooms

957. Your "Personal Records" file should include:

- Your full legal name and Social Security number
- The title to your car
- Proof of legal residence—mortgage documents, utility bills addressed to you, a voter's registration or a library card
- Names and addresses of living spouse and children
- Names and addresses of close friends, relatives, doctors, lawyers, and financial advisers
- The original copy of your will; funeral and burial preferences and/or arrangements
- Death certificates of parents or other close relatives
- Location of passport, trust documents, birth and marriage certificates, divorce and citizenship papers
- List of employers and dates of employment
- Educational and military records
- Religious affiliation, names of institutions and clergy

- Membership in organizations and awards received

958. You might want to store some items in a safe-deposit box. These would include citizenship papers, adoption papers, deeds for property, titles, and mortgages, savings bonds, securities, court decrees, family jewelry, and irreplaceable photographs. Don't store cash in a safe-deposit box. It won't earn interest, and it will be taxed on the death of the box owner.

959. Your safe-deposit box will be sealed upon your death. Keep that in mind when deciding what to keep there. Check with your bank to see if your survivors have access to your safe-deposit box, or if access can be given to others in an emergency. Don't put anything in a safe-deposit box that you might need quickly, or when the bank is closed.

Some important documents that should *not* be in your safe-deposit box are: signed originals of wills, life insurance policies, burial instructions, cemetery plot deeds, living wills, or instructions for organ donation.

960. Here are some common legal and financial terms relating to estate planning.

Conservator: a person or institution designated to protect and manage the financial assets of an incapacitated person
Durable power of attorney: a type of "power of attorney" that gives another the power to take care of your personal and

financial affairs if you become incompetent

Fiduciary responsibility: the holding of something (usually money) in trust for another.

Guardian: a person given authority to make decisions, including financial ones, in behalf of another

Incompetence: a legally designated condition in which a person cannot make decisions for himself. It is usually caused by medical conditions that accompany physical or mental illness, aging, or accidents.

961. Some other important terms:

Legal advocate: a lawyer, legal consultant, or organization that represents the interests of an individual

Living trust: a signed authorization to manage a person's affairs if he or she becomes disabled or incompetent; it is also a way to avoid probate.

Living will: a signed, dated, and witnessed document transmitting a person's wishes regarding the use of medical procedures to sustain life. (See items 709–711.)

Probate: the legal process of gathering and distributing the property of an estate, and being sure that the deceased's debts are paid and that remaining property gets to its new owners

Trust: a legal entity, used before and/or after death, that provides for the distribution of a person's assets for the benefit of that person or others; a trust is administered by a trustee.

Estate Planning with Taxes in Mind

962. Besides the federal estate tax (see item 951), your estate is subject to two other taxes.
They are:

- Inheritance tax. This tax is levied on the amount that an heir receives. The tax applies to all transfers of both property and money at death, and to transfers made in contemplation of death (that is, those made within two years prior to death).
- Pickup tax. This is a state tax that applies only to those estates subject to federal estate tax (that is, estates worth over $600,000). The estate *does* pay a state tax, but not directly. It pays the federal estate tax, and then the state takes—or "picks up"—some of that directly from the feds.

963. One of the biggest mistakes made in estate planning is forgetting that a retirement fund, such as a tax-deferred 401(k), has not yet been taxed.

Not only do you have to pay income taxes on this money when you withdraw it, but the amount that remains in the retirement fund is subject to estate taxes at death. A third tax of 15 percent—called a success tax—is also imposed on such funds.

964. Being generous while you're alive is the easiest way to reduce estate taxes after you die.
Besides, you get to see the joy created by your largesse.

Federal tax laws allow you to give $10,000 a year to as many individuals as you'd like without having to pay gift taxes—up to a total of $600,000 in your lifetime. Your spouse can do the same.

965. You can also save taxes by helping out with education and medical expenses. Besides the $10,000 annually, you can pay tuition expenses for, say, a grandchild. The contributions are tax exempt provided they are paid directly to the educational institution. The same is true for medical bills, as long as they are paid directly to the health care provider.

Legal Advice

966. Get a lawyer to help you through the thicket of estate planning—even if you only want a simple will. Find an attorney who specializes in the subject. Your accountant and financially savvy friends may know of someone; or contact your state's bar association, or law schools in your area, and ask for their lawyer referral services.

Your accountant—and financial planner, if you have one—will also have some thoughts on your estate and should be consulted as you plan.

967. When deciding among attorneys, ask them these questions:

• Do you handle many estates similar in size and degree of complexity to mine?

• Do you do the work yourself, or is most of it done by a paralegal under your supervision?

• What are your billing practices? How much do you charge per hour, or per fraction of an hour? (A flat fee is often used for certain routine work, such as probate, title searches, and simple wills.)

• How long will specific work—a will, for example—take?

968. There is an entire legal specialty, called elder law, devoted to the affairs of older adults.

It deals with tax and estate planning, aging in general, incapacity, planning for dealing with serious illness and long-term care, government benefit programs, protective services, and guardianship.

To find an attorney in your community who specializes in elder law, contact:

National Academy of Elder Law Attorneys
655 N. Alvernon, Suite 108
Tucson, AZ 85771
602-881-4005

969. These legal documents form the foundation of good estate planning:

• A will spells out how your assets will be distributed at your death and provides instructions for the care of minor children.

• Durable power of attorney specifies who can handle your personal and financial affairs, especially should you become incompetent.

• A living will provides written instructions for medical care during terminal illness. It is often joined with a health care power of attorney, specifying who can make medical decisions in your behalf. (See items 709–711 for more information.)

• A living trust helps provide a backup source of asset management during your life, especially should you become incompetent. It can also help avoid probate after your death.

Wills

970. Is a will necessary? Apparently, many people don't think so, since over half of the 2 million Americans who die each year don't have wills.

Some believe they don't own enough property to require a will; others think that life insurance or joint ownership arrangements are all that is needed. Still others assume their spouse will inherit everything automatically. Sometimes people who have no children feel there is no need for a will. But most people simply put off making a will.

971. When a person dies without a will, state laws go into action. The state will appoint an administrator—someone who doesn't know you or your family—to distribute your estate. Such an arrangement is undesirable, especially when it comes to providing for surviving minor children, because the administrator doesn't know your wishes, especially regarding guardianship of the children. And, need-

less to say, the administrator cannot make bequests to charities and friends whom you may have wanted to give money to.

972. A will can save probate costs. Estate taxes can be reduced through wills and other estate planning. A husband and wife should have separate wills. These can complement each other—such as naming heirs if both spouses die at the same time—and also take into account any special gifts to other family members or special friends. The smaller the estate, the more important that it be settled quickly, because delays mean paying more legal fees. Having a will makes things go faster.

973. Learn the lingo of wills. Here's a short glossary of words often used.

Appraisal: the process of determining the value of property owned by the deceased
Bequest or *legacy:* gift of personal property (such as jewelry and artwork) or real property (such as real estate, cars)
Creditor: person to whom the deceased owes a debt
Estate tax: a tax on the estate of the deceased
Executor: a person who makes sure that the terms of a will are carried out
Heir: a person who inherits property, with or without a will
Inheritance tax: a tax imposed on the heir receiving property from an estate
Intestate: a situation wherein no valid will exists
Testate: a situation wherein the deceased left a will

974. Go prepared when meeting with your attorney to draw up a will. Take lists of your property, separated into broad categories such as "real estate," "stocks and bonds," "retirement funds," "life insurance," and "cash." Also indicate which property is owned jointly. You should also bring your recent tax records and your Veterans' Administration number.

Be ready to discuss whom you would like to be the executor of your estate, or to act as guardian if you have young children. Discuss any other relationships you want to provide for.

Getting organized to talk to your attorney will help you figure out what you want in your will. It can also save you money, since your attorney will have to spend less time interviewing you and sifting through your records.

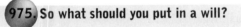 **975. So what should you put in a will?**

Anything you like—or dislike. The best advice is to list your wishes specifically. For example, if you want to disinherit a child, stating so in your will enables it to hold up in court. It is very difficult to disinherit a spouse, though. Most courts give surviving spouses access to at least a third of an estate.

If you must provide for minor children or dependent parents, you may want their caretaker or guardian to be different from their financial manager. And if you do not specify how and when minor children are to inherit your assets, a court will oversee the assets until they are 18 or 21.

Many people set up trusts for children, specifying how the trustees are to spend the money and when or if the children will eventually manage it themselves. Most experts these days advise the children not to receive the assets until they are 40 years of age.

976. You may want to write your own will. It's possible, but be sure you adhere to all rules and regulations, or your will could be declared invalid in court.

If you'd like to give writing your own will a try, the U.S. Department of Agriculture's Extension Service offers information on the process. A local law school can help, too (see item 903 for more information).

977. Your executor carries out the terms of your will after your death. It is a position with legal standing. You can name your spouse, a relative, or a friend, or a bank or other professional organization to be your executor. (Be sure to get permission from the person or institution first.)

An executor can be paid a fee for the work. The fee is usually based upon the size of the estate and is paid out of the estate. A spouse, friend, or beneficiary may waive such compensation.

If your executor dies before you do, the court may appoint someone else to administrate your estate. It's a good idea to name an alternate executor who is young and in good health. The trust department of a bank is also a good choice.

978. Being an executor is a time-consuming job. Some of the responsibilities are:

- Obtaining the death certificate and providing copies to your insurance companies, Social Security office, and others
  - Presenting the will to probate court
  - Completing and filing state and federal tax returns
  - Establishing any trusts created by the will and making any payments due them
  - Arranging for appraisal of all property
  - Safeguarding the property
  - Disposing of property according to will instructions
  - Collecting debts due to the estate and paying any owed
  - Providing interim management of business interests

979. Have a will-signing party. In many states, two witnesses are required at the signing of a will. To be a witness, a person must be competent, may not know the contents of the will, and may not be a beneficiary of the will. Some people like to make a small party of signing a will at an attorney's office, and bring along champagne for the event.

980. Even the most carefully worded will can become outdated. Perhaps you'll move from one state to another after you retire. That usually doesn't invalidate a will (since there is reciprocity between states), but it's a good idea to have it reviewed by a lawyer in your new location.

Changes in your number of children or grandchildren, your marital status or financial status, or the health of your executor or those named in your will can affect its contents. Again, check with your attorney. Up-

dating a will doesn't always require rewriting it. Changes can often be made with an amendment called a *codicil.*

981. For more information about wills and probate, contact:

Consumer Affairs Section
Program Coordination and Development Department
American Association of Retired Persons
601 E St. NW
Washington, DC 20049
Ask for "A Consumer's Guide to Probate" (D13822).

Legal Counsel for the Elderly
601 E St. NW
Washington, DC 20049

Legal Service Corporation
750 1st St. NE, 11th Floor
Washington, DC 20002
It will send a listing of attorneys and legal support services for the elderly in your county.

Association of Funeral and Memorial Societies
20001 S St.
Washington, DC 20009
202-745-0634

Nolo Press
950 Parker St.
Berkeley, CA 94710
510-549-1976
Publishes how-to books designed to help

people avoid legal fees, including a workbook on preparing a will yourself.

National Academy of Elder Law Attorneys
655 N. Alvernon, Suite 108
Tucson, AZ 85771
602-881-4005

Trusts

982. A trust is not a will, but trusts are often included in wills. They are being used more and more to sort out the affairs of blended families (second spouses, stepchildren, etc), to provide for longer life spans and impaired abilities, and to protect the vulnerable, such as minor children or spouses inexperienced in financial matters. Trusts can also be used to alleviate taxes on estates worth over $600,000.

A financial adviser or institution (such as a bank) uses assets in the trust for the benefit of the people named in it. Sometimes the creator of the trust administers it himself or herself before death.

983. There are two forms of trusts. Those that can be changed are called *revocable,* and those that cannot are called *irrevocable.*

If you set up a *revocable* trust, you are usually both its trustee and its beneficiary. This form of trust is often created to reduce taxes; you will have to declare the trust when you file your personal income taxes. *Irrevocable* trusts are tax entities in and of themselves (in much the same way that a small

business is its own tax entity). Any money the trust earns that is not paid out to the beneficiaries of the trust is taxed at a high rate.

There are many variations on both types of trusts, the most common of which will be discussed in items below.

984. Remember that living trust mentioned above? It's a revocable trust usually set up to take care of a person if he or she becomes ill or incompetent; it is often structured to turn into several other trusts upon the death of the person setting it up.

As one financial planner explained in *Fortune* magazine, such a trust sets out the wishes of the person creating it, requiring the trustee to follow those directions. By contrast, a power of attorney authorizes the agent to act as he or she wishes in behalf of the ill or incompetent person.

985. You can leave more than $600,000 tax free to your children if you set up a bypass trust. Also called a credit-shelter trust, this is the most common trust for estate planning purposes. Under federal tax laws, married couples can leave everything to each other tax free. But only the first $600,000 of an estate is tax free when assets are passed to children or others. A bypass trust allows the surviving spouse to benefit from the estate during his or her lifetime while allowing the children to eventually share an inheritance of more than $600,000 tax free.

986. Here's how a bypass trust works: If a couple has a joint estate of, say, $1.2 million and no bypass trust, the estate of the one who dies first would pass to the surviving spouse tax free. When the surviving spouse dies and the estate is passed to the couple's children, everything over $600,000 will be taxed. If the couple parks $600,000 in a bypass trust designated to go to the children eventually, but benefiting the surviving spouse until his or her death, the money will pass to the children tax free on the death of the surviving spouse. And the remaining $600,000 exemption from tax applies to any other assets outside the trust—in other words, the entire estate is now tax free (600,000 + 600,000 = 1.2 million).

987. If you've left money to your wife, what happens to it when she dies if she remarried after your death? This scenario is the reason some people put monies not only into a bypass trust but also into a "marital deduction trust." Such a trust is tax free because it qualifies for the marital deduction. Its function is to be sure that your money stays in your family after both your and your spouse's deaths. A marital deduction trust lets your spouse use the assets during her lifetime, but you designate what happens to them after your spouse's death.

If the surviving spouse is very inexperienced in financial matters, a financial professional can be named trustee instead of the spouse.

988. A "Q-TIP" is a marital trust used by couples with children from previous marriages.

Q-TIP stands for "qualified terminable interest property," and is another way of letting a surviving spouse benefit from an estate during his or her lifetime while allowing you to direct the eventual dispersal to certain children.

In other words, this type of setup prevents your stepchildren from inheriting your money after you die, while enabling your new spouse to benefit from it while you are still living; when you die, your estate then passes to the children you wish it to go to.

989. Some information bandied about in magazine articles is only for the very rich. There's a certain life insurance trust designed to save estate taxes on the policy.

Here's how it works: An individual with a large life insurance policy puts it into an irrevocable trust for his or her spouse. After the individual's death, the spouse would have the use of the funds from the insurance throughout his or her life; upon the spouse's death, the remaining money would go to the couple's children tax free.

There are several catches, of course. If you transfer an existing insurance policy into this sort of trust, you must live three years before it is out of your estate for tax purposes. The policy can also run afoul of federal gift taxes if the trust is not constructed carefully.

990. A trust that helps you leave a lot of money to your grandchildren, without a big tax bite, is also for the wealthy. It's called a generation-skipping trust. Operating on the theory that Uncle Sam won't get to tax one generation if assets are given to the next, the federal government takes 55 percent of everything in excess of $1 million left to the grandchildren.

A generation-skipping trust is set up by a married couple (in much the same way as a bypass trust) to preserve $1 million before the generational tax sets in. If, say, several hundred thousand dollars is put in such a trust early on, and grows to exceed $1 million before your death, the full amount is saved from the generation-skipping tax, even though it exceeds $1 million.

991. A QPRT can help you take an expensive house or vacation home out of the taxman's clutches. QPRT stands for "qualified personal residence trust." It allows you to put a house into a trust while retaining the right to live in it for a specified number of years.

At the end of that period, ownership of the house goes to the trust or its beneficiaries. You save some gift tax by continuing to live in the house, because your living there reduces its value. The catch is that if you die before the term of residence is finished, the house remains part of your estate.

992. Contributions to charity via a trust can be structured to give you income during life, and a tax break, too. One such mechanism is a *charitable remainder trust.* Most large charities can help you and your attorney set one up.

Such a trust works best for people whose assets have appreciated significantly (for instance, due to stocks that did very well, or land that has become very valuable). To sell such assets would cause a large capital gains tax bite—but they can be given to a charity through a charitable remainder trust, thereby avoiding tax. The charity sells the assets and sets up an annuity fund that pays the donor regular income through his or her life. The drawback is that on the death of the donor, the asset belongs to the charity and is not available for your family to inherit.

993. A CHARITABLE LEAD trust is the opposite of a charitable remainder trust. Once again, assets are placed in a trust, but this time the trust pays the *charity* income for a specific number of years. At the end of the period, the donor's beneficiaries get the principal and pay reduced estate or gift taxes on it.

Costs of setup and operation are high; experts say that this trust works best for the very rich.

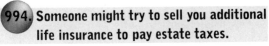

994. Someone might try to sell you additional life insurance to pay estate taxes.

This is a hot marketing campaign aimed at older adults. Think carefully and consult your financial and estate planning advisers before purchasing such insurance.

If your estate will not top $600,000 (which is when federal taxes kick in), or if your estate will go to your spouse tax free, you do not need such insurance. You also do not need it if much of your wealth is in stocks and bonds that can be sold easily for cash, or if you have established the kinds of trusts that help you avoid estate taxes.

If much of your wealth is tied up in a small business, or in hard-to-sell real estate, such insurance might be helpful as a way to get cash to pay taxes. There may also be income tax advantages to passing on your wealth via life insurance.

Gifts to Charity

995. Proportional to their income, the 65-and-over set give the most to charity. They donate more than 3 percent of their income to charitable causes.

Americans are generous in general. In a recent year we gave over $100 billion to individuals, $10 billion to foundations, and $6 billion to organizations.

Research shows that three out of four households gave money to charitable causes in recent years. According to one source, the proportion of households that give peaks through age 64, with more than 80 percent of households contributing to charity.

996. Your age does not affect tax rules applying to charitable contributions. If you itemize deductions on your federal income tax, your charitable contributions can equal half your adjusted gross income. (It can equal less than that if you're donating appreciated property or giving to veteran's organizations, cemeteries, or fraternal organizations.)

Donations of over $250 should be documented with a receipt, and if you give more than $75 to an organization while receiving something in return—an art print or theater tickets, for example—you should obtain a statement from the charity saying how much of the donation is tax deductible.

Most large charities and educational institutions have staff dedicated to helping you plan and document your gifts, so you should feel free to consult them.

997. Most large charities and educational institutions offer help with "planned giving." Services include helping you or your attorney figure out estate planning strategies that involve charitable remainder trusts, or gifts of real estate that will eventually benefit their institutions.

998. Giving shouldn't mean being taken. Con artists know that older adults can be softhearted, so a common scam is to solicit for charities that don't exist.

If you believe a particular organization may not be operating for charitable purposes, or is making misleading solicitations, write: Correspondence Branch, Federal Trade Commission, Washington, DC 20580. You can also call the National Fraud Information Center's Consumer Assistance Hotline at 800-876-7060.

999. Here are some tips for screening requests for charitable gifts.

• If you receive a phone or in-person solicitation, ask questions—and be persistent until you are satisfied with the answers.

• Don't be pressured into giving money on the spot.

• Contribute by check, not cash; make the check out to the charity, not the individual collecting the donation.

• Mail appeals should clearly identify the charity and describe its programs.

• Keep records of your donations, by a receipt, canceled check, or bank statement. You will need this information at tax time.

1000. A very common scam is to use a name that sounds like that of a reputable charity. Don't be fooled by impressive-sounding names, and be wary of copycat charities whose names sound like (or whose logos are similar to) those of familiar charities.

Another common trick is to send an unsolicited invoice for a contribution. Appeals should not be disguised as bills or invoices. In fact, it's illegal to mail such an invoice without an obvious disclaimer.

It is also illegal to demand payment for unordered merchandise. You are under no obligation to pay for or return items such as seals, stamps, cards, or pens enclosed with an appeal.

1001. If you want to know more about charitable giving and avoiding charitable fraud, contact:

Philanthropy Advisory Service
4200 Wilson Blvd., Suite 800
Arlington, VA 22203
703-276-0100

National Charities Information Bureau
19 Union Square W
New York, NY 10003
212-929-6300

Council of Better Business Bureaus
Publications Department
4200 Wilson Blvd., Suite 800
Arlington, VA 22203

Index